VICTORIA'S UPHILL

Donald Brown

Uphill Village Society

www.uphillvillage.org.uk

Also by Donald Brown:
Somerset versus Hitler
Uphill's Great War

This publication has been generously supported by sponsorship from
Bristol Water Works

ISBN 1 901 084 53 1

Printed and
bound by

Woodspring Resource Centre

Locking, Weston-super-Mare
Tel: 01934 820800

Contents

Victoria's Uphill

Uphill's railway station was bedecked with flags and flowers when Queen Victoria's royal train passed through on the way to the far south-west of her kingdom. She may have waved at cheering children, but it is unlikely that she gave much thought to just another village along the line.

This narrative tells of what it was like to live in Uphill during the 19th century, the lifetime of Queen Victoria. It draws on information from many local books, North Somerset Museum, Somerset Record Office, Uphill Village Society Archive and Weston Library's Local Studies Department. Most direct quotations of dialogues and background detail come from the excellent contemporary Weston *Mercury* reports. The writer is grateful for all the help given by the people in those organisations.

Sources are listed in the Bibliography. As some of them expressed personal viewpoints and memories, absolute accuracy cannot be guaranteed, but from those old newspapers and documents emerges a clear picture of a living and developing village inhabited by people like us.

The book's progress to the printer has been greatly helped by the support and efforts of family and friends as well as by the printer himself. Uphill Village Society, generously supported by sponsors, has financed publication so that today's villagers may know more of their heritage.

The book refers to Victorian currency, weights and measures.

Money came in pounds (£), shillings (s) and pence (d). There were 12 pence in one shilling and 20 shillings in a pound.

Equivalent decimal units are 10 shillings = 50 pence, 1s 6d = 7½p, 1s = 5p, 6d = 2.5p, 3d = 1p.

The basic unit of weight was the pound (lb).

1 lb = 0.5 kg, 14lb = 6.5 kg, 28 lb = 12.5 kg.

112 pounds were called a hundredweight (cwt) = 50 kg. 20 cwt or 2,240 lbs made a ton.

Liquids came in pints.

1 pint was about half a litre. 8 pints made a gallon, about 4.5 litres.

Lengths were measured in inches. 1 inch = 25 mm.

12 inches made one foot = about 300 mm.

3 feet made 1 yard = just under a metre.

Distances were measured in miles:

1 mile = about 1.5 km.

Areas were in acres:

1 acre = about 0.5 hectare.

Part 1:   Pastoral Parish 1800 – 1840

Chapter 1.   1800: New Century, New Princess

View from Weston 1805   *[NSM]*

> Population: 144
> Rector: Rev Thomas Deacle BA
> Lord of the Manor: Simon Payne of Uphill House

When the hilltop bells of St Nicholas rang in the first New Year of the 19th century, 144 people lived in 39 houses in Uphill. By the time the bells rang for the birth of Princess Victoria in 1819, the population had doubled to 270 people, still in 39 houses. They were not the same 39 houses, as workers' homes in those days were not built to last. Records of other Somerset villages show that most families lived in overcrowded one-room shacks of driftwood and clay, thatched with reeds. Water was carried from wherever it sprang from the ground and sanitation was the surrounding soil. Unsurprisingly, workers were ragged and dirty although the gentry wore well-tailored elegant clothes. Everyone had bad teeth and bad breath. Medical care depended on traditional folk remedies. Infant mortality was common and life expectancy short.

Working life was harsh, dulled by heavy cider and beer drinking by both sexes. Children ran wild. Crime was unchecked by severe punishments, including public executions, the pillory,

transportation, long sentences of hard labour and floggings for all ages. Over 200 capital offences included wearing disguise on a highway, cutting down young trees, shooting rabbits, poaching at night, stealing goods worth 5 shillings from a person or shop or 40 shillings from a house. Prisoners defended themselves in court without legal advice. Outdoor bare-fist fighting remained a popular entertainment but bull-baiting, badger-baiting, dog-fighting and cock-fighting were gradually being prohibited.

People depended on open wood fires for warmth and cooking and on candles for light, although the big houses enjoyed coal and paraffin. With no artificial lighting out of doors, "the moon was the parish lantern", glow-worms gleamed along grassy banks and the night sky blazed with the light of constellations, planets, rings round the moon, shooting stars and sometimes the shimmering curtains of the Northern Lights. The land was so quiet that a man hammering nails on Steep Holm could clearly be heard on Uphill beach.

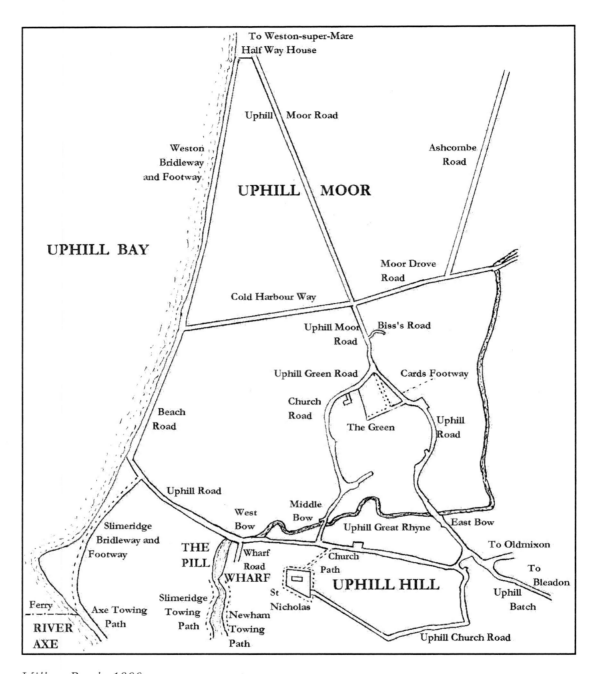

Village Roads 1800

Uphill's roads were unsurfaced cart-tracks 20 to 30 feet wide, caked with animal dung. Moor Road, today's Uphill Road North, crossed Uphill Moor, a salt-marsh between Uphill and Weston. It entered Uphill and forked at Uphill Green which covered today's Church Copse, Old Rectory, Donkey Field and some Manor grounds. When the Jubilee of George III was celebrated there in 1810, it was described as "a small field adjoining the Rectory garden which was then common land". Uphill Road continued on the line of today's Uphill Road South, Uphill Way and Links Road to the beach. The right fork was Uphill Green Road, passing the original Rectory which covered today's St Aubyn's Avenue, becoming Church Road.

Uphill's first Rectory   *[UVS]*

At the south end of the Rectory gardens, an arched gateway – still there – opened onto Rector's Way along the edge of the Green past today's church hall to where the church now stands.

Rectory   gateway

Green Way footpath across the Green remains as today's path along the fence between the Rectory and Church Copse.

Uphill Church Road, now Folly Lane, climbed up to the church and churchyard. A sycamore tree, planted by the path in 1810 to mark George III's Jubilee, still stood in 1900. Church Path was the direct footpath and Churchyard Path ran round the churchyard for the purpose of repairing or storing materials for the wall.

Wharf Road gave access to moorings on the Pill. From there, boats were towed to the Axe along Newham Towing Path. On the other side of the Pill, a public bridleway and footway led along Slimeridge Towing Path to the Axe Towing Path. Beach Road went north along the beach to the end of Cold Harbour Way which is today's footpath across the golf course. From there it became Weston Bridleway and Footway, continuing on the beach to meet Moor Road at the inn Halfway House, on the site of today's Royal Sands.

Today's Devonshire Road was Ashcombe Road to Ashcombe in Weston. Moor Drove Road is now Windwhistle Road and Jury Path is Windwhistle Lane. Biss's Road crossed today's Manor grounds: a hilltop gravestone records the burial of William and Mary Biss in 1804.

By the turn of the century some substantial stone houses had been built where there was a good independent water supply. A "Cottage and tenement at West Bow" – today's sluice – was sold in 1806 by the Rev Jonathan Gegg of Loxton to Thomas Jones of Uphill, Mariner, and by him to Thomas T Knyfton, who already owned the Ship Inn. The Ship, older than any pub in Weston, had opened its doors in 1713 as the Crowne, to be renamed the Lamb in 1751 and the Ship in 1799. Shortly after the Queen's accession, Thomas Chaplin died there on 16th April 1837. The circumstances are not known but must have been noteworthy as his ghost lingered on.

A hundred yards away, in 1720 or earlier, the West Inn, later renamed the Dolphin, had opened on the site of today's canoe shop. It was a low building with a thatched roof like most houses in the village. Its thatch caught fire and the building burned down but was rebuilt in its present location, absorbing a ship's chandler's and two cottages. Every year at May Day the Uphill Revel filled the road between the inns and a impromptu band paraded raucously round the village.

From Middle Bow bridge over the rhyne, Church Road passed Walnut Cottage, The Cottage, the tithe barn, Sherwell House and Frogmore Cottage, then just one dwelling, back to the Rectory. The Rev WT Bowles, rector from 1769 to 1787, was a keen gardener. He planted climbers on trellis on the Rectory walls and laid out wide lawns and shrubberies. The next Rector, Thomas Deacle, extended the building, adding a large dining-room in 1820. Opposite the Rectory, Park Cottage was probably the local home of the Knyftons.

Children of the gentry were educated at home by private tutors until the boys were old enough to be sent to a boarding school. Girls stayed at home, learning the arts of genteel living from governesses. Village girls stayed at home as well, but in their case they cared for babies and ran the house, allowing their mothers to work. Their brothers worked in the fields. There was no compulsory schooling and the majority of country folk were illiterate. Uphill however was one of the villages that had a Parish Schoolroom where a local literate person taught whoever cared to turn up with a penny fee and where the -

good old discipline of Father Stick and his children, Cat o' Nine Tails, Rope's End, Strap, Birch, Ferrule, and Cane was wholesomely maintained.

The school was based in an 18th century thatched cottage, now Cardes Cottage, alongside the Green in what became Uphill Castle grounds. The footpath past it was Cards Footway. The school was probably established by the indomitable Somerset educationist Hannah More who was living next door in Rose Cottage in 1793. Rose Cottage stood on the site of an earlier cottage, dating from 1695.

Before the Enclosure Acts, gypsies could camp on any waste or common land for up to a year after which they were liable to the death penalty. One gypsy family, the Joules, lived almost permanently on a quarry between Uphill and Bleadon. Isaac Joules, a knife-grinder always called "Old Isaac", was reputed to be a farmer's son who had left home to marry Merrily, a beautiful girl from a gipsy family of healers and fortune-tellers and a range of other supernatural powers. He was also said to be king of the gypsies, with the power to cure ailing farm animals, or, if need be, put the Evil Eye on anyone foolish enough to cross him.

Isaac and Merrily raised a large family of daughters as beautiful as their mother and known in the village as always kind and courteous. Merrily died in 1827 and Isaac in 1841 at the age of 70.

Isaac Joules   [NSM]

Their grand-daughter Druscilla Joules died in 1929 aged 94 having lived at Bleadon for over 50 years. She smoked a short clay pipe while making brushes and pegs for sale.

Isaac and Merrily were buried in Yatton where Merrily's tombstone reads:

> Here lies Betsy Joules, a beauty bright,
> Who left Isaac Joules her heart's delight.

Uphill Batch, a steep cart-track, led up to Bleadon Hill. A toll-gate controlled access to the Bridgwater Road, a turnpike maintained by tolls levied on wagons and stage-coaches. Two farmhouses stood on the Batch. The lower, Uphill Farm, was rebuilt in the 1830s with a Tudor style front door and leaded windows. Manor Farm, occupied by Noah Wilmott in 1824, was rebuilt at the same time by Simon Payne using local stone recovered from Uphill's 16th century manor house. Thomas Tutton Knyfton bought both farms in 1853.

Once a week the postman came through Uphill, wearing a red coat, riding on a donkey and blowing a horn as long as his arm. He carried letters for the gentry and, at a time when newspapers were limited to London, news of the outside world. But ordinary people wrote no letters and kept no diaries and so left no written records of ordinary life. Some, however, had good memories and their recollections were recorded later in the century by the Weston *Mercury*. AM Griffin was one, describing the scene in 1803:

> From Uphill to Weston Hill and Ashcombe extended an open moor devoid of trees and with scarcely a shrub to break the monotony of the scene. There were no regular roads and although some attempts had been made to drain the moor, a great part of it was every winter under water. Sand tots (dunes) stretched all along the sea front where the esplanade now is and the fishing nets were spread out on them to dry. The entrance to the beach was where the Sanatorium now stands. Weston consisted of five farm houses, a new house built by Mr Hancock, the Rectory and about 13 fishermen's and labourers' cottages. The population was about 300. Uphill was the larger place, to which the Westonians went for that gaiety and company they could not find in their small village; as a proof of its greater importance, the bay is called Uphill Bay.

> In the moor, large flocks of geese fed, and wild duck, widgeon and teal abounded in the neighbourhood, also some birds called by the inhabitants "sepoys" which had their habitat in an outer sea wall of which no trace now remains, it having all been swept away by the tides. Sometimes flocks of wild geese flew overhead in such numbers that three have been brought down by one shot. Fish was plentiful — salmon, salmon-peel, soles, sand-dabs, conger eels &c — and shrimps and sprats were so abundant that the former could be bought for 1d per pound and the latter at ½d.

Weston's "Very Oldest Inhabitant" recalled the Norvills:

> …In about 1812 or 1813 the Norvills came in from Uphill. Mrs Norvill took in washing and ironing and her husband was a shoemaker and "dealer in tea, coffee, tobacco and snuff." There was a pigstye against the house, and children played all round about. No one complained of the drains, as there were none.

Samuel Norvill was at Old Harse's wedding in Uphill:

> The Rev Stiddard Jenkins drove the wedding party along the sands to the Halfway House. They joined the road which began there, drove to the foot of the hill and walked up to the church. Thinking we were late, the Rev Jenkins looked in his fob for his watch but couldn't find it. After fumbling about he discovered it in his small clothes at his knee. Turning to me he said, "That's what it is to have an industrious wife to mend your clothes." At the church he said to Harse, "I don't know whether I can marry you after all as I haven't got leave. The wedding did take place however in spite of all the difficulties.

Samuel Norvill also knew about the fishing. The first salmon taken in the bay had to be given to Weston's Lord of the Manor, the Rev Wadham Piggott living at Brockley. In 1815:

> I took him one weighing 32½ lbs caught in a net between two poles off Knightstone. The next tide we took a few more of only half the weight.

Wild-fowlers squatted silently on the Axe mud each evening on bundles of straw known as brawlers or billies. Each held a bonny box, a lantern with two candles shining out through a bull's eye lens. Wild geese and duck settled on the flats to feed but could not see past the light, allowing the fowler to crawl close to his target.

From Black Rock to Birnbeck, fishermen stretched their nets between poles across the bay's clockwise tidal current so that fish swam into the mesh. At low tide they went out in flat punts to collect the catch but, as the tide fell, gulls had to be scared away:

Edward Harse, the Knightstone gull-yeller, could be heard at Congresbury.

Samuel Norvill continued:

> A cart-track ran northward from Uphill along the beach which was called The Strand, before turning through drifting sand dunes to Weston-super-Mare. Weston had no road system and no public buildings, its 34 houses being dotted round a pattern of fields and along a single muddy lane known as The Street. Its postal address was Weston-super-Mare, near Cross.
>
> We walked to Uphill along a high pebble beach and inside that an artificial mud bank to keep the sea out, known as the sea-wall. This had a path along the top and ran all the way to Uphill where part remains. It was kept in repair by owners of the adjoining auster tenements (small cottages with rights to common land). Marker stones bore their initials and the distance in feet they maintained.
>
> The road from Weston to Halfway House was built with stone from Bristol Road batch. Until then, travellers from Bridgwater had to stop at Halfway House if the tide was in and wait until the sand was firm and dry before they could drive in. There used to be a signpost there, with two arms, one saying Uphill and the other Weston. Sand drifted so high that only the arms were visible for years. Now they have been buried but must still be there under the sand.

Riding from Weston to Banwell in 1826, the Rev John Skinner passed Halfway House, the site of today's Royal Sands apartments. Its first landlord was John Harris whose customers were itinerant labourers and smugglers rather than visitors:

> We rode gently along the beach towards Uphill, stopping by the way to look at the foundations of a new hotel just emerging from the sand. What saith the Parable on this head? Is he not a foolish man who buildeth his house on such a foundation? ... what can possibly induce such myriads to visit this nasty place to broil on a loose sand during the dog days with no other view to amuse them but the muddy expanse of a turbid estuary?

The Rev Skinner may have had had no eye for tourist potential, but back in 1797, Bonner & Middleton's *Bristol Journal* had advertised:

FOR HEALTH AND SEA BATHING.

At Uphill in Somersetshire. Jane Biss and Son most respectfully inform the public that they have fitted up two commodious Houses for the reception of Families or Single Persons during the summer. The situation at Uphill is universally allowed to be healthy and pleasant.

Pleasure boats and Passage Vessels to the Holmes or Welsh Coast.

The enterprise failed as did the Somerset Sea Bathing Infirmary established in 1826 at Uphill by the Bishop of Bath & Wells "to cure the Scrofula in Poor Persons". It provided five patients with "board, lodging and warm baths for 3 shillings per week" but closed after two years for lack of support. A new stage-coach service from Bristol put Weston firmly on the tourism map in 1814 but Uphill remained a simple rural parish where the peaceful landscape, sea airs and fine views attracted a few wealthy families to settle.

Robert Wolfe, a nephew of General Wolfe who captured Quebec, was one of these. With his wife and two daughters he retired to Somerset after service as Accountant-General to the East India Company and bought or rented the new Uphill Castle. His wife Anna Maria was the daughter of famous miniaturist John Smart and a portrait of the daughters labelled "The Misses Wolfe of Uphill Castle" was reputedly by George Romney, fashionable London painter. Mrs Anna Wolfe died aged 47 in November 1813 and was buried in Clifton. One of the girls, Sophia Anna, married Joseph Baker Grindon in St Nicholas Church on 28th September 1815. The Parish Clerk spelled her name Woolf but gave her address as Uphill Castle.

The Wolfe sisters   *[UVS]*

Chapter 2.   Payne, Gegg and Knyfton

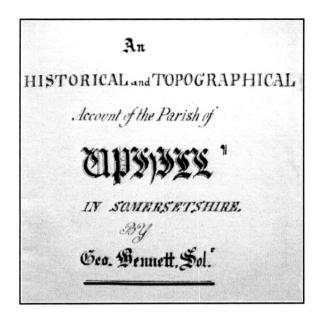

An

HISTORICAL and TOPOGRAPHICAL

Account of the Parish of

Uphill [1]

IN SOMERSETSHIRE.

By

Geo. Bennett, Sol[r]

George Bennett, Solicitor, visiting the village of Weston for the health of his family, described Uphill in a letter. Headed with a sketch of hilltop St Nicholas, this was reprinted in the *Gentleman's Magazine* of May 14th 1828. It opened:

> The parish of Uphill is situate in the Hundred of Winterstoke 8 miles west-north-west from Axbridge and 138 miles from London, at the conflux of the River Axe and the Bristol Channel.

After a history of the parish from earliest times, the writer came up to date:

> ... Simon Payne Esq married Hester Gegg, spinster, only Daughter and Heiress of the late Revd Jonathan Gegg of Axbridge who built the handsome House on the summit of the Hill above the village, called Uphill House, which commands very extensive and picturesque prospects to the South and North. Mr Payne has built several new Houses in the Village, which are let as Lodging Houses and also a good House in the fantastic or modern Antique Stile at the end of Uphill green, called the Castle.

> There are two tolerably decent Inns at this place, one called "The Ship" and the other "The Dolphin";

> The widow of TT Knyfton Esq has a comfortable Summer residence at this place, with Shrubberies laid out and planted in a tastefully rural and truly pleasing manner. The Clergyman's House is neat and commodious by an extensive

> Shrubbery intermingled with Forest Trees of larger growth.

> This village is much frequented in the summer and autumn for the benefit of Bathing in the Salt water.

Bennett named three families: the Paynes and Geggs who were investing heavily in property, and the Knyftons who owned property in the village and estates across Somerset.

Jonathan Gegg was born in 1724, the son of Jonathan Gegg of Kings Standley, Gloucestershire. He took Holy Orders and moved to a living in Axbridge establishing himself as a wealthy land-owner with property in Axbridge, Loxton and Uphill. He married Susan Timbrel and they had a son John Henry Gegg. When Susan died, the Rev Jonathan married Hannah Richardson of Uphill House, today's Grange, "a farm-house on the village's southern hillside, in 9 acres of mature woodland with views". He moved in, enlarged the estate and had the house rebuilt. Their only child, Hester, was born there in 1770.

Rev Jonathan Gegg   *[SRO]*

Jonathan Gegg died aged 66 in 1790 and Hannah died in 1797. They were buried in a Gegg vault beneath the chancel of St Nicholas, but the original named stone was damaged and replaced with a plain slab.

Simon Payne was a business associate of the Rev Jonathan Gegg. Although an attorney-at-law, he was not rich and, with an eye on the future, he asked for permission to marry Hester.

Hester Gegg [SRO]

The perceptive parson, however, demanded that Simon first establish a personal annual income of £300. Payne achieved this by persuading his mother and sister to give him all their money against a promise that he would provide for their futures. Gegg died in 1790 and Simon, now 37, married the 20-year old Hester (1770-1842) and her fortune and moved into her Uphill House where their first son Charles Henry Payne was born a year later. Uphill House was today's Grange.

Now the wealthiest man in Uphill, Simon Payne purchased the title Lord of the Manor of Uphill-cum-Christon. This title had been held by his family until ceded to the Crown in 1553 in settlement of debt. It returned to private ownership and in August 1790 William Burridge inherited all the Manor lands and tenancies. Keeping only Oldmixon Farm, he immediately sold the lot to Payne.

In 1764 the Rev Jonathan Gegg had built Mulletts, a dwelling house "adjacent to Uphill Green". Simon Payne's next big investment was to build

a grand new house in the grounds of Mulletts in 1805, adapting the original building as its coach house and stables. This became known as Uphill Castle, now Uphill Manor.

Simon Payne [SRO]

At a humbler but still profitable level, Payne spotted a growing market in mobile labour and built several new lodging-houses. More land came his way as Lord of the Manor when the Uphill Enclosure Act of 1813 awarded him sectors of the village's common land. But a law-suit against him for defaulting on payments for the maintenance of Uphill Rhyne reached the King's Bench and by 1814 he had exhausted his wife's money. As his debts grew he had to mortgage the Castle and the Lordship of the Manor along with more of his estates to stave off bankruptcy before he died in 1830.

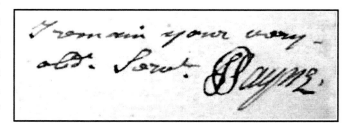

Simon Payne signature 1804
[Permission kindly given by SRO to use the image of
a signature from file C/GP/MISC/5]

Uphill Castle   *[Permission kindly given by Col Frith to use the image from SRO file A\AEH\19\9]*

The same Enclosure Act allocated to John Henry Gegg, Gentleman of Uphill, 6 acres of Uphill Moor, on the north side of the village. John Henry Gegg was the son of Rev Jonathan Gegg's first marriage and thus half-brother to Simon Payne's wife Hester. On 1st March 1812 he married a Welsh cousin Eliza Gegg and they settled in Uphill where nine children were baptised. Henry William in 1813, Thomas in 1814 and Robert Edward in 1815 were followed by a fourth son, Robert, born in 1818 and buried six years later in old St Nicholas graveyard. Triplet sons were born in 1819: John Henry, Francis Thomas and Joseph. Two daughters were baptised, Ann/Eliza in 1821 and Susan Timbrel in 1823.

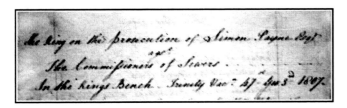

Simon Payne prosecution 1807   *[SRO]*

In about 1818, John Henry Gegg entered Holy Orders. He bought Uphill Castle, which had come on the market as a result of Simon Payne's debts,

where he set up "a respectable Boarding School for young gentlemen". Years later AM Griffin recalled the school for the *Mercury*:

> There was a large boys' school at Uphill kept by Mr Gegg. The boys used frequently to camp among the sand tots making a fire of driftwood and amusing themselves with watching the porpoises which gambolled unmolested close to the shore. Now and then a wild swan would put in an appearance and once the boys caught one and cooked it but found it decidedly tough eating.

> The Weston Rector was the Rev Wadham Pigott, a friend of Mr Gegg's and happy was the boy who was chosen to take a note or message across the moor to the Rectory where he was duly rewarded with cake and wine by the kind-hearted old gentleman.

Gegg planned to extend the Castle towards the sea across land acquired under the Enclosure Act. He began building a school chapel beyond Coldharbour Bank formed by sand drifting against his boundary hedge. But a new boy joined the school from the West Indies where his father was a sea captain. His luggage carried germs of yellow fever, infecting other pupils who were sent home. Rather than wait for transport, one boy walked fifteen miles to his parents' farm at Nempnett Thrubwell. Thirsty, he drank a mug of farm cider before going to bed. His survival was naturally attributed to that cider.

The school closed and the Rev John Henry Gegg went bankrupt in 1825 and fled to Jamaica. His assignees in bankruptcy sold Uphill Castle in 1830 to a Daniel Beaumont Payne and two brothers optimistically named Hope, but it was too much for them and they also went bankrupt. No Geggs were recorded as baptised or buried at St Nicholas after 1837. John Henry Gegg eventually returned from Jamaica to Somerset to buy land and build houses in a new development at Moorland Road where he lived in one of his own villas. He revisited the Castle, by then named the Manor, to call on Mrs Knyfton. Of his large family, his fifth son, also John Henry Gegg, died aged 93 in Weston-super-Mare on 12th October 1911.

Meanwhile, as Simon Payne sank into bankruptcy, his son and heir Charles Henry Payne persuaded his mother Hester to give him Uphill House.

Charles Henry Payne   [SRO]

Although himself a barrister and a Commissioner in Bankruptcy, Charles Henry followed the family pattern and filed for bankruptcy only two years later. Nevertheless, in 1835 Isambard Kingdom Brunel dealt with him as Lord of Manor and owner of land required for the new Bristol and Exeter Railway. This rescued him and the 1841 Census records him as a 45 year-old Barrister-at-Law still living in Uphill House with

his wife Ann Payne, also 45, and three servants, George Haynes (40), Sarah Pim (20) and Ann Gad (20). His mother died in 1842.

But on 20th October 1847 Charles Henry Payne was again declared a debtor. He put some of his Uphill estates including Uphill House and Farm on sale and moved to 75 Albany Street, London. In November he was consigned to Marshalsea Debtors' Prison and declared bankrupt:

> CH Payne, bankrupt debtor, estate for sale 20 Oct 1847.

> Uphill House and Farm for sale 6 Nov 1847 he now being in debtors prison.

In spite of all this, he had returned to Uphill House by 1851 where he employed a bailiff named Way. He redeemed his father's mortgage on Manor Farm and the Lordship of the Manor, but they were again sold two years later by his assignees in bankruptcy. Charles Henry Payne does not appear in the 1851 or 1861 Uphill Census. He died in 1863 but is not listed in the St Nicholas Burial Record.

> Notice of Sale of manor 1832
>   by order of Assignees of Daniel Beaumont Payne, Henry Hope, George Hulbert Hope, Bankrupts...
>
> Mansion called The Castle
>   7 cottages with bakehouse, blacksmith, and carpenter's shop
>   The Dolphin Inn
>   New house Slimeridge and land
>   Various pieces of land with Good Water
>   Various fields: The Sale Piece, Payne's Eleven Acres, Gould's Six Acres, Gould's Four Acres, Gould's Five Acres, Payne's Ten Acres.

In its first thirty years, the Castle had brought nothing but disaster to the Geggs and Paynes. Somerset land-owner Thomas Tutton Knyfton now bought the place, establishing a Knyfton dynasty in the village that would last for one and a half centuries.

The Knyfton family had been dispossessed of a baronetcy in Derbyshire in the 1650s after supporting King Charles I in the Civil War. In 1698 George Knyfton arrived in Uphill, married Mary Hobbs and within the next hundred years the family energetically expanded as major Somerset land-owners with estates around Uphill, Wedmore and Westbury-sub-Mendip. They were Lords of the Manor of Westbury from 1791 until 1847 owning homes there and in Uphill. George's great grandson was Thomas Tutton Knyfton, born in Uphill on 29th October 1798, educated privately and at Trinity College, Cambridge, graduating BA in 1821 and MA 1824.

Although Thomas Knyfton bought Uphill Castle in 1832, he did not live there. On 15th December 1836 aged 38, he married Eliza Maria daughter of Maj Gen Sir Love Jones Parry of Caernarvon but their marriage lasted less than two years. She died on 29th September 1838 aged 28, six days after the birth of their son. He was baptised Thomas Parry Knyfton but survived only two weeks, dying on 13th October. Both were buried in the family vault within St Nicholas church.

❑ ❑ ❑ ❑ ❑

Chapter 3. St Nicholas Renewed

St Nicholas Church 1828   *[George Bennett]*

When Princess Victoria was born in 1819 she was fifth in the line of royal succession and no-one thought she would ever become queen. Nevertheless, the loyal villagers of Uphill rang a peal of celebration for her birth from the belfry of St Nicholas Church. The bells were inscribed:

> THOMAS KNYFTON CHURCHWARDEN
> WILLIAM BILBIE FECIT 1775

William Bilbie was a Chewstoke bell-founder and the churchwarden was Uphill's first Thomas Tutton Knyfton. The tenor bell measured 29 inches in diameter and was inscribed:

> I to the church the living call and to the grave summon all.

On a death in the village, the sexton tolled this bell for an hour: once every minute for a man, twice a minute for a woman and three times a minute for a child. At the end of the hour, he tolled another 20 chimes, the signal for St Peter to open heaven's gates to receive the departed's soul. A week later, on the day of the funeral, the bell chimed again, once every minute from the moment the coffin left the house until it was carried into the church for the funeral service. As it was carried out to the grave, a further 20 chimes signalled to St Peter that the funeral was over. The sexton was paid a penny a chime.

Burials meant carrying the coffin up the rocky path to St Nicholas Church where successive generations went into the same family grave to avoid the labour of digging in bed-rock. A local carpenter knocked up wooden coffins and wooden crosses for those who couldn't make their own. Villagers also walked up the hill for Sunday services, weddings and baptisms. On 14th January 1806 for example, the Rev Thomas Deacle christened Jane, the fifteenth and final child of Ezekiel and Mary Jones.

On 20th June 1837 Victoria did come to the throne and on 10th February 1840 she married her German cousin Prince Albert. Cracked celebratory peals demonstrated that the third bell needed recasting and the Churchwardens recorded the expense:

1840 Easter. Hauling the Bell to Bristol	£ 0	6s	0d
Pd for Beer for men taking down and hanging the Bell	£ 0	6s	3d
Pd for Re-casting the Bell	£15	3s	4d
Pd for hauling it home	£ 0	6s	0d

The church's five bells had hung on their oak frame for 65 years but the hill-top building was already 700 years old and later that year the Church Vestry Meeting resolved:

... that, considering the very dilapidated condition and inconvenient situation of the present church, this Vestry is of opinion that it is highly desirable to provide a new church in a situation more convenient to the inhabitants generally, provided adequate funds can be procured for such purpose.

£1,510 was the estimated cost and of this, £1,110 was immediately promised through private subscriptions. The Patron of the living, John Fisher Esq of Langford, donated the site.

The new church was built in an Early English style with walls of local limestone, a freestone tower and a slate roof. Inside, a ceiling of open timbers spanned a broad nave with no aisles. Mrs John Fisher, the Rector's wife, laid an uninscribed stone at the south-east corner of the nave.

The building was consecrated and opened for worship on June 3rd 1844. In the new graveyard, village undertaker Robert Minifie built burial vaults of brick, painted the traditional white.

Both St.Nicholas Churches and the old Rectory, 1844   [UVS]

Both churches continued in use with services in each on alternate Sundays until 5th April 1846 when restoration of the old church began.

A "beautiful Norman priest's door" in the south wall was built up, leaving no trace. A Vestry Meeting on 5th November 1847 resolved to:

Wall up the South window nearest the West end;

Wall up the archway between the body of the church and the tower;

Take down the partition between the chancel and the tower into the belfry;

Wall up the present chancel door (near the East end, now only visible from the outside);

As the present door is not wide enough to carry in a coffin, open a wider door at an old window entrance previously closed up;

Repair the roof of the chancel and tower.

From then on, the old church was used only as a burying chapel for the old churchyard. The next problem came with the porch. This had been re-roofed in 1780, not with tiles of Uphill clay, but with slabs of Cornish granite. After 70 years, their weight was making the foundations sink and the roof bend like a horse-shoe. As the Rev F Warre reported to the Somerset Archaeological Society in 1849:

Owing to this subsidence the crown of the arch is much depressed, which is the cause of its present very uncommon shape..... The porch is an interesting relic of ancient days, which is rapidly falling into decay, and which in the course of a few short years will probably be entirely destroyed.

St Nicholas before restoration   [UVS]

□ □ □ □ □

Chapter 4.   Parish Government

Since the Dissolution of Monasteries in the 16th Century, local administration had been the duty of parish churches. Chaired by the priest, committees and officials were elected at the Easter Vestry Meeting. Voting was restricted to the gentry and landowners whose rates provided parish funds. They appointed Churchwardens who administered church affairs, Overseers of the Poor who provided work or relief as needed, Waywardens who maintained roads and Constables of the Law who kept the peace with an official truncheon.

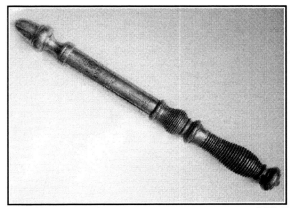

Uphill's   truncheon   *[NSM]*

Any failure of duty was a legal offence for which the culprit appeared at the County Quarter Sessions.

In 1832, 14 men were listed as Uphill parish electors. Four of these lived outside the village but owned land in the parish:

8556 Bradford, William
8567 Briffett, John Stowey
8558 Collings, Thomas
8559 Deacle, Rev Thomas
8560 Every, George
8561 Haynes, George
8562 Hancock, Joseph
8563 Jones, John
8564 Jones, John
8565 Knyfton, Tutton Thomas
8566 Norman, Joseph
8567 Rogers, Thomas Oliver Weston-s-Mare
8568 Richardson, John Blackford, Wedmore
8569 Symes, John Oldmixon, Hutton

In 1821 the Churchwardens' Book was introduced, charging a Parish Rate to all householders. All property was valued and a rate of between 1½d and 3d in the £ was charged.

Payment was unenthusiastic, but most eventually paid up. Uphill's Churchwardens' Book listed all valuations and rates until 1870.

The parish rating system also identified villagers to serve on juries in the law courts. Their qualifications included social status, type of property-holding, and liability for windows tax and poor rate. Gentry dominated Uphill's list until 1821, with Joseph Hancock as the only farmer. Thereafter, shopkeepers and yeomen were drawn in. The Paynes left the list in 1816 and the Geggs in 1818; TT Knyfton appeared in 1835 after buying the Castle. Jurymen were listed annually: the names Hancock, Harse, Haynes and Knyfton were to run on through the history of the village.

1810   Simon Payne Esq; John Croft Esq; John Gegg, Gent; Thomas Richardson Gent; Joseph Hancock Farmer; Elias Mansell Innkeeper.

1811   Simon Payne Esq 56, Freeholder; John H Gegg, Gent 28, Freeholder; Thomas Richardson, Gent 60, Freeholder; Joseph Hancock Farmer 50, Copyholder. Signed Thomas Isgar, Tythingman.

1812-16 Simon Payne 57, Freeholder; Robert Woolf 56, Leaseholder; Thomas Richardson, Gent 60, Freeholder; John Henry Gegg, Gent 28, Freeholder; Joseph Hancock Farmer, Copyholder.

1817   John Henry Gegg, Gent, member of th University; Joseph Hancock Farmer 51, Copyholder.

1818   Thomas Richardson, Gent 60, Freeholder (crossed out) Dead; John Henry Gegg 33, Clerk. Signed Jacob Tripp, Tythingman.

1819   Joseph Hancock Farmer 60, Copyholder.

1821   James Booleage 45, Farmer; Joseph Harse 62, Farmer, Constable.

1822   Joseph Hancock Farmer (the Elder) Yeoman; Thomas Collins, Yeoman.

1823   1822 Joseph Hancock Farmer – infirm; Thomas Collins, Yeoman.

1825   Henry Jones, Yeoman, Freeholder. Signed Joseph Hancock, Churchwarden; Thomas Payne, Overseer of the Poor.

1828-31 John Jones, Tailor.

1832   John Jones, Taylor; Thomas Yeatman, Shopkeeper, Freeholder.

1833   Joseph Hancock, Farmer; James Taylor, Bailiff; Thomas Yeatman, Shopkeeper, Freeholder.

1835   Joseph Saunders, Freeholder; John Sergeant, Lodging House Keeper, Windows; Thomas Yeatman, Shopkeeper, Freeholder; Thomas Tutton Knyfton Esq, Freeholder;

1836   Joseph Saunders, Freeholder; Thomas Yeatman, Shopkeeper, Freeholder; Thomas Tutton Knyfton Esq, Freeholder;

1837   William Jones, Innkeeper, Windows and Poor Rate; Joseph Saunders, Yeoman.

Chapter 5.   Underground Uphill

Cross-section of Uphill Caves, 1820   *[UVS]*

Villagers had always quarried their own stone on common land, creating the rock faces along the northern foot of the hill. Following the Enclosure Acts, commercial quarrying arrived in the 1820s. Chris Richards of North Somerset Museum Service:

The earliest rock faces show that rock was broken out by gunpowder placed in shot-holes made by a steel drill and sledge-hammer. The drill was about 1¼ inches diameter with a cutting edge at one end. The quarryman decided the position, angle and depth of the shot-hole to gain maximum effect. He held the edge of the drill against the rock while his mate beat the other end with a hammer. After each blow he turned the drill about a third of its circumference and thus   laboriously chipped out a shot-hole. He made his fuse from wheat straw or a goose-quill filled with crushed gunpowder and inserted it with the gunpowder into the shot-hole. He rammed in fine stones to contain the blast, sounded a warning and lit the fuse. A shot-hole 6 feet to 8 feet deep produced a rock-pile of 10 to 30 tons. After 1830 factory-made fuses were available, proving more reliable and safer.

The warning was sounded on a special bugle which emitted only a single note. When blasting was to take place three quarrymen stood just outside the perimeter of the working and each simultaneously sounded a prescribed number of bugle calls for Alert and All Clear.

About 30 feet below the cemetery, quarrymen blasted into the hill's carboniferous limestone and opened up a fissure littered with bones. These attracted the interest of David Williams, vicar of Bleadon who, like many churchmen, was an amateur historian and archaeologist. He said the bones were of "animals of a country and climate differing from ours," mostly spotted hyena, and the gnawed and broken bones of their prey. Although cave hyenas could crunch, swallow and digest the largest bones, enough remained to show that woolly rhinoceros, cave bear, oxen, horses and other animals had found refuge in Uphill's caves. Over the millennia, climates had ranged from the tropical to the glacial, attracting the hyena during hot periods, the horse in more temperate times and the woolly rhinoceros in the ice ages.

Another cave 20 feet lower down the hill was larger, about 40 feet long and 12 feet wide. Some good stalactites hung from the roof which went up to 20 feet high, and fossils studded the limestone walls. Polished rock showed where foxes had squeezed through the cave's narrow access. Inside they left the bones of sheep, birds and cuttle-fish. Buried among the debris lay a fragment of Roman pottery and a coin of the Roman Emperor Julian.

Twenty years later a new shaft upwards into this cave revealed a pot of the coins. The quarrymen closed the cave with a door and used it as an explosive store. The bones went to Bristol Museum and the Roman coins – 200 denarii – were not seen again.

An 1834 estate map shows a small field called Coal Pit Ground between the top of today's A370 road cutting and the railway. Similar rocks are at Hutton where references to coal go back to the 1780s. In Upper Canada Coombe, Billy Jones' Coal Mine cut into thin seams of soft coal which burned well. Fortunately for Uphill and Hutton, if not for the land-owners, there was not enough coal to be commercially profitable and Uphill's coal-pit survived on a later map only as a pond.

Pottery   fragment   *[NSM]*

Chapter 6.   Rhyne, River and Sea

The pure waters of Ashcombe Stream once meandered from Ashcombe spring through a basin of marshland to Uphill. During the 18th century the stream had been engineered into Uphill Great Rhyne, the main outlet of a pattern of rhynes or drains. The rhyne needed constant maintenance to protect its banks, to prevent silting and to control flooding. This duty fell to the Hutton Jury of Sewers, an elected committee that levied payments from landowners whose lands abutted the rhyne. They paid according to the length of their frontage which was marked by stones bearing their initials.

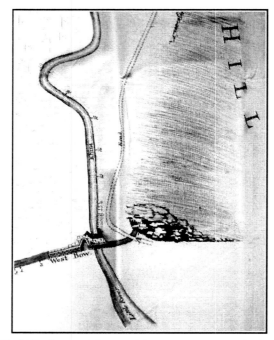

Uphill Great Rhyne 1804   *[SRO]*

A roll of those responsible for maintenance in 1804 included:

Rev Deacle Rector of Uphill;

TT Knyfton in respect of Ship Inn;

TT Knyfton in respect of a tenement late of Widow Knyfton;

S. Payne in respect of the Manor called Uphill-cum-Christon, late Burridges;

S. Payne Esq proprietor of Mulletts, occupied in 1824 by Mr Thomas Gegg;

S. Payne Esq proprietor of Manor Farm, occupied by Noah Wilmott;

S. Payne Esq proprietor of Dolphin Inn, occupied by William Morris;

S. Payne Esq as Lord of the Manor of Uphill-cum-Christon.

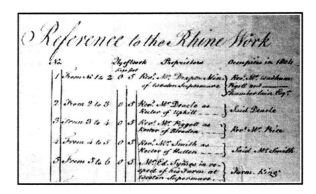

Rhyne landowners 1804   *[SRO]*

Not all paid up. In 1800 Simon Payne asked the Jury to install "a hatchway at the East Eye of the West Bow of Uphill Rhyne to prevent salt water from running inland". Typically, he did not pay for this and by 1807 the sum due reached £204 8s 4½d. The debt was still unpaid in 1811 and Simon Payne was taken to court. The case eventually reached the King's Bench and was part of his eventual financial downfall.

The 1804 map showed three bridges over the rhyne: East Bow, beside today's Little Orchard, Middle Bow otherwise Church Bow beside today's Walnut Cottage and West Bow where the rhyne emptied into "the Little River" between the sea wall and rocks and so along the Pill to the River Axe.

Uphill's long history was determined by its position at the mouth of this estuary. The west wall of its hilltop church was whitewashed as a navigational marker. Although small, tidal and muddy, the River Axe nevertheless provided a harbour sheltered from the open sea as well as a route inland through the flooded Somerset Levels.

Fishermen sailed out from it to net the rich waters beneath Brean Down. A village ferry had crossed the Axe since at least 1637 and the river remained navigable as far as Axbridge until floodgates were built at Bleadon under the Axe Drainage Act of 1802.

Before the days of newspapers, sailors kept Uphill informed about the world. From St Nicholas Church on the hill, people were accustomed to watching the sails of ships following the international marine highway of the Bristol Channel into Wales and England.

The main business of Uphill's sea-going trade was in livestock, shipping in oxen, sheep and pigs from South Wales to be driven overland in great herds to cattle fairs in Bristol and Exeter. They moved along ancient green lanes such as Uphill Drove, now Drove Road. This trade continued throughout the 19th century until coal became a more profitable cargo. In 1832 a mail ferry was contemplated between Sully in Wales and Uphill.

Uphill harbour   *["Warden of the Road"]*

In the churchyard lay the bodies of shipwrecked mariners lost to the dangers of shoals, rocks, currents and gales. A stone marked the grave of:

> John Bliss, of this parish, Mariner, who died Sept 29th 1792, aged 58 years.
>
> Also of Thomas, son of the above John Bliss who died Dec 24th 1801, aged 32 years.
>
> "The boist'rous winds, and Neptune's waves
>
> Have tossed us to and fro.
>
> In spite of both, by God's decree,
>
> We harbour here below,
>
> Where at anchor we do ride
>
> With many of our fleet.
>
> Yet once again shall we set sail
>
> Our Admiral, Christ, to meet."

We don't know if any Uphill seamen fought at Trafalgar in 1805 but four years after the battle Cyrus Purnell of Lympsham auctioned the sloop *Delight*, originally the French boat *Elisabeth* captured by HMS *Iphigenia* during the Napoleonic Wars and "now used in the coal trade in the Uphill river." Sea-going ships were built, bought and sold on the Axe. Shipwright John Blanin of Axbridge built the 18 ton sloop *Hope* at Uphill in 1802 and John Gill Hawkins auctioned at Hobb's Boat in 1812 "the sloop *Friends*, 47 tons register, also a coal barge of 11 tons and a pleasure boat almost new". Village residents in 1818 included three captains of coal sloops and four seamen.

While Uphill Bay offered little scope for the deliberate wrecking of ships, everyone was quick to turn beachcomber when a ship ran ashore and shed its cargo. In 1812, the West Indiaman *Rebecca* foundered off Steep Holm. Her cargo of rum was washed ashore and spread along the beach Although Weston's Lord of the Manor claimed salvage rights, the people got there first. They emptied rum barrels into buckets, basins, jugs and bowls while farmers filled churns. Innkeepers simply rolled the casks into their cellars. Customs Officer Jones from Uphill investigated and confiscated what little was left.

Customs Officers had watched the Axe from as early as 1685. Riding Officers and Surveyors supervised the Customs men; Land Waiters controlled imports and exports. Charles Green was Riding Surveyor at Uphill and Land Waiter at Bristol Port. High duties on imported goods made it profitable to smuggle Dutch gin, French brandy and wine, Caribbean rum, tobacco, silk, tea and coffee. Even starch, vinegar, soap, candles, and sail cloth were worth running in. Brandy and rum came in barrels of varying size: puncheons held 100 gallons, ankers held 7½ gallons. Tobacco was often concealed by being twisted into coils to resemble rope, or cut into shapes to look like leather. When Customs men closed down the English Channel coast, smugglers based themselves on Steep Holm, Flat Holm and Lundy.

As Riding Officers patrolled on horseback from Uphill to Kewstoke, signal lights shone between Uphill Hill, Half Way House inn, Worlebury Hill and St Thomas' Head at Kewstoke. In came the smugglers to dump their contraband in the dunes or to sink their cargo offshore beneath a marker buoy to be collected later. One French skipper sailed in at midnight and cast his contraband overboard. Uphill's excisemen found him still there at dawn, trapped by the rapidly falling tide, his boat surrounded by barrels. Coastguards pursued a boat into the Axe where the smugglers abandoned it and fled along ditches and down lanes to Bleadon, over the hill to Hutton and then across the moor to home, glad to escape. Their boat had no name painted on it and could not be identified. The coastguard followed normal practice and sawed it in three so that it could not be used again and repair was impossible.

Gentry with big houses often allowed kegs to be left in cellars or buried under garden paths. Most houses had a secret storage place. But the Customs men kept a constant watch and contraband often had to be left hidden for a long time. One cargo was buried in Uphill for a complete winter before it could be shifted. A man was seen burying a keg in the sand dunes and walking away until it was safe to collect it. The watchers gleefully dug it up and carried it home where they hid it under the thatch of a hayrick. But when they went for it, the keg had gone: the original man had let them do the dangerous carrying away and had then recovered it. When workmen building the new St Nicholas church found two barrels of brandy under a stack of timber, they knew enough to leave them there and after a few days the barrels had gone.

Smugglers regularly carried contraband brandy in a 4-horse hearse. Sometimes they used a gig with a fast trotting horse. As carts had to display the name and address of the owner, the driver kept a stock of boards showing different names and residences, switching them round in every village so that he could not be identified or traced.

Uphill Parish Wharf, such as it was, lay along the banks of the Pill, a tiny tributary that ran barely 500 yards into the Axe. Ancient fishermen's rights, rather like common land, meant that no harbour dues could be charged for this, making Uphill one of very few free ports in England. As a result, there was no profit in building a proper commercial wharf until the developing 19th century coal trade made it worthwhile. The mooring place had never even been defined until 1813 when the Enclosure Commissioners met in the Ship:

Uphill Enclosure Act 1813. Public Wharf.

> ... the said Gabriel Stone, Joseph Wollen and Young Sturge agreeably to the directions of the said Act did set out and allot as and for a Public Wharf for the use of the public and of all and every person and persons whomsoever who might have occasion to use the same for landing loading and unloading coals and other goods brought in or carried out of the Port of Uphill aforesaid ...

> All that one piece or parcel of land part of Newham Warth aforesaid adjoining the West Bow containing by admeasurements two Roods and numbered 54 on the said Plan bounded on the East by an Allotment of Land Numbered 55 and by the Wharf Road on the West and South by Uphill Pill and on the North by the Sea Wall.

The second Uphill Enclosure Act of 30th September 1818 specified:

> Newham Warth adjoining the West Bow not exceeding one half acre for a public wharf for landing, loading and unloading coals and other goods brought in or carried out of the Port of Uphill.

Pony gig   [RBC]

The new Parish Wharf was built where Wharfe Farm now stands. As trade increased, hard standings or staithes developed along both sides of the Pill for a hundred or so yards. The Enclosure Act maps the position of the ferry but makes no mention of it in the text. When the Rev John Skinner visited the Bishop in Banwell in October 1826, he wrote:

> … I met Captain St Clare or Sinclair, who told me that a vessel had been found yesterday in the Channel with a lading of oil and hides without anyone on board and that they brought her into Uphill. We drove to Uphill to see the vessel which was found near the Flat Holme. It seems by her papers she was on her way from Newfoundland to Bristol. They suppose that she must have foundered on Tuesday night, and that her crew left her at that time, as the log book was brought up to 12 o'clock Tuesday morning when she was off Padstow, in Cornwall. It is ascertained that there was a woman and child on board. Her cargo was fish oil, her rudder when she grounded was unshipped and a hole stove in her stern. It is supposed that there were seven or eight men on board, and that they took to the boat which was upset, but nothing has been heard of any bodies washed up on shore.

Not all shipwrecked bodies were lost. A tombstone in the churchyard near the south wall of the tower was inscribed:

In memory of William Webber, son of George and Charity Webber of Porlock, who was drowned in Bristol Channel, Sept 5 1830, aged 28 years.

In the cold stream my limbs were chill'd
My blood with deadly horror thrill'd
My feeble veins forgot to play,
I fainted, sunk, and died away.
All means were tried my life to save,
But could not keep me from the grave.

❑ ❑ ❑ ❑ ❑

Chapter 7.   Changing Times

In 1803, 31 of Uphill's 51 families worked on the land. Fertile riverside meadows, known as "warths", had been reclaimed from the River Axe's salt marshes when the Somerset Levels were drained during the 17th century. Rich land-owners worked land around their manors and farms, while villagers lived humbly but independently, working their own patches and strips of common land. The Lord of the Manor owned the land but commoners had the legal right to graze animals there. They could fish his stream, take pigs to forage in woodland, collect brushwood for animal bedding and collect fallen wood for domestic fuel. Common soil rights allowed them to take clay and to quarry stone for their own use. They also enjoyed a different common law right to fish the bay and tidal waters.

Samuel Norvill recalled that farmers worked in smock frocks in those days. He added:

> Everyone kept geese on common land at little cost to them. Once a year they plucked the feathers from the living birds and sold them. These feathers were said to be better quality than from dead birds.

Arable crops grew on the surrounding land and on Brean Down. Corn was grown tall, providing long-stemmed straw for thatch. Grain was brought to the windmill on Uphill hill in wooden-axled carts, known as putts, drawn by oxen. A map of 1782 marks a building where the mill tower still stands. A Royal Exchange fire insurance policy dated August 11th 1789 valued the mill at £100, named the owner as "Mr John Marchant of Uphill and the Company of Somerset Yeoman" and described it as:

Geese on the rhyne   [UVS]

a windmill situated on an eminence near the church in Uphill aforesaid and known by the name of Uphill Mill.

Forty years later:

> The truncated tower of this windmill is now used as an observation platform, its exposed site giving good views over Weston Bay and the Bristol Channel. The parallel-sided tower is built of random coursed limestone blocks, 17'2" high to the present parapet level, 12'2" 4'3" inside diameter, with 2'2" 6'3" thick walls.

This mill was derelict by 1829.

Derelict mill tower   [UVS]

The Uphill Enclosure Act of 1813 handed large areas of common land over to private ownership. New owners took over about 340 acres from the tenants of small cottages known as tenements or austers in an area defined as "Uphill Moor, Uphill Hill, Uphill Green, New Ham Warth, Slimeridge, the point and Slimeridge Warth". For instance:

> ... to John Henry Gegg, Gentleman of Uphill, 6 acres of Uphill Moor between Ashcombe Road to the west and Moor Drove Road to the south ... also about 44 acres of open and unenclosed arable lands to the east and West Fields.

Simon Payne, as "Lord of the Manor of Uphill and of Uphill and Christon" was:

... entitled to the soil of said open and common pastures ... but was allotted one-twentieth of the land in lieu of his rights to the soil.

He also received:

... an ancient inclosure on the North side of Uphill Hill commonly called Jones's Garden.

Setting the tone for the forthcoming century of Victorian progress, the new masters profitably consolidated scores of inefficient patches and strips of land into large fenced fields while villagers lost their ancient commons rights, turning overnight from independent peasants into hired farm-hands with no security at all.

While eagerly fencing their new possessions, Uphill's landowners read of Wellington's victory in 1815 over Napoleon at Waterloo. Their London newspapers arrived by local carrier from the nearest coaching stage at Cross. But while London rejoiced at victory, the people grumbled at the rising price of bread, an economic factor that was revolutionising rural life across the country and would do the same in Uphill.

Mechanical innovation such as threshing machines and steam power provoked fears of unemployment. Rioters broke up new machines and were transported or hanged. Thousands of soldiers and sailors disbanded after Waterloo had no work. A severe winter brought sixteen weeks of frost; snow reached the hedge tops in Uphill. 1816 was worse. Called "the year without a summer", it rained almost every day and snow fell in London in May. Low temperatures ruined the harvest and grain prices soared. But landowners dominated government, passing Corn Laws that protected their profits by keeping up the price of grain. Starvation was widespread, mass emigration to North America began and in Somerset bread rioters were dispersed by armed soldiers. Poverty, hunger and total exclusion from political power fostered deep discontent among the people.

George III died in 1820, old, blind and incapable, to be succeeded by his frivolous spendthrift son George IV. Conspirators plotted to murder the Cabinet, seize London and form a provisional People's Government. The leaders were betrayed and hanged or transported, but with memories of the French Revolution still fresh, change had to come. The Reform Bill of 1832 opened parliamentary seats to the rising richer middle classes who organised themselves into the Conservative and Liberal parties. At local level, the same rate-paying middle classes stood for election on to councils instead of allowing rich landowners to co-opt each other.

The shift from an agricultural to a capitalist industrial economy accelerated. Wars had enriched farmers, manufacturers and land-owners. Those with money rushed to invest it, aided by cheap loans and paper money. In spite of widespread bankruptcies, industrial progress flourished and banks used the new Post Office to send more invitations to customers to invest. In Uphill, some families — the Knyftons — prospered, while others — the Paynes and the Geggs — were ruined.

Part 2:   Ancient & Modern, 1840 - 1850

Chapter 8.   Uphill in 1840

Panorama   1840   *[UVS]*

Population 400: 193 females + 207 males

Rector: Rev John Thomas Fisher BL

Wesleyan Minister: Leonard Tilley

Parish Clerk: George Haynes; Relieving Officer: Samuel Norman;
Schoolmaster: Edward Cowdell

Lord of the Manor: Charles Henry Payne of Uphill House

Forty years into the 19th century, the accession of Queen Victoria was followed by the first national Census. This recorded 68 families in Uphill, totalling 400 people living in 64 houses. In the whole village, only one dwelling was empty and one was occupied while still being built. 337 (84%) of the villagers had been born in Somerset, 59 elsewhere in England, 3 in Ireland and 1 in Jersey.

Men and boys had 19 different Christian names between them, the favourites being John, William, James and George. Female names came from a range of 32, with Elizabeth, Mary, Ann and Sarah the most popular. The oldest inhabitants were Thomas Collings (83), Jane Isgar (81), Jane Hancock and Sarah Harris, both 80.

Of 193 females, 56 (29%) were housewives with 76 (39%) young daughters still at home. 28 (14.5%) aged between 13 and 37, worked as female servants. The big houses each employed three or four, but many farmers and small businesses needed a maid. At least seventeen women (9%) were widows, ten living with their families and four on Poor Relief. Two widows, aged 55 and 50, ran farms and another, aged 50 with 3 children, kept a lodging house with 8 lodgers. 11 women were classified as financially independent. 29-year old Mrs Mary Thomas, with three sons and a daughter registered as an Army wife: her husband could have been serving in Afghanistan with the Somerset Light Infantry.

There is no mention of Hester Payne, whose money still subsidised the uncertain finances of the Payne family. She died in 1842 aged 72.

66 (32%) of 207 men worked as labourers: 46 for Uphill's 8 farmers, 4 building the railway and 2 making bricks in Uphill's clay-pit. The richer families employed a coachman and four manservants. Two blacksmiths shared the farrier trade. House building and maintenance occupied ten carpenters and two masons, but no quarrymen. One plumber-glazier had enough business to take on an apprentice. Three cobblers with two young trainees made heavy leather lace-up boots with iron-nailed soles and a tailor made men's clothes. Surprisingly, no men registered as sailors, fishermen or excise men.

Villagers were served by one baker, one coal merchant and five publicans: John Mathews in Halfway House, John Yeoman in the Ship, John Harris in the Dolphin, James Curry in a beer-house in the village and John Bond in a Totterdown beer-house. Schoolmaster 31-year old Edward Cowdell came from Jersey, married a local woman and lodged with their family in an agricultural labourer's house.

Business had grown enough to attract an accountant to Uphill, James Lyddon, who lodged with one of the shoemakers.

Hillside Cottages 1846   *[NSM]*

Thomas Knyfton appeared as a 41-year old magistrate living in Uphill Lodge. He shared it with his widowed mother Betsy Knyfton (65), Mary Graves (35) his recently widowed sister and her children Robert (3) and Albert (5 months).

Other gentry included Charles Payne, barrister, in Uphill House; John Lloyd retired Naval officer; William Godley, retired Army officer; and the Rev John Fisher in the Rectory. Married four years earlier, John Fisher had just been elevated from his position as Uphill's curate.

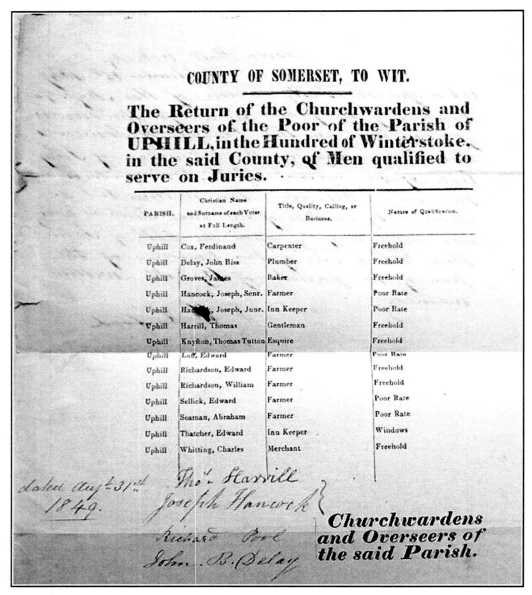

COUNTY OF SOMERSET, TO WIT.

The Return of the Churchwardens and Overseers of the Poor of the Parish of UPHILL, in the Hundred of Winterstoke, in the said County, of Men qualified to serve on Juries.

PARISH.	Christian Name and Surname of each Voter at Full Length.	Title, Quality, Calling, or Business.	Nature of Qualification.
Uphill	Cox, Ferdinand	Carpenter	Freehold
Uphill	Delay, John Biss	Plumber	Freehold
Uphill	Groves, James	Baker	Freehold
Uphill	Hancock, Joseph, Senr.	Farmer	Poor Rate
Uphill	Hancock, Joseph, Junr.	Inn Keeper	Poor Rate
Uphill	Harrill, Thomas	Gentleman	Freehold
Uphill	Knyfton, Thomas Tutton	Esquire	Freehold
Uphill	Luff, Edward	Farmer	Poor Rate
Uphill	Richardson, Edward	Farmer	Freehold
Uphill	Richardson, William	Farmer	Freehold
Uphill	Sellick, Edward	Farmer	Poor Rate
Uphill	Seaman, Abraham	Farmer	Poor Rate
Uphill	Thatcher, Edward	Inn Keeper	Windows
Uphill	Whitting, Charles	Merchant	Freehold

dated Augt 31st 1849.

Thos Harrill
Joseph Hancock
Richard Pool
John B Delay

Churchwardens and Overseers of the said Parish.

Jurors' Roll 1849   [Permission kindly given by SRO to use the image from file Q/RJL/42/21]

From 1840, eligibility for jury service varied every year, reflecting changes of wealth. Thomas Knyfton's name was often added to the list in different ink, as if he were resident for only part of the year:

1838 Henry Parker Hurford, Yeoman; Thomas Tutton Knyfton Esq, Freeholder;
John Matthews, Innkeeper, Windows.
1839 Henry Parker Hurford, Yeoman; John Yeatman, innkeeper; Harry Giblett, Freeholder; George Eavery, Freeholder; John Evans, Freeholder; Thomas Tutton Knyfton Esq, Freeholder.
1840 Thomas Tutton Knyfton Esq, Freeholder; Henry Parker Hurford, Yeoman; John Matthews, Innkeeper, Windows. ...
1848 Charles Whitting Brick and Coal Merchant.

The nearest court was in Weston where town constables enforced order in the streets, especially at night when violence spilled out of the many beer-houses. Some of these jurors may have sat on a trial in 1844 of the assailant of Constable Hill who was stabbed while quelling a drunken disturbance. Judges and juries took a vigorous view of such behaviour and the culprit was speedily transported to Australia.

Uphill had little crime, although when Obadiah Miles got drunk in the Dolphin, a Mr Mounter stole his purse, left the inn and stole some of his employer's tools. Mounter, also known as Smith, worked for Abraham Palmer, one of Uphill's shoemakers.

Juvenile crime showed a similar pattern. With no schools and limited employment, Weston had a large under-class of what the *Mercury* called "street Arabs" – wildly unruly boys whose judicial punishments included immediate flogging with a birch or cat o' nine tails by a policeman. Uphill was spared this problem as boys worked with or for their fathers. Thomas Bailey, William Goss and William Hill were charged with setting fire to the sedge at the side of Uphill Road but they were not villagers.

With police confining its underclass to the back streets, Weston continued to attract holiday visitors, many renting villas or hotel suites for the season.

Progress came with them. Town Commissioners were established by Parliament to levy rates, borrow money, light, pave and drain the town. The town had three doctors, including Dr Robert E Gegg, perhaps a member of the Uphill family.

By 1841, a gas works served fifty private subscribers and illuminated forty-two street lamps; a printing press opened; and the first local newspaper *The Westonian* appeared in 1843. The big attractions of Weston were its healthy air, pure water, sea-swimming and local drives to picturesque spots such as Uphill, still unlit, unpaved and undrained.

Panoramic sketch 1846 [NSM]

❑ ❑ ❑ ❑ ❑

Chapter 9. Field Names

In a tiny rural parish, names of houses and roads were unnecessary, but every field had a name, still used in 1843 when they were recorded in Uphill's Tithe Apportionment. Tithes were an annual tax of 10% of the value of property paid by land-holders to the parish church. Every field name told a story of location, area, quality, crop or possession. Although the stories are forgotten, a few of the names remain. Slimeridge Warth and Newnham Warth were fenced pastures reclaimed from the river bank. Walborough, where the Pill joins the Axe, sounds Roman as does Cold Harbour, the patch of woodland by the track across the golf course. Brick Close was the clay-pit and brickyard at today's Beach End Road. Sandcroft gave its name to Sandcroft Cottages, House and Avenue.

Rural communities had a Pound or Point where stray animals were secured pending payment of a fine. The Point was where the Pill runs into the Axe, then an island. Two fields were called Manor Pound and Pound Paddock, suggesting pounds near Manor Farm. Pendennis could mean "animal pen on the Down". Folly House and Garden were on the right going up Folly Lane. Crook meant a hill, Hay an enclosure and Leaze a pasture. The list was long:

The Warth	Walborough	Strowd Leaze
Eben Warth	Great Ham	East Georges Leaze
Slimeridge Warth	Cobblers Ham	Moor Leaze
Newnham Warth	In Great Ship Ham	Rhyne Furlong
Belwicks	Little Ship Ham	Stream Furlong
Tankard	New Close	East Stream Furlong
Holcombes	Bow Close	Manor Pound
Snite Hays	Brick Close	Pound Paddock
Jordans Ass	Symes Close	Mushell Paddock
Gore	Saltwicks	Folly House and Paddock
Priddy	Tynings	The Point
Cold Harbour	New Tyning	Hitchens
Pendennis	Tyning in Upper Way	Bartletts
Black Acre	Barton	Maltlands
Poplar Acre	In Meers	Oatland
Ham Six Acres	Strand Hotel	Crook
East Townsend Acre	Godney	Elm Hay Orchard
West Townsend Acre	East Field	Stars Ground
East Home 12 Acres	Common Mead	Roses
The 12 Acres	Sandcroft	East Roses
Poor Five Acres	Upcroft	West Roses
	East Leaze	

❑ ❑ ❑ ❑ ❑

Chapter 10. Brunel's Railway

In 1835 these ancient fields were pillaged by Britain's new industrial age. Isambard Kingdom Brunel planned the route of the Bristol and Exeter Railway to run from Bristol, past Weston and between Uphill and Bleadon.

The work was done by hand with picks, shovels and wheelbarrows, augmented by gunpowder. The foreman or ganger started work with a blast on a whistle and the shout "Blow-up, blow-up" and ended it with the shout "Yo-ho, yo-ho". Each man shovelled 20 tons of earth a day into wagons. For this he could earn 5 shillings, much more than any other manual worker. But there were no safety procedures and no compensation for death or injury. Two were buried in Uphill in March 1840: Charles Jenkins (16) and Henry Brean (15).

Known as navvies, the workmen tramped in gangs between jobs, living in crowded and unsanitary rough huts alongside the track although a few found lodgings nearby. In their distinctive clothing of moleskin trousers, canvas shirts and coloured waistcoats, they earned a reputation for fighting, hard living and hard drinking. Respectable people feared them as a threat to social order.

This was the army that camped in Uphill's fields bringing the biggest social upheaval since the Enclosures. Mr WM Peniston was Brunel's resident site engineer; a rail contractor Robert Chesterfield and his wife Ann boarded in the village with publican John Harris; three labourers, William Brown, John Brown, Joseph Gilbert and his wife Elizabeth lodged with publican John Yeatman; and John Jackson rented a room with James Groves the baker.

Railway Navvies

Railways meant big money for investors, landowners and traders. One of the owners of the land required was Lord of the Manor Charles Henry Payne of Uphill House. The bankrupt Payne seized this opportunity to rescue his finances by selling land. At the same time he asserted his social position by demanding his own station platform on the new line. Brunel agreed and went ahead with a cutting 69 feet deep between Uphill Hill and Bleadon Hill. As this split farms and separated communities, he bridged the cutting with the highest single-span brick arch in the country. The arch spanned 110 feet, 63 feet above the line and was supported during building on a semi-circular structure of timber.

On the Weston side of the bridge stood a small elevated platform, Mr Payne's personal railway station.

Building an arched railway bridge

The railway company paid its labourers a month in arrears and credited wages to selected suppliers who set their own inflated prices. The prospect of good wages had attracted Mendip miners to join the Uphill navvies. Notoriously independent and murderously tough, the miners went on strike until they had full payment in cash. Brunel was on the site and agreed to look into their demands, but the men were too angry to trust him and the strike looked like escalating into a riot. With no political representation, no trades unions and no rights, exploited workers turned readily to rioting to express their discontent. Employers responded by invoking the Riot Act which enforced dispersal within one hour of any gathering of over 12 persons on the order of a magistrate. Brunel sent for the nearest magistrate, Thomas Tutton Knyfton of Uphill Lodge. In his *Seaboard of Mendip* Francis Knight wrote:

> Without loss of time Mr Knyfton started for the scene of action, and taking the Riot Act in his hand, passed into the thick of the crowd, where he was greeted with menacing language and uplifted pick-axes. With calmness he talked to the men, telling them that law was stronger than force, and that all would be well if they acted in the spirit of their contract; if otherwise, a troop of cavalry from Horfield Barracks would probably be marching on Uphill. The navvies grew calmer, and, by the tact, good temper and resolution on the part of this ruler of the district, peace prevailed and the frightened village shopkeepers were reassured.

The cavalry that Mr Knyfton could have deployed were the North Somerset Yeomanry, squads of volunteer farmers riding their own horses. First formed to fight Napoleon, they now quelled Somerset's growing industrial unrest. As employers themselves, they were ready to be involved. Their tactic was to ride among demonstrators dispersing them with blows from the flat of their sabres, but as everyone in Uphill knew very well from Welsh sailors in the harbour, troops had recently shot dead 22 rioters in Newport.

The strikers were silenced, work resumed and the railway opened between Bristol and Bridgwater on 9th June 1841. To mark the occasion a special train from Bridgwater called at each station to take local gentry and share-holders to a grand dinner in Bristol. Mr and Mrs Payne, formally dressed for the occasion, stood on their personal platform and waited for the train. It came and it whistled but it did not stop and for Charles Henry Payne it never did. The agreement had been to build the platform, not to stop trains for him. Furious, he turned to the law for redress. He lost his case and his money and fell again into bankruptcy. But he is remembered. His temper earned him the local nickname of "Devil" Payne and the bridge over the cutting is still known as Devil's Bridge.

We may assume that Magistrate Thomas Knyfton had a place of honour at the Bristol and Exeter dinner table and perhaps also on its board of directors.

Isambard   Kingdom   Brunel

Cheaper and quicker, the railways replaced travel by stage coach and, without turnpike tolls, road surfaces decayed. Ironically, Uphill Toll-Gate stood between Brunel's cutting and Payne's station. The rail journey for 1st class passengers from Bristol to London took 9½ hours.

In 1844 the Cheap Trains Act introduced 3rd class travel at a penny a mile in open carriages attached to goods trains with no guaranteed time of arrival. Cheap day-trips brought a new class of holidaymaker to the sea-side. Uphill's farmers found that the noise and steam of passing engines did not cause cattle to abort or dry up as feared. They could get their produce to market quickly and cheaply while fish from Uphill Bay had a direct line to London's markets and restaurants. What's more, punctual trains brought accurate time-keeping to a community that had never needed clocks or watches.

The railway bridged the Axe at Lympsham, closing it to navigation and diverting all cargoes to Uphill Wharf. Progressive industrialists built an iron steamer at Bristol for a sea-route "between Cardiff and Uphill designed to unite the Taff and Exeter Railways", but the service never materialised. The nearest approach was an advertisement in 1844 for:

> Boat trips to Cardiff etc from Uphill Landing stage
> – Capt Stone

Nevertheless, Uphill's seaborne trade became sufficient for the appointment of Customs Officer JB Adams as a Tide Waiter to collect import duties. He was killed in a fall from his horse in June 1850. Coastguard Cottages, with their distinctive gothic windows, were built at about this time. As smugglers still worked the Channel coast, Coastguard John Prankard had a Revenue cutter moored on the Pill. He was supported by three part-time preventive men who had off-duty jobs as farm-hand, barber and shoemaker.

The sea still took its toll. The Churchwardens' Accounts in 1847 recorded:

> Paid to George Gould for picking up a dead body on the Strand   £0 5s 0d

❑ ❑ ❑ ❑ ❑

Chapter 11. The Methodists

While navvies rioted and the Church of England planned a new parish church, a fresh force for change reached the village. In December 1840, 62-year old farmer John Evans sold a plot of land for £5 to a group of small businessmen: draper Matthew Day, builder John Palmer, butcher William Smart, yeoman George Ewens, mason Benjamin Brice, painter John Williams and cordwainers (shoemakers) George Vowles and Leonard Tilley.

They were Methodist Trustees and within a year they had built their Chapel next door to the new church. The entrance opened directly from Uphill Road into a single stone-floored room with a pulpit in the centre in front of the choir.

This simple architectural directness grew from Methodism's reliance on vigorous preaching of the Christian faith and its practical expression in care for the poor, for widows and orphans, for social outcasts, even for prisoners. These attitudes attracted large congregations of working people away from the formal rituals of the class-conscious established church.

In 1851 Leonard Tilley, the 45-year old shoemaker, became Uphill's Methodist minister, assisted by visiting lay preachers. Lay preachers were working men with little formal education but with intelligence and faith, who had learned to speak effectively in public. Across the country such men were using their skills in a new form of politics, forming trades unions to protect exploited workers. In London, they compelled the government to bring down food prices and then demanded reform of Parliament, including universal secret voting for all men over 21. This was too much: the government filled the streets with troops, barricades and cannon, blocking these first small steps towards democracy. All this took place in London but, on Brunel's railway, London was now only 12 hours from Uphill, mechanised printing presses spread the new political doctrines to all who could read and the Methodists ensured that their congregations could read.

Wesleyan Chapel Sign

□ □ □ □ □

Part 3:   Life and Death 1850 - 1860

Chapter 12.   Uphill in 1850

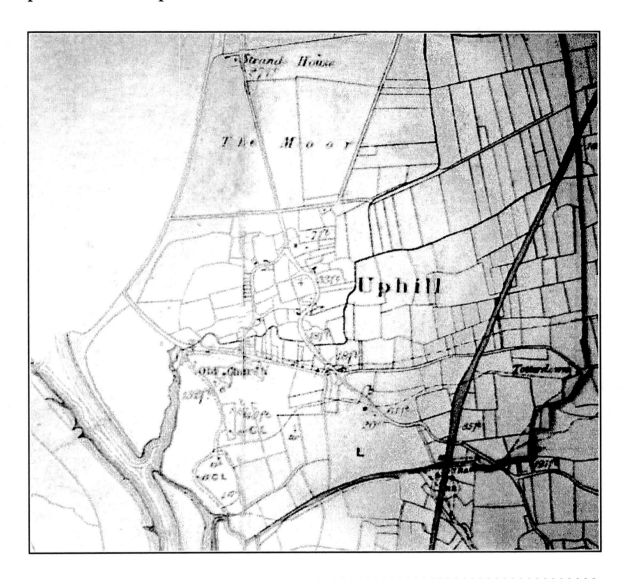

Population 422: 205 male + 217 female

Rector: Rev John Thomas Fisher; 1854 Rev Frederick Trevor MA
Curate: Rev George Cuff
Methodist Minister: Leonard Tilley
Parish Clerk and Sexton: George Haynes;
Parish Registrar: Samuel Norman; Post Office Receiver: John Biss Delay
Schoolmaster: John Jones
Lord of the Manor: Charles Henry Payne of Uphill House

Only 30% of Uphill's inhabitants in 1851 had been born in the village. Although almost all the rest did come from Somerset, some sailors, customs men and servants of the gentry had moved in from other counties. Ten heads of family were villagers, with six surnames between them: John Delay, Robert Every and John Jones; Thomas and Richard Russell; Henry and Richard Poole; Samuel, Jesse and Joseph Norman. Only two complete families, parents and children, were born in the village: Richard and Sarah Poole, and John and Maryann Jones. The Pooles were farmers and their baby son Obed was to play an important part in village life. John Jones was the village tailor. With his wife Maryann he also taught and lived in the Parish Day School, the thatched schoolhouse and cottage in Uphill Castle grounds.

At a time when the average life span was 40 years, Uphill's oldest inhabitants were widows Jane Isgar (91) and Elizabeth Binding (80), parish clerk George Haynes and his wife Hannah, both 80 and John Curry (80), gentleman's gardener. Villagers in their 70s included Ann Taylor (78), Jane Delay (74), Jacob (74) and Hannah (72) Tripp, Thomas Follett (72) and 70-year olds Samuel Bailey, Daniel Jones and Samuel Clarke. Youngest recorded workers were Mary Crandon, a 13-year old live-in house servant at the Dolphin, and John Vowells, an agricultural labourer at 12.

A boarding school met the demands of the rising middle classes for private education. Like the Rev John Henry Gegg's original boarding school thirty years earlier, it was probably based in the Castle, owned but not yet occupied by the Knyftons. Thomas Warton was the schoolmaster, helped by his wife Hester, her sister Charlotte Camm, a housemaid and a cook. They had 18 boys on roll, mostly from the south-west but some from as far away as Yorkshire and Neath. One pupil was Henry William Payne aged 16 from Tetbury, Gloucesterhire. It may be coincidence, but the Gegg family had originated in Gloucestershire, there had been a Henry William born to the Rev John Henry Gegg in Uphill in 1813, and families did keep using the same Christian names. Although the school closed in 1852, schoolmaster Thomas Warton remained registered as a village juror.

The Census recorded 422 people, 22 more than in 1841. They lived in 72 houses instead of 64 but many old properties had been rebuilt. This is evident from the building tradesmen: four brickmakers, three masons, three mason's labourers, two carpenters, a plasterer, a painter and apprentice and — a real sign of progress — a plumber. He was John Biss Delay and the business was big enough to employ two assistants. This still left him time to work as the Post Office Receiver: mail came to him from Weston-super-Mare and he distributed it round the village. Victorian progress was also signalled by eight resident railway workers.

With cheap mass-produced cotton cloth replacing home-woven fabrics, village women found the need for six dressmakers, while the men had one part-time tailor. Two shoemakers and an apprentice made and repaired footwear. Four women described themselves as laundresses and three as washerwomen. Master baker James Groves (48) provided bread for the village. His day's work began at midnight when he made the dough. Fast, hard work in the oven-heat of the bakery filled the rest of the night. At dawn he delivered his bread round the village, while his wife sold it from the bakery door. William Counsell, one of the stonemasons, had a house big enough to accommodate his wife Maria's general shop, their two young daughters, William's unmarried brother Robert, also a mason, a lodger and a servant, 14-year old Caroline Hunt, to help Mrs Counsell clean and cook.

Resident domestic service was the main occupation for women and girls. Of 50 working females aged 13 to 65, 21 were maidservants, 4 cooks, 1 housekeeper, 2 nursemaids and a nurse. Working from their own homes were two more nurses. With no medical services available, country people turned to old women who were well versed in practical midwifery and traditional remedies. Some big houses included one such nurse in the domestic establishment. Although they were termed "nurse" the word "witch" could well have been whispered. As late as 1867, the *Mercury* ran a leader on witchcraft in Somerset, referring to Ann Davis, a "witch" at Axbridge. One of Uphill's three nurses was Elizabeth Binding who shared a cottage with Jane Isgar. Both were farm-worker's widows, registered paupers living on payments from the parish rate. Known as Old Jenny, Jane had "all faculties perfect" on her 92nd birthday in April 1851.

Uphill's 205 men and boys shared 34 different Christian names, 13 of them Biblical. Most popular were John 29, James 21, Thomas 21, William 19, Joseph 15 and George 14. The 217 females shared 38 names, 8 Biblical. Favourites were Mary 32 (of which 11 were Mary Ann), Elizabeth 26 (and another 12 Eliza), Ann 24, Jane 15 and Sarah 14. One young lady was christened Temperance and another Olympia.

35% of employed males – 37 men and boys aged between 12 and 80 – worked on the land. Their employers included 9 farmers: Joseph Hancock, his son Joseph and his son-in-law Richard Poole; Miss Mary Hancock, Edward Luff, John Quick, Edward Sellick, Robert Every and James Evans. James Fisher ran a poultry business from his market garden and made enough to pay two maids and a boy servant. Another market gardener, 70-year old Samuel Clarke, put his son and grandson out to work while his wife took in lodgers. Two blacksmiths, James Parker and John Wilde, made and mended machinery and equipment and provided farrier services for horses.

But carpenter Ferdinand Cox spotted the needs of an ambitious gentry and branched out into the new business of coach building. He employed two assistants who lodged with him: Michael Collings as coach painter and Solomon Smith as apprentice wheelwright, their board and keep being part of their wage. His wife had a servant-girl to help look after their two young children, his aunt and his mother-in-law Hannah Taylor. She ran a grocer's and draper's shop licensed to sell beer. Unsurprisingly, Ferdinand Cox was soon earning enough to qualify as a ratepayer and juror.

The village had the same three inns, with Halfway House now also known as Strand House. Mrs Ann Every was landlady of the Dolphin while her husband Thomas was away as captain of a collier bringing in Welsh coal for his coal merchant's business. Farmer Joseph Hancock ran the Ship Inn with his wife Charlotte as landlady and Eliza Bishop as resident barmaid. He sold it in 1858, but magistrates in the Victuallers' Licensing Court refused a certificate:

> in consequence of some informalities in the transfer to Mr H Seaman, who has recently entered upon the premises.

❑ ❑ ❑ ❑ ❑

Chapter 13. Social pyramid

Uphill's gentry sat on top of a Victorian social pyramid. They were land-owners, investing inherited wealth in new industrial ventures, foreign trade and insurance. Their homes were manor houses embellished with coats of arms and surrounded by elaborate formal gardens. Domestic staff met every need.

Ladies looked elegant in crinoline skirts, supported on wire cages or bustles to make them stand out at the back, below slender waists held in by tightly-laced corsets.

Gentlemen wore knee-length frock coats in silk or velvet, silk waistcoats and shirts with starched high collars and cravats. Woollen vests and long underpants kept them warm in their draughty houses. They wore top hats or perhaps the newly fashionable bowler hats and carried fine canes. Beards and side-boards were universal. Young children of both sexes wore fashionable dresses with pinafores. Daughters were still educated at home by governesses. Sons went to boarding school and university, acquiring an education that was scholarly rather than practical, a public school accent and a strict code of gentlemanly conduct. This code entailed a strong sense of responsibility for those less fortunate, while firmly keeping them in their social place. The eldest son inherited the estate; failing a son, the inheritance went to the nearest male relative.

Such privileged lives set a standard for the socially ambitious whose income was earned rather than inherited:

yeoman farmers, master tradesmen, businessmen, physicians and surgeons, solicitors. They learned social rules from Mrs Beeton's book *Household Management*. Some gave themselves the nomination of Gent or Esq when they retired. Thomas Follett, a 72-year old widower, did this when he moved to Uphill. He had been one of the first public chemists, socially somewhere between a doctor and a shopkeeper. His son moved a step up the ladder to deal in property as a conveyancer. His two unmarried daughters in their thirties were helped in their domestic tasks by a resident cook and a 14-year old errand boy. By 1854, the Jurors' list named innkeeper Charles Tutton and baker Josiah Coles as Gentlemen.

This rising middle class wanted status, bigger houses, more ostentatious possessions, personal servants, public schools for their sons and pretty social accomplishments to help their daughters marry into the landed gentry. All this cost money which meant lower wages for their employees already living in unhealthy squalor with little future save the parish dole or the workhouse, brightened by the prospect of celestial glory as promised in church and chapel. Mrs S Whitting Wheatstone House.or and chief landowner of the soil.llick, Thmoas Whitting*; arrill, Thomas Lear, Rev F Trevor,

Workers who aspired to a little independence were easily kept in firm legal check by their masters:

TERMS FOR RENTING A PLOT OF GARDEN GROUND,

SITUATE IN THE PARISH OF UPHILL IN THE COUNTY OF SOMERSET.

First – *Robert Arthur Kinglake of Weston-super-Mare in the County of Somerset Esquire* agrees to Let, and *Uriah Baker of the same place* agrees to take, All *those three acres of Garden Ground being part of a Field situate near the Drove in the Parish of Uphill*

From the *Twenty first* day of *December next* and so from year to year, until either the Landlord or Tenant shall give Six Calendar Months' Notice in Writing to the other of *his* intention to terminate the Tenancy on the Twenty ninth day of September then next.

Second – The Rent to be the Sum of *Eight Pounds* Sterling per annum to be payable on the Twenty-fourth day of June in every year during the said Tenancy, the first payment to be made on the Twenty-fourth day of June next.

Third – The Landlord, without any previous Notice, to have power to expel and turn out the Tenant from the possession of the said Plot of Land, in case the Rent demanded and not paid on the said Twenty-fourth day of June in any year, or if the Tenant shall be guilty of wilful encroachment, or shall be convicted of any offence by way of trespass against his neighbour in respect of his Allotment, or shall become a Bankrupt, or Insolvent, or suffer an Execution to be made or levied on any part of his Premises. The standing Crops, in the event of either of the above cases to be forfeited, and become the property of the Landlord, and to be dealt with as he may think proper.

Fourth – The Tenant shall keep up and repair, in a manner satisfactory to the Landlord, all Fences bounding or lying opposite to his Land, either

of Walling or Quick Fence, under the penalty of Expulsion set out in the third clause.

Fifth – The ground to be cultivated only as a garden, and in a good and husbandlike manner, and to be well and sufficiently Manured. No Hemp, Flax or Teasels to be grown on any part thereof.

Sixth – The Landlord to pay all Rates, Taxes, Assessments, and Rent-Charge in lieu of Tithes.

Seventh – The Tenant to yield up immediate possession, if required, for Building purposes, when Crops shall be valued by Arbitration.

Witness the hands of the parties the *Thirtieth* day of *November* One Thousand Eight Hundred and *Fifty-nine.*

The mark of   +   Uriah Baker   A

Signed by the within named by making his mark thereto of Uriah Baker and William Smith in the presence of MH Norris.

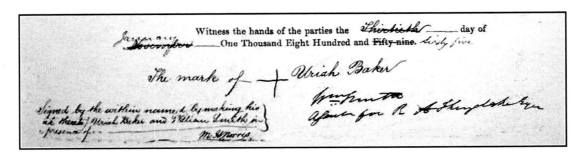

Uriah Baker's mark, 1865

Chapter 14. Thomas Knyfton's new Castle

The widowed Thomas Knyfton, aged 51, was firmly established in high society. In 1851 he owned the Castle but still lived in Castle Lodge, served by a resident staff of butler, housekeeper, cook and housemaid, while his coachman occupied a cottage next door. He had another home in his birthplace, Westbury-sub-Mendip, where he owned land and was Lord of the Manor. Thomas Knyfton had risen fast through the County hierarchy: a Deputy Lieutenant of Somerset when only 34, he was now High Sheriff. In 1853 he finally displaced the Paynes from Uphill's gentry when he bought the Lordship of the Manor — and Manor Farm — from Charles Henry Payne's assignees in bankruptcy for £500.

Striking architecture with intricate stone work and decorative stencilling followed the style of Pugin, the fashionable and influential Victorian architect. Pugin was an eccentric genius whose designs, based on the medieval pointed arch, had recently been used in the new Houses of Parliament. A tower rose above the Castle's roof and a north porch replaced the original southern entrance.

The magnificent new drawing room, 30 feet long and 22 feet wide, looked east through a large window. Its vaulted and panelled ceiling was decorated with medallions and a multi-coloured stencilled design. The walls were covered with

Thomas Tutton Knyfton   [UVS]

Georgiana Knyfton   [UVS]

A brass plate in the new village church recorded Thomas Knyfton's second marriage. On 12th July 1855 he married Georgiana Sophia Colston, daughter of the Rev William Hungerford Colston DD, well-known Bristolian and Deputy Lieutenant of Somerset.

Across the road from the church, he extended the Castle as a wedding present and also as a statement of his powerful social and economic status. Timber scaffolding and stacks of stone bordered the way into Uphill as the work proceeded.

newly fashionable wallpaper that not only looked splendid but absorbed the effect of smoke from the great cast iron fireplace. Oak panels walled the dining room and a smoking room provided a retreat for the gentlemen. Carved oak book-cases lined a fine library. An octagonal hall and windows of stained glass followed Pugin's gothic style. New staff quarters and cellars provided service areas to meet the family's domestic needs.

In all, the Knyfton home extended to seven bedrooms, two dressing rooms, a nursery, and a bathroom. While Uphill could provide the stone

Uphill Castle mid-century
[Permission kindly given by Col Frith to use the image from SRO file A\AEH/19/9]

masons and labourers to meet the architect's demands, the London firm JG Grace & Co was brought in to work on the interior. Grace's specialised in Pugin's designs and came fresh from decorating the new Houses of Parliament.

A high stone wall with grand Lodge gates enclosed a coach house and stables and a dozen acres of gardens and ground. Gardeners cultivated exotic flowers and fruit in a heated conservatory tiled in colours reminiscent of medieval church flooring.

Although involved in village affairs for the next three decades, Thomas Knyfton was frequently away from his grand Uphill home.

Uphill Castle Lodge   *[UVS]*

In Westbury-sub-Mendip, the Manor passed to the Church but he remained one of the chief landowners and the family had a memorial in the church. The Post Office Directory of 1859 has no address for the Knyftons in either Uphill or Westbury. The 1861 Census records no residents in the Castle and no Knyftons in Uphill. The residents in the Castle for the 1871 Census were Miss Penelope Brice (85) identified as "aunt of Head of House", her woman companion, a butler and footman, the cook Mrs Mary Ann Keen (53), and four women servants. In the 1881 Census, a new cook, Miss Harriet Elizabeth Seward (35), took over occupancy of the Castle, aided by three domestic servants, Elizabeth Redwood (46), Elizabeth Cox (17) and Annie Davis (21).

The Knyfton crest over the Lodge gates   [UVS]

❏ ❏ ❏ ❏ ❏

Chapter 15. The Whitting family

Another powerful family appeared in Uphill's 1851 Census. Charles Whitting was born in 1813 in Bristol, son of another Charles Whitting, Master Plumber and WC Manufacturer, and Mary Bliss (1772-1844), daughter of Mariner John Bliss of Uphill. In 1845 the younger Charles Whitting joined the gentry when he married 25-year old Anne Harris Morgan Williams, daughter of Edward Morgan Williams a landowner and magistrate in Glamorgan. A son Charles Edward was born the same year and a daughter Anne in 1847.

The family moved to Uphill in the late 1840s where another daughter Mary Gwenllian and a second son Edward Morgan were born. Charles Edward, however, was brought up by his maternal grandparents in Wales, returning to Uphill when they died in 1860. Now aged 38, Charles Whitting's wealth came from a variety of sources. He first qualified as an Uphill Juror in 1848 as a Brick and Coal Merchant. By 1851, the Census described him as a land owner, coal merchant and brick maker, employing 16 men. His domestic establishment included his wife and children, a nurse, a nursemaid, a maidservant and a manservant. Charles Whitting's jury qualification now classified him as Gentleman as well as Merchant. He built the palatial Sandcroft House as the Whitting family home and by 1863 was included in Burke's *Landed Gentry* and had acquired a coat of arms.

Charles Whitting's uncle George Whitting retired from the East India Service, the organisation that governed Queen Victoria's Indian Empire, and came to lodge in the village with William Counsell. In 1854 a Thomas Whitting, Coal Dealer – perhaps George's son – joined the jurors' roll. As *The Times* commented:

> What is most coveted in this country, more than wealth, more than talent, more than fame, more even than power, is aristocratic position, to obtain which other things are sought only as the means.

Charles Harrill, a house proprietor, lived next door to Sandcroft. His brother Thomas, another land owner, lived in Walnut Cottage next door to their widowed mother Jane, also a landed lady. A neighbour was Robert Counsell, whose daughter was his servant. Another landed proprietor was Thomas Macy Leir, with wife, 3 children a grand-daughter; a resident cook and a groom.

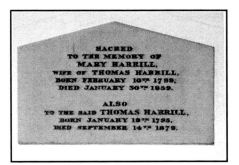

SACRED
TO THE MEMORY OF
MARY HARRILL,
WIFE OF THOMAS HARRILL,
BORN FEBRUARY 10TH 1799;
DIED JANUARY 30TH 1859.

ALSO
TO THE SAID THOMAS HARRILL,
BORN JANUARY 18TH 1795,
DIED SEPTEMBER 14TH 1879.

Sandcroft   House   *[UVS]*

Chapter 16. Uphill House

Uphill House renovated   *[UVS]*

John Monson Carrow Esq of Stoberry bought Uphill House in 1853 from Charles Henry Payne's bankrupt estate. His widowed mother, Mrs Mary Carrow of Weston-super-Mare, gave him a block of investments to help pay for major restoration, the first since Jonathan Gegg had moved in 75 years earlier.

Within a year, builder John Perry of Weston-super-Mare transformed the place creating the building now known as Uphill Grange. He moved an outer wall to extend the drawing room, rebuilt the entire roof, opened a new private entrance in the South Front which he faced with stucco, renewed floors, windows and doors throughout, "removed the mould and constructed a new floor in Mr Carrow's room to create an air flow beneath", laid a Pennant Stone floor in the back kitchens, larder and pantry and improved the boot house, coal house and servants' privy. Updated plumbing included "two new pan water-closets, one in the main bedroom". As there was no mains water or drainage, rain-water was pumped to flush the WCs into a soakaway. Domestic water came from wells – sunk alongside the soakaways – or from rain-water channelled from the roof into cisterns. The kitchen cistern was built into the pantry roof, keeping it cool. Tanks, pipes and gutters were made of lead. For this work John Perry was paid £1,420.

The rough-cast on the North Front, East and West Ends was replaced in 1853-4 at a cost of £164 12s. When a new garden wall was built, the mason recommended stone from the grounds to ensure good quality, as "stone from the quarry opened by Mr Whitting near the Plantation will not produce proper materials". Finally, grand new iron entrance gates closed the road into the grounds.

Uphill House Gates   *[UVS]*

John Carrow did not live to enjoy his magnificent mansion and the following year his widow, Mrs Frances Gertrude Carrow, prepared to sell. The inventory defined the rooms as:

> Drawing Room, Boudoir, Dining Room, Morning Room, Entrance Hall and WC, Closet, Landing, NE Bedroom no 1, SE Bedroom no 2, Dressing Room, SW Bedroom no 3, West Dressing Room, NW Bedroom no 4, WC, Staircase and Landing, SE Attic no 1, SW attic no 2, Closet, No 3, No 4, No 5, Butler's Room, Kitchen, Scullery, Larder, Passage, Cellars, Stable, Harness Room, Bedroom over, Yard, Lawn.

In 1855, the Rev William Robert Crotch, a 61-year old widower and retired clergyman, bought Uphill House. He moved in with his son William Duppe Crotch (22) and daughters Catharine (17) and Charlotte (11). Their household staff comprised three unmarried women: a cook, Sarah Ann Test, and two housemaids, Mary Rainsford and Emily Sparks, as well as a married couple, Thomas Griffin, from Hutton, the coachman, and his wife Charlotte, another housemaid.

Like many 19th century clergymen, the Rev Crotch was an enthusiastic amateur antiquarian and archaeologist. Uphill provided plenty of scope. In May 1859, Weston-super-Mare Natural History Society spent a morning at the Uphill cutting of the new railway where they examined the "remarkable position of the strata there exposed". They moved on to Uphill House to inspect the "valuable and extensive museum of the Rev Mr Crotch", before walking down to explore Uphill Cliff Caverns.

Clergymen were wealthy members of the gentry with social obligations to local people. When Uphill villagers felt there was something to celebrate, they marched in procession behind a brass band round the big houses where the owners:

> vied with each other in placing before their unexpected, but nevertheless most welcome guests, "substantials" not forgetting full frothing flagons of "genuine home brew'd" and brimming bumpers of cider to wash down the edibles.

William Crotch soon found that Uphill House was on this hospitality route. He joined such other benefactors as the Knyfton and Whitting families in paying for "most substantial and excellent dinner prepared in prime style for the poorer classes" at the Dolphin and Ship inns at Easter and Christmas.

But villagers were not averse to giving hints and "A Churchgoer" wrote anonymously to the *Mercury*:

> Uphill Parish Church has been much improved of late years and we are indebted to the Rector for this good work; but how is it that with a number of wealthy inhabitants they cannot give the poor old parishioners a little fire-place in the church during winter months. The music is very good, and better than in some larger churches; but if Mr Crotch and some of the parishioners would give us an organ it would be better than the little harmonium.

Uphill House was home to the Rev Crotch until 1870.

❑ ❑ ❑ ❑ ❑

Chapter 17. The Rectory and William Lisle Bowles

The Rectory

[UVS]

Born in Langford, the 47-year old Rector of the parish, the Rev John Thomas Fisher, lived in the Rectory with his 36-year old wife Eliza. Their three daughters and a son, all born in Uphill, were taught at home by governess Miss Anne Lea. Two maids lived in to do the housework. A Weston Guide-book of 1852 described their home, now built over as St Aubyn's Avenue:

> Near the church is the snug parsonage, thickly covered with roses, jasmine, myrtles and vines, and mantled with festoons of various plants; its russet-thatched roof relieved by luxuriant masses of foliage – a true picture of English home scenery, which in the wide world for comfort and tranquillity is not surpassed.

A high stone wall round the grounds enclosed a conservatory, greenhouses, vineries and kitchen gardens, outhouses and sheds as well as stables and a coach house for the Rector's carriage and pair.

Splendid shrubberies had been planted by the Rev William Thomas Bowles, Rector from 1769 to 1786. His son, William Lisle Bowles, after a childhood in Uphill Rectory, followed his father into the church eventually becoming a Canon of Salisbury Cathedral. He established himself as a poet, recalling the view from Uphill:

> Behind that windmill, sailing round and round
> Like days on end revolving,
> Bleadon lies, ...
> And Weston there, where I remember a few cottages.
> Sprinkling the sands, uplifts its tower, and shines,
> As if in conscious beauty, o'er the scene. ...
> And yet that hill, the sight is to my eyes
> Familiar as those sister isles that sit
> In the mid Channel.

In his eighties, Bowles described his childhood at Uphill:

> Was it but yesterday I heard the roar
> Of these white coursing waves, and trod the shore,
> A young and playful child – but yesterday?
> Now I return with locks of scattered grey
> And wasted strength; for many, many years
> Have passed, some marked by joy, and some by tears, Since last we parted. As I gaze around
> I think of Time's fleet step that makes no sound.
> In yonder vale, beneath the hill-top tower,
> My father decked the village pastor's bower;
> Now he, and all beneath whose knees I played,
> Cold in the narrow cell of death are laid.

He praised Uphill's gentry and their benevolence in the modern world of greedy industrialism:

How false the charge, how foul the calumny
On England's generous aristocracy,
That, wrapped in sordid selfish apathy,
They feel not for the poor!
      Ask is it true?
Lord of the whirling wheels, the charge is false!
Ten thousand charities adorn the land,
Beyond thy bold conception, from this source.
What cottage child but has been neatly clad,
And taught its earliest lesson from their care?
Witness that schoolhouse, mantled with festoon
Of various plants, which fancifully wreath
Its mullion windows, and that rustic porch,
Whence the low hum of infant voices blend
With airs of spring, without. Now, all alive
The greensward rings with play, among the shrubs
Hushed the long murmur of the morning's task,
Before the pensive matron's desk!

John Betjeman said of the poem:

> He is describing the village school of his childhood at Uphill, Somerset, within sound of the Severn sea. And he goes on to picture old people, almsmen and almswomen, pensioned by private charities of the past.

A stone in the floor of Salisbury Cathedral commemorates:

> The Reverend
> WILLIAM LISLE BOWLES
> M.A
> Canon Residentiary of
> this Cathedral
> Born Sept 25th 1762
> Died April 7th 1850

❑ ❑ ❑ ❑ ❑

Chapter 18. Sea Trade

With the quarries clattering and blasting away in the background, Uphill Wharf was a dirty, noisy place where men and horses sweated to provide power for block and tackle, windlass and derrick. Sloops of around 25 tons brought in coal, timber and salt, sailing out with cargoes of Uphill bricks, tiles and lime. As these were all sailing vessels, reaching the Wharf from the River Axe via the Pill required a technique known as "drudging". The boat came in on the flood tide, stern first, dragging an anchor to control speed so that the rudder would still operate. Once at the Pill, the boat was warped or towed to the Wharf by a horse or local lads.

The bulk of the coal came from Wales, with some from the Forest of Dean loaded at Lydney. Captain Cann was master of the best known coal-carrier, *Arabella*, later lost off Ilfracombe. Half a dozen barges at a time would arrive to unload into a yard with an officially calibrated weighbridge. The best coal sold for 10d a hundredweight. Local people bought their own, taking it away in a donkey cart. The poorest bought a pound weight at a time, carting it home in a wheel-barrow. Coal went by the cart-load into Weston for domestic use. The carts came back full of cinders and ash to be sifted and re-sold as ash-blocks and mortar for builders.

By the middle of the 19th century, 16,500 tons of Welsh coal came into Uphill every year. Nearly half a million tons went to other Bristol Channel ports while over 100,000 tons took the long sea-route round Land's End to the major English Channel harbours. Her Majesty's Customs kept an eye on things, Mr Carter replacing Mr SG Deeble as Chief Customs Officer in 1858.

In those confidently expansive times, such trade attracted the attention of big business. A proposal in the 1850s envisaged Welsh passenger ferries sailing into the channel of the Axe to dock at a pontoon pier floating from Black Rock. From there, a causeway to the Uphill bank of the Axe would meet a new ¾-mile rail link with Uphill station. Warehouses and cranes would line the Axe. The Weston-super-Mare Pier, Steam Ferry and Railway Company raised £20,000 in £10 shares, many held by Weston Water Works and local businessmen. On August Bank Holiday 1854, Uphill village turned out to watch a trial run as the paddle-boat *Taliesin,* loaded with Welsh

holiday-makers, steamed into the Axe – and safely out again. Experts in the Dolphin and the Ship remained unconvinced. They were right; the idea came to nothing and within a month Uphill's pontoon pier had gone.

In May 1858 the *Mercury* announced to summer visitors:

> UPHILL - We are pleased to find that Capt Every has again placed two capital boats upon the Axe Ferry, crossing from this village to Brean Down. There are few more romantic or pretty rambles on this coast than on Brean Down....

A few months later, under the headline:

CONTEMPLATED DOCKS AT UPHILL

Weston's businessmen read how "the importance and utility of such a scheme, and the lucrative trade" made it "work of paramount importance". There would be a direct line of railway from Uphill to Wells to join the East Somerset line and also:

> direct communication with Southampton so that steamship companies may be supplied with coal from the Principality – a coal so superior in quality to all others for steam navigation purposes. The success of the undertaking is so certain ... that shares to the amount of nearly £100,000 have already been applied for.

Mindful of Weston's needs, where "trippers and trade have to land over rough stones and mire at Anchor Head" the *Mercury* insisted:

> The Docks at Uphill will not remove the necessity of a proper landing-place at Weston.

As businessmen looked at their ledgers, seamen still watched the weather. In February 1859:

> UPHILL - A few days since, part of the wreck of a ship floated in here, apparently one of the yards, upon which it is calculated that upwards of two tons weight of barnacles were attached. These extraordinary creatures were clustered in thousands, varying in length from the minutest measure to upwards of 30 inches. Various speculations of the time the timber must have been tossed in the water before getting such an accumulation of life were hazarded. Several gentlemen here and in Weston have obtained specimens to place in their collections.

And in April:

> LOSS OF THE SLOOP "AFFO" - This vessel, the property of and commanded by Mr William Coles of Sidney House in this town during her voyage from Lydney to Uphill, laden with coals, went down. The coastguard report that the vessel left Lydney and whilst proceeding down the Severn struck upon a bank or rock which completely stove in her keel causing her to sink immediately, giving Capt Coles, his son, a mate and pilot who were on board, barely time to escape in the small boat attached to the sloop. The vessel, which had been recently overhauled and thoroughly repaired, was not insured....

But a week later:

> THE "AFFO" - This vessel arrived at Uphill river on Wednesday, consequently our informant was incorrect last week. The vessel has received considerable damage; as for the cargo, it has been nearly all lost.

The following autumn the bay was hit by the worst storm for 50 years, followed by heavy snow.

❑ ❑ ❑ ❑ ❑

Chapter 19. Life in the Village

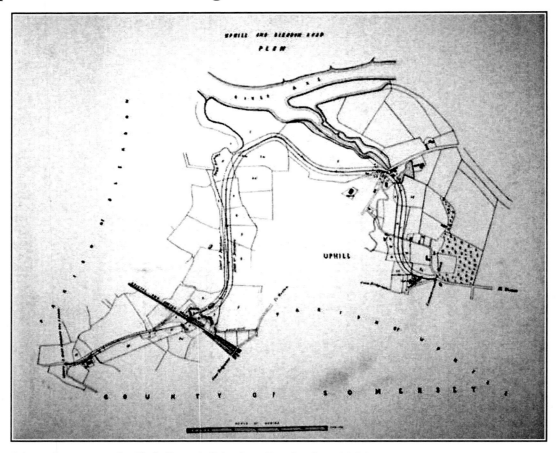

Planned new road: Uphill and Bleadon Road plan 1854
[Permission kindly given by SRO to use image from file Q/RUP/243]

The Batch, a steep narrow road, climbed out of Uphill to Bleadon. In 1854 a new road was planned to bypass this hill, running through the middle of the village from the Castle, between St Nicholas and the Rectory, across today's playing-field, down today's St Nicholas Road, along the north bank of the rhyne to the sluice, past the quarries and along today's bridle tracks to the toll-gate and railway bridge. The engineer's reference book for the project identified the owners of land that would be required, all familiar names. The pasture and plantation where the road would start was church land, bequeathed to "the Rector of the Parish" in the will of the Rev JT Fisher. Charles Whitting owned the stone quarries, lime-kiln and the Public Wharf. Thomas Whitting, his cousin, owned the second quarry. Charles also owned the coal yard with stable and pig strip, which were occupied by Thomas. Charles owned the clay pit which was occupied by John Drake a brickyard labourer. Land beside the rhyne was owned by TT Knyfton, named as Lord of the Manor. The scheme came to nothing although public rights of way still run along the route.

Slimeridge Farm was rebuilt, "with a graded slate roof" instead of the original thatch.

Slimeridge Farm
[Permission kindly given by SRO to use the image from file DD\X\VZ/5]

- 48 -

The *Mercury* reported approvingly in 1858:

> The whole of Uphill parish seems to be going through a thorough renovation. The drains are being repaired and extended: the roads widened by pulling down old intruding walls, and placing new ones in their stead; overhanging trees are being lopped, and many of the hedgerows nicely trimmed. A further improvement could be effected by shearing up an ornamental hedge or two, not far from the admired rectory, that have lately been allowed to grow wild. A taste for the useful and beautiful appears in healthy growth in the village and we trust all will cultivate and assist it.

And, like William Lisle Bowles, the paper acknowledged generosity:

> TT Knyfton Esq, of Uphill Castle, near this town, with his usual liberality, forwarded to RA Kinglake Esq the sum of £5 for organising the Working Men's Institute at Weston-super-Mare.

Thomas Knyfton allowed the newly formed Weston Cricket Club to practise on his meadow near the Strand Hotel, the old Halfway House. Uphill men enjoyed an older sport, that of Pigeon and Sparrow Shooting, won in 1859 by James Jones, Royal Navy Coastguard. Village fishermen with rods took eels, roach, tench and an occasional pike from the rhyne while boys netted minnows, tadpoles and newts.

A grislier activity entertained a Somerset crowd on 16th January 1858 when John William Beale, guilty of a murder in Leigh Woods, was hanged on a gallows in front of the county gaol in Taunton. Newspapers carried a detailed description of the scene for those unable to be there. In April 1872 the *Mercury* headlined:

BRUTAL WIFE MURDER NEAR BLAGDON

above the story of "the Charterhouse Murderer", William Lace, a Mendip miner who was sentenced to death at Wells Assize and executed at Taunton Prison. A black flag flew over the gaol entrance and the prison bell tolled throughout. Although an Act of 1868 had ordered capital punishment to be carried out privately, this did not exclude the Press which published full details of the whole process.

Uphill's crimes were less gruesome. The *Mercury* reported:

A FORAGER FORGIVEN

Ann Hayes, of Uphill, was charged by Joseph Hancock of the same place, with having stolen some lugs (logs) of wood from a field in his occupation. He cut down some trees in the field and had them made up for firewood. He had since missed a number of the lugs. A witness living next door to the woman saw her and her children take away some of the lugs, ten or twelve times. Mr Hancock did not press the charge. The woman paid his expenses and promised not to repeat the felony.

Joseph Hancock was from an old Uphill farming family and also landlord of the Ship. It was common practice for landowners to make their point by taking petty thieves to court and then not pressing the charge. In the street, however, points were made more robustly. On 21st August 1855 Thomas Whitting of Uphill was fined 10s "for beating H Martin". And two months later:

> Henry Smith, a labourer of Uphill, was charged by Mr Thos Whitting of Uphill with threatening to stab him and swearing he would "rip up his gizzard." He was also charged with assaulting PC 152 whilst in the execution of his duty. Henry Smith was committed to Shepton Mallett prison for six weeks' hard labour.

Early the next year, Weston County Court heard the case of Whitting v Castle:

> The plaintiff, a coal merchant of Uphill, sued the defendant who resides at Hutton for £3 1s 4d, balance of an account for coal, cider, bricks and lime, supplied to the defendant's mother who died in August last. Castle had taken possession of all his mother's effects, which comprised furniture, valued at £30, a horse and cart and a number of laundry requisites. The judge therefore observed that the defendant having acted as executor was bound to pay his mother's debts.

Henry Maine of Uphill appeared at Weston Petty Sessions on a charge of assaulting his wife as she had left him and would not return to him. Although not punished for the assault, he was ordered to pay her 5s a week maintenance. Another maintenance case saw John Vowles summonsed by the Overseers of the Parish of Uphill for leaving his wife and child chargeable to the parish.

Vowles and his wife had gone to Ireland as servants with Mr Fry and there got married. They returned, but not having a home, the wife went to live with her father at Hutton, but from illness became chargeable to the parish. She had received 7s 6d from the relieving officer. Vowles said he was willing to repay the 7s 6d and he was in treaty for renting a house at Uphill to make a home for his wife and child. Under these circumstances he was ordered to pay the 7s 6d and discharged.

Disputes over pay were taken to court. At Weston Petty Sessions:

Mr Michael Duckett, a farmer of Uphill, was ordered to pay his servant Sarah Wood £1 4s 8d, wages due to her.

When quarry owners tried to cut pay in April 1858:

the Committee of Operative Masons called a strike over pay and conditions in quarries.

The *Mercury* letter columns provided a powerful forum for complaints. In February 1858, Uphill correspondents grumbled about newcomers taking jobs; stone-throwing by youths at Bleadon; no sight of police on the road at the toll-gate for two months; and no response by the police to a robbery.

In January 1859 they also found fault with their new Rector, the Rev F Trevor, and Curate, the Rev George Cuff:

UPHILL *Refusing baptism* - On Sunday, a platelayer on the Bristol and Exeter Railway, named Fear, who resides in this village, had arranged to have his infant child christened at the parish church, and had invited "godfathers and godmothers". The nurse, baby and sponsors and parents were all gathered in the church and collected round the font. Both rector and curate were at hand; the latter, however (upon whom the duty should devolve) hastily left the church on the plea that he had to read the burial service at a grave in the old church yard on the hill and therefore could not wait to receive a child into membership of Christ's church.

Whatever their motivation, some church members were less than inclusive. In April 1859 the *Mercury* published a "Letter from An Inhabitant of Uphill to the Rector and Churchwardens of Uphill":

Gentlemen – There has been of late much complaint by several parties who attend our parish church of the occasional appearance of a singular new attendant, whose manners and movements attract the attention of the female members of the congregation.

Cannot some arrangement be made to accommodate the newcomer with a seat in a part of the edifice where his peculiarities would be less observed?

❑ ❑ ❑ ❑ ❑

Chapter 20. Private Medicine

Most grandmothers knew that the best treatment for a child's cold was to rub the patient's chest vigorously with goose grease thinned with turpentine. Adults preferred tea brewed from dried, powdered cuckoo-pint leaves, sold by gypsies as a cold cure. Other teas were brews of relaxing vervaine or scented lemon balm. Meadowsweet tea was a pain-killer, feverfew helped migraine and St John's Wort dulled depression.

Agrimony, known by its descriptive country name "church steeples", was good for diarrhoea, yarrow soothed varicose veins and staunched wounds. Herbs were infused in tallow to make ointments. A dirty sock wrapped round the neck eased a sore throat, a mole's foot hung round the neck helped children with teething trouble and a thimble rubbed on the gums helped new teeth through. Fleabane trodden into the earth floor repelled fleas, while repeated soakings with paraffin shifted head lice.

Even less scientific remedies involved carrying a sick child through three parishes, while a child with respiratory disease had also to be carried through a flock of sheep. Treatment for whooping cough entailed the father of the family, and no-one else, placing the head of the sick child in a hole in a meadow at dusk. Failing that, the cough could be eased by feeding the hair of the child to a dog in a churchyard. Believing that a seventh son and seventh daughter in one family had miraculous powers, mothers asked them to touch a sickly child.

A pill of aloes and strychnine eased constipation., but the real remedy was regularity:

> After a drink of cold water before breakfast, the patient should go regularly after breakfast, and take plenty of time to complete the act. Every house should have a comfortable closet, free from bad smells. If in the country, where there are no sewers, the privy should be well built, the outside wall boarded up and battened and the inside lathed and plastered so as to keep out the wind.

A fatal fever commonly followed childbirth, the result of unsterile instruments and germs on the midwife's hands. Infant death was common, usually recorded by the coroner as "debility", "lack of breast milk" or "starvation": the outcome of poverty, overcrowding and ignorance.

Although Uphill's village nurses kept no records, they knew that overworked mothers used patent medicines to soothe crying babies. The most popular was Godfrey's Cordial made of opium, treacle and spices. Another "quietener" was poppy tea brewed from penny opium sticks sold by village shops for "veterinarian" uses. They did the trick but suppressed the baby's appetite causing death from malnutrition.

Serious illness was diagnosed as "fever". Smallpox, consumption (tuberculosis) and scarlatina (scarlet fever) were not easily treated although some believed that smoking a pipe of dried cow dung helped consumptives, especially if they inhaled. Influenza was sweated out by breathing steam while wrapped in flannel.

The ague (malaria) needed other treatments such as swallowing a cobweb rolled into a ball or applying a dead chicken to the patient's bare feet. Washing in water from the church font was beneficial but some preferred to buy gypsy charms which hung round the neck with such messages as:

> Ague farewell
> Till we meet in hell.

Some sewed a snail in a bag and hung that round the neck while others believed they should "Catch a large spider and shut it in a box. As it pines the ague will go." Doctors prescribed quinine, but opium was cheaper.

❑ ❑ ❑ ❑ ❑

Chapter 21. Death by Cholera

Cholera arrived in Exeter in 1832 and Wells in 1866. A foul and fearsome disease, it killed tens of thousands across the country without warning or explanation: two-thirds of those infected died horribly within a day. One useless treatment prescribed:

> ... full doses of laudanum together with acetate of lead and bismuth ... or a quarter grain of morphine after every movement of the bowels.

Infection was blamed on "miasma", the stench that hung over ditches and cess-pits. There was plenty of that as humbler folk used outdoor privies dropping into cess-pits while smarter families with indoor closets piped their sewage into their own cellars. The invention of WCs simply accelerated the flow. Astute men smelt profit in this, paying "night soil men" to empty privies in Weston, carrying their buckets through the house and on open carts to a dump on Hopkins Street. When the stench there became intolerable the sewage was carted to old brick pits in Locking Road, mixed with ash and sold to farmers as fertiliser. They spread it on their fields where, the experts claimed, weathering provided effective cleansing. The only limitation was to grow surface crops for the first year and root crops thereafter. Domestic urine was collected separately and recycled to make ammonia for industry.

This highly profitable business continued until cholera was shown to result not from foul air but from polluted drinking water drawn from sources adjacent to cess-pits and sewage dumps. Weston latched on fast and the *Mercury* told its summer visitors:

Weston-super-Mare Water Works Company mains are laid all over the town. The water rises to the tops of the houses and supplies Baths and Water Closets in the most effectual manner. Being drawn from a copious spring about a mile from the town, it is *perfectly free from Sewage and all other Impurities,* so productive of diseases.

The Town Commissioners firmly identified the problem:

> ... the town has an excellent supply of water; ... the drainage seems at present the *great* plague the town has to contend with.

They solved it by running a sewer into Uphill Great Rhyne which conveniently flowed through Uphill to the sea. They also built the town's first public slaughter house where it could drain into the rhyne. To meet Government legislation, sewage was eventually pumped into disinfecting tanks on Drove Road before overflowing into the rhyne. Economy with disinfectant combined with a slow-moving water-course and hot summers to turn the rhyne into a mile of solid stinking sludge. A public meeting in Uphill in 1850 had voiced complaints about this "severe nuisance" and when the Commissioners met

in 1859 to discuss Weston's drainage, Thomas T Knyfton wrote them a formal letter from Uphill Castle stating his:

> determination to oppose, as far as the law would allow, the drainage of Weston coming into the parish of Uphill at all.

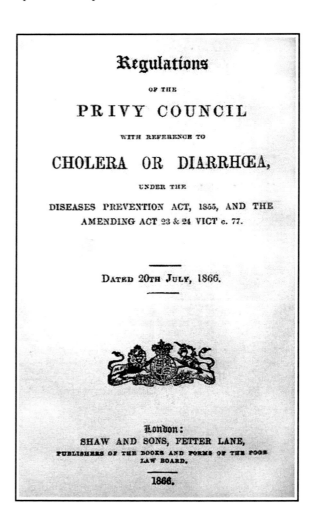

Part 4:   Progress 1860 - 1870

Chapter 22.   Uphill in 1860

> Population 439: 217 male + 222 female
> Rector: Rev Stephen Bennett MA; Curate: Rev CF Hawkins
> Wesleyan Minister: Thomas Gould
> Parish Clerk, Overseer, Rate Collector: Robert Counsell; 1867: Harry Hancock
> Sextoness: Mrs Hannah Haynes; Organist: T Edwards
> School teacher: Miss Jane Hackett;
> Post Office Receiver: John Delay; Letter Carrier: Silas Goodby
> Lord of the Manor: Thomas Tutton Knyfton JP MA of Uphill Castle

The 1861 Census defined the parish as including "Uphill Hill, a Farm House in Uphill Drove, Totterdown Farm, Strand or Halfway House". The number of inhabited houses had gone up by 25% to 85 whereas the population had risen by only 4% to 439 showing that fewer people were living in each house. Thomas Knyfton and Charles Whitting owned most of the land, drawing rents from farmers and householders.

Charles Whitting used his Militia rank of Lieutenant and lived in his grand new mansion, Sandcroft, with his wife Anne and their two daughters. The girls were brought up at home by a governess and a schoolmistress Miss Jane Hackett who had her own cottage. A butler, a footman, a housekeeper and three maids completed the household.

Charles Whitting's cousin Thomas illustrated the blurring of social lines. Thomas lived on Wharf Farm, renting land for farming, but he made his money from Uphill clay-pits, manufacturing and selling housebricks. Meeting new needs in bigger houses he developed lines in drainpipes and firebricks.

Thomas Whitting also imported coal and salt to the Wharf, storing the salt in his Salt House from which he supplied cheese manufacturers and shops. He demonstrated his commercial status by adding "& Co" to his business name, while his social credentials merited an "Esq" in Kelly's Directory. When he died in December 1870, he was classed as "yeoman". He owned Wheatstone House near the Ship which he left to be sold for his widow Sarah, children and grandchildren. The building comprised two houses, No 1 occupied by Elizabeth Smart and No 2 by Sarah.

Thomas Whitting's dealings around the wharf were watched by Customs Officer Daniel Henry Frederick Carter, usefully based in the Strand House Inn, Coastguard James Jones and Customs Officer William Burdwood.

Only two mariners now lived in the village. One was James Robert Smart whose family was to keep the maritime link well into the twentieth century. By comparison, six men worked on railway track maintenance.

Fire-dog from Uphill Brickyard   [NSM]

Village gentry included Montgomery Gladstone, Charles Harrill and Thomas Harrill, Thomas Macie Leir and Thomas Kington Leir and Miss Salmon. Uphill was well provided with churchmen. The Rev WR Crotch MA still lived in Uphill House. The Rev Stephen Bennett MA, Oriel College, Oxford replaced the Rev Frederick Trevor as Rector in 1862, with the Rev George Cuff as Curate. Thomas Gould preached as a minister in the Wesleyan Chapel, having returned with his wife and family from his calling as a Baptist missionary in Jamaica.

30% of the residents were born in Uphill and twelve surnames went back to the 1841 Census: Cavill, Counsell, Delay, Evans, Every, Groves, Hancock, Haynes, Norman, Poole, Russell and Vowles. William Counsell ran the grocery shop, perhaps on the site of today's newsagent. His brother Robert aged 35 was now married with a two-year old son Oliver. Still a stonemason, he also worked as Uphill Parish Clerk and Rate Collector. Their brother James aged 42 had joined them from Mark and was farming 75 acres at Totterdown, part of Uphill. With his wife Mary Ann he had 5 sons and 7 daughters aged from 7 months to 19 years. Other long-established families included farmers James Evans and the Hancocks; baker James Groves; and John Delay, still the Post Office Receiver as well as a plumber and market gardener. Uphill had six other farmers: William Fear, John Harse, Edward Luff, Joseph Norman, John Roydon and Abraham James who also retailed beer. Hannah Haynes (92) and Jacob Tripp (85) were the oldest villagers.

Excluding gentry and clergy, 99 Uphill men had jobs. 20% were listed simply as labourers, 20% worked specifically on the land, 14% in building trades, 12% in shops or pubs and 12% were in domestic service. The oldest labourer was 85 and the youngest 13. The village supported two bakers: James Groves and John Masters. In 1869, Josiah Coles and Henry Millier set up shop as baker and grocer while George Skinner and Robert Wills sold milk from their own dairies.

By now, some of Uphill's five dressmakers had the new Singer sewing-machine, but milliner Eliza Payne still sewed her creations by hand. 31 women were employed, half in domestic service, one-third in service industries and one-tenth in agriculture. Their ages ranged from Miss Mary Hancock, still farming at 70, to little Elizabeth Marshman aged 9, employed as a resident servant by blacksmith James Williams. Two other smiths served the community, brothers William (20) and Robert (15) Minifie, living with their widowed mother Mary. They came from Devon and were to play a big role in the development of the village. Full of drive they advertised:

Messrs Minifie,
Uphill Shoeing Forge and General Smithy —
have added to their usual business
that of Wheelwright.

and, expanding:

William Minifie, Uphill,
requires to rent a Country Smith's shop in
Weston-super-Mare.

In 1864 Arthur Stone bought Thomas Whitting's coal business at the Wharf:

UPHILL COAL WHARF

ARTHUR STONE, COAL MERCHANT,

in returning his sincere thanks to the Inhabitants and Visitors of Weston-super-Mare and its vicinity for the kind support he has received while he carried on his business in Weston-super-Mare, begs to state that he has taken on the above Coal Wharf, where he trusts to be favoured with a continuance of their patronage, assuring them that it will still be his study to supply none but Coals of the best quality and to render them at the lowest remunerating prices.
Orders will receive prompt attention.

Robert Vowles, a 50-year old labourer, lived with his wife Sarah between James Groves' bakery and Thomas Russell's tailor's shop. Their eldest son George was a carpenter and 13-year old William a labourer. Daughter Hannah worked as an ironer but 12-year old Alice went to school.

The family also found room for two lodgers. One of these was James Heath, born in Uphill in 1794 and now a widower. His only son, Robert, had quit work as a farm labourer twenty years earlier to seek a better life in Australia. Now, at 72, James no longer made enough as a plasterer to pay his rent and was therefore committed to Axbridge Union workhouse. He died on 31st October 1866 and his body was released to Uphill for burial. Back in his old lodgings, Robert and Sarah Vowles wondered what to do with the locked box of clothes which he had left there.

As they pondered, the box, in their words, "flew open" revealing a roll of multi-coloured papers under the clothes. The papers turned out to be cheques sent to the old man by his son who had made his fortune in Australia. Robert Vowles sent the cheques, worth over £40, to the London office of the bank, requesting payment to him. But the cheques were returned for James Heath's signature and Robert Vowles sent them back to the Australian son. The *Mercury* commented:

> The question arises whether the poor old man from ignorance was aware of the value of the highly coloured and decorated pieces of paper sent by his worthy son, or whether through penurious habits he chose to live and die in a workhouse rather than part with the money.

❑ ❑ ❑ ❑ ❑

Chapter 23. Ferdinand Cox and the Dolphin

In ten years of Victorian prosperity, Ferdinand Cox had progressed from carpenter to property-owning businessman. He owned the Dolphin which he now sought to elevate from its basic status as a beer-house. Beer-houses were licensed by HM Excise to any property-owner covered by two sureties who were housekeepers, regardless of any criminal record. In September 1860 Mr Cox applied for an hotelier's licence and Mr W Smith represented him at Axbridge Licensed Victuallers Court as reported in the *Mercury*:

> The Dolphin was formerly a licensed house, but the licence was taken to another house called the Strand Hotel in the same parish but has now been given up for some time. Mr Cox's house has been improved and now contains five sitting-rooms, eight bedrooms and every convenience for a respectable inn. It is very near the River Axe where the landing place will be for packets plying between Cardiff, Weston and Uphill; in fact the Cardiff Steam Navigation Company has just purchased the landing-slip. Mr Cox has resided in Uphill 20 years; has kept the Dolphin Inn which is his own property as a beer-house for 16 years and there has never been the slightest complaint against him.

Unsurprisingly, Mr Thomas Every of the Ship opposed the application. He had extended his coal import business by purchasing the Ship Inn from Joseph Hancock and now claimed "… there is just bread and cheese for one house, not for two; it is a small parish not numbering over 250 inhabitants." He ridiculed the idea of a packet station: "A steamer plied between Cardiff and Uphill for three weeks during this summer and only carried one passenger." In spite of his pleas, a licence was granted to the Dolphin.

Ferdinand Cox immediately "provided a dinner with wines at his expense to thirty friends in celebration." His good fortune seemed to have run out when an accident stopped him working; but only the day before the accident he had taken out an insurance policy which paid £6 a week during his illness. At Christmas he marked his movement up the social ladder by "giving a dinner to thirty or forty working men".

In Weston the new Gaslight Company was extending illumination to more streets, but Uphill's roads remained in darkness despite a plea that:

> Gas light serves both as policeman and citizen, raises the value of house property and would prove a real comfort to inhabitants.

Ferdinand Cox took note and in November 1861 the *Mercury* reported:

> Another proof of the public spirit of Mr Cox proprietor of the Dolphin Hotel was apparent when the establishment was brilliantly lighted up with gas, manufactured on the premises. Mr Cox had long felt the want of some better mode of lighting up than that afforded by tallow, wax or oil, and therefore determined on the erection of a small gas apparatus. The bright light of the worthy host so far outshines that of his neighbours "as daylight doth a lamp". The entire work has been carried out by Mr T Llewellyn, gas-fitter of Bristol.

In further celebration, Ferdinand Cox gave a Christmas Eve supper to his friends and customers and in March 1863 edged closer to the gentry, when:

> about 70 of the poorer classes sat down to a most substantial and excellent dinner prepared in prime style by the host and hostess of the Dolphin Inn, Mr and Mrs Cox. The chair was taken by the Rev Stephen Bennett and the chief subscribers to the feast were TT Knyfton Esq, Charles Whitting Esq and the Rev Dr Crotch. An excellent dinner was also prepared and partaken of at the Ship Inn.

In the mid-sixties Albert Amesbury took over the Dolphin but not Ferdinand Cox's good luck. Whether or not the private gas-works was to blame is not clear, but in August 1868:

> Mr and Mrs Amesbury awoke with a sense of suffocation. They found the room in flames with the bed curtains, bedsteads and the bed itself on fire. The neighbours were aroused and with a good supply of water at hand the fire was put out. Mr Amesbury suffered slight burns on the leg and his trousers containing £30 in notes were partly destroyed.

Chapter 24. Halfway to Convalescence

Although the Dolphin raised its standards, the Strand House remained at beer-house level. In September 1865 landlord James Moore went out for an hour, leaving his 20-month old son Albert Edward with his mother Charlotte. Having no servant, she got on with her work while the boy played with the dog. She missed him and searched the garden and sands behind the house before crossing the Uphill Road where she found the child drowned in a pond 40 yards from the house. An inquest found there was no blame, but James and Charlotte Moore moved away.

Peter Phillips took over in 1866 and the Strand reverted to its old name of Halfway House. As a beer-house, the inn was not subject to approval by the magistrates which was fortunate for Phillips as he soon appeared before them to be fined 5 shillings for allowing his horse to stray on the highway twice in one week. Shortly after this, his daughter Bella, described as "a little girl", was summonsed for "cruelly treating a horse" and Peter Phillips was charged with "knowingly permitting the torture to be inflicted". Mr Bullen of Bristol Animal Friends Society gave evidence that he saw a horse on the sands near Uphill in a most wretched condition. The little girl was driving it with its legs tied and blood was coming from cuts caused by the rope. The Bench dismissed the summons against the girl but fined her father 10s and costs.

A "Letter from An Invalid" to the *Mercury* in August 1867 complained about the inn:

> I enjoy the pretty drive in a carriage to Uphill and round through Hutton and Locking and back to Weston. But premises halfway between Weston and Uphill have such a horrid and insufferable stench that it is almost impossible to pass along the road. Should it long continue, some malady will present itself.

The problem did not long continue. Five years earlier, the Bishop of Bath and Wells had chaired a meeting to discuss "the best method of establishing a Sea Bathing Infirmary on the coats of Uphill or Weston-super-Mare, for affording relief to diseased objects of Charity" but there was no progress. In 1868, fearing an influx of "diseased objects", villagers opposed a new proposal for a County Sanatorium within Uphill Parish and TT Knyfton withdrew his earlier offer of financial support. Although Halfway House was within the parish, it was far enough away to be acceptable and, within a few months:

> The old Halfway House between Uphill and Weston affords a most eligible site for a new West of England Sanatorium or Convalescent Home. Its patron, Mr Swete, says it will shortly, with alterations and additions, be ready for patients. It will offer recreation and bathing — and being a mile from Weston keeps patients from the many sources of temptation.

Halfway House rebuilt as the Sanatorium   [UVS]

The *Mercury* reported the official opening in November 1868:

> The old Halfway House was a roadside tavern which had become almost disused and was rapidly falling into dilapidation. It has been completely gutted and transformed into a cheerful pleasant cosy home in which few would recognise the Strand House Inn of last summer. The house stands some little distance back from the turnpike road, fronted with a neat line of railings.
>
> A large Conservatory stands behind the house. The garden at the rear leads down to a few feet from high water mark. There are attractive gravel walks in the garden and a terrace with views of Weston. The plan is to build a raised esplanade with a bathing house beneath. Patients will adopt the bathing costume used at Llandudno and other fashionable watering places and thus not need a bathing machine.
>
> A chamber over the fire grate in the hall transmits heat back into the room instead of wasting it up the chimney. The central dining hall measures 34 feet by 15 feet. Patients are in bedrooms not wards. Light coloured decorations give the appearance of a most comfortable home, not an institution. All this has been done in six months and 13 patients are already there.
>
> There will be no admission of anyone suffering from a disease. All patients are here to recuperate in salubrious and restorative air after long spells in hospital.
>
> The Sanatorium visiting day is Wednesday from 2-4 pm.

The reference to bathing costumes and machines reflected attitudes to sea-bathing where a balance was required between the sensitivities of residents and the need to sell the benefits of salt water to holidaymakers. A sign on the beach near Halfway House ordered bathers on the Weston side of the board to enter the sea from bathing-machines. The machine proprietors provided suitable dresses for swimming. Bathers changed inside enclosed carts which were then dragged by horses into the sea where they descended steps into the water. Boats were not allowed within 200 yards on the seaward side of the machines.

On the Uphill side of the board, well away from houses, men could bathe naked. Even that freedom was restricted by a new bye-law in August 1869 requiring men to wear bathing costumes everywhere on the beach. At the same time the *Mercury* published a complaint about young women who chose to bathe "in loose gowns which blew up in the breeze", even when men were close by. The correspondent thought women should be compelled to wear loose trousers on the beach and forbidden to swim if men were near.

❑ ❑ ❑ ❑ ❑

Chapter 25. Village Crime

Gentlefolk averted their eyes from bathers on the beach and certainly never ventured into Weston's back streets. By March 1861 attacks on the police had become so serious that constables on night duty were armed with cutlasses. Residents were plagued by numbers of ragged hungry boys, sent out early in the morning by their parents to beg from door to door. So many of these turned to crime that a benefactor opened a school to feed and train them. Uphill did better for its youngsters and the Diocesan Inspector of Schools reported creditably on the work of Mistress Hillier in the village schoolroom. But Uphill youths did misbehave. John Bailey, Henry Davey, William Davis, George Stone and Isaac Hardacre all belonging to Uphill were charged with disorderly conduct at Weston Petty Sessions in August 1861. The court heard that:

on a Sunday afternoon they had been hollering and swearing to such an extent as to annoy the people in church. Twenty or thirty boys were in the habit of playing at ball every Sunday evening and had been frequently cautioned. The Bench reprimanded them, informing them that they were liable to be imprisoned with hard labour. They were fined 2s 6d each.

The *Mercury* of 24th August 1867 reported a different form of rowdiness, the rough justice of skimmity, a traditional rural mockery of suspected misconduct:

A "rough band" – both instruments and performers were rough – paraded through the village in the evening to the cottage of a woman who appeared to have been on terms too familiar with a man employed on Brean Down. They played some music including "Cat's Quadrilles" and then marched to the man's lodging and played again. The concert was repeated the next evening. The woman is a mother of five or six children and her husband is a hard-working, industrious and steady man.

The village had its share of criminal activities at various levels. Andrew Comer lived in Wheatstone House between the Dolphin and the Ship. In February 1860:

WANTON ACT

Within the last week some mischievous party has knocked off the lock and forced open and damaged the door of a stable belonging to Mr Andrew Comer. In order to discover the offender, Mr Comer has offered a reward of two guineas.

In January 1866:

WILFUL DAMAGE

As some evil-disposed person or persons have on several occasions damaged the walls on the road between Weston and Uphill, a reward of £1 has been offered for information. We sincerely hope the perpetrators of these dastardly acts will be brought to justice and receive the punishment they deserve.

When Mr William Shaw's windows were broken, labourer John Palmer was charged and found not guilty. In December 1867:

Miscreants threw a stone through the window of the cottage of Mr Joseph Norman. He has offered a reward of £2.

Charlotte Brewer took her lodger, John Little, a baker, to court, charging him with shaking her child, "using exceedingly bad language and threatening to knock her b–y brains out". John Little told the court that her boy, who was dreaded by all the children in the neighbourhood, had thrown a stone at his two-year old son, cutting his head and causing it to bleed. Furthermore she had called him a thief. The case was dismissed.

Two respectable local farmers clashed rather more violently when William Fear was charged with assaulting James Counsell. The two men were at Congresbury Fair and got into an argument over a bet. James Counsell told the court "Fear called me a thief and struck me violently on the face". The magistrate told Mr Fear he ought to be very sorry and had made himself liable to a heavy fine. But he went on helpfully to suggest finding a "mutual friend" to settle the matter less expensively out of court. The two men agreed and the case was dismissed. The magistrate was less forgiving when James Axen knocked down John Jones for refusing to lend him a shilling after an evening in the Dolphin. Axen was fined 5s for assault.

Straightforward thieving brought some to court. 18-year old John Madge was a mason's labourer living with his parents in Uphill. He was charged with stealing £8 14s from the till of the White Hart Inn in Hopkins Street. He had bought two pints of cider in the inn, paying 3d for it. Then he went into the shop part of the premises and asked for a quarter of a pound of cheese. When he paid for it, the landlady Mrs Palmer discovered the coin was counterfeit and returned it. John Madge told her he had no money upon which Mrs Palmer kindly allowed him to take the cheese. But she then found that the entire contents of the till had also gone. Madge bolted through the back door but police arrested him. A search showed he had about £6 10s in gold and £1 0s 6d in silver. He was sentenced to ten months hard labour.

In Weston, William Wilkins of Uphill bought a waistcoat from Mr Darling's shop for 8s. He put it in his pocket, went into the Swan Inn for a drink and sat next to Mary Coles. He later missed the waistcoat and reported Mary Coles to the police for theft. In court, the waistcoat was handed back to him by James Gould who said a man had taken it, not the woman. In view of the confused evidence, the case was dismissed. When the same James Gould opened as Uphill's coal merchant, he put up six fowls value one guinea as prizes in the skittle alley. Rather unsportingly, labourers David Bailey of Bleadon and Charles Laney from Weston snatched the prize without playing skittles and were duly charged with theft.

As affluence and social aspirations developed, so did targets of theft. Landlord of the Dolphin Albert Amesbury and his wife set about smartening the place up and labourer John Baker could not resist the temptation. He broke in and stole an electro-plated coffee pot with a matching cream jug, a gold brooch set with pink stones, a work box, a pair of women's new boots and a clothes brush, valued together at £5 3s. The court heard that Samuel Travis, butcher of Uphill, had bought the jug for 5s not knowing it was stolen.

The enclosure of common lands and the expansion of housing had left travelling gypsies with fewer traditional sites. Although Uphill's own gypsy family the Joules remained in their quarry on the Bridgwater road near Devil Payne's railway station, others of the family kept travelling. One, Josiah Joules, was spotted by Police Sergeant Ross in the act of breaking down and stealing some garden fencing and "after a sharp race of some distance he apprehended the defendant". Finding Josiah guilty and fining him £1, the magistrate said he was surprised to find "a tribe of gypsies disgracing the town by taking up their abode on the beach".

Whatever their social position, not everyone paid their bills. Thomas Every claimed £6 6s 2d from Thomas Kington Leir Esq for coal delivered to his father Thomas Macie Leir Esq, now deceased, both of the same address. He won his case, shaming the defendant by pleading, "I am a dealer in coals residing at Uphill and Mr Leir is a gentleman".

After winning his case against Mr Leir, Thomas Every was in his turn taken to court by a mariner named Jones who sought £2 3s 6d from him for unpaid wages. When Every claimed that Jones owed him more than that amount, the judge split the difference and awarded Jones 8s.

William Henry Underdown similarly refused to pay a boy Joseph Browning his due wages of 11s 9d. Joseph's mother, Sexa Browning, had made an agreement for her son to work at the rate of 5s per month plus food, subject to notice of one month if he did not suit, but he had been dismissed without pay and without even a day's notice. Joseph's story was that Mr Underdown had given him 3s to buy oatmeal in Weston but it was after 7 pm, too late to go into Weston, and he said he would go the next morning. Mr Underdown claimed that he had told the boy to buy the meal in Uphill not Weston. Although magistrates might have been expected to favour fellow employers, they ordered William Underdown to pay 9s 9d to Joseph, with costs.

The lack of protection for employees roused factory workers to violence elsewhere in Somerset and mobs of hungry women and boys seized bread from bakers' shops in Chard and Ilminster. Fears also spread of terrorism from the Fenians, Irish nationalists.

Weston and Uphill were understandably nervous when word went round that Irish labourers working on the new fort and harbour on Brean Down were rising in rebellion and marching on the town. But it was all a hoax. The Irish were indeed crossing to Uphill and walking into Weston, but it was just pay day and they all behaved well.

Joules' gypsy camp   *[UVS]*

Chapter 26. Roads and Buildings

Weston traders placed stone slabs to help shoppers cross the unpaved muddy roads. Ladies stitched on dress suspenders to lift their skirts clear of the mud. The road at Uphill Bridge was so rough that the horse of a Royal Mail cart fell, breaking its shafts and delaying the mail on its way from Weston to Cheddar. The *Mercury* demanded improvement:

SOUTH OF THE SANATORIUM.

A correspondent calls our attention to the very bad and dangerous state of the footpaths leading from the Atlantic House in Ellenborough Park Road South towards Uphill, which should be one of the most pleasant walks of the town. We can fully endorse his remarks, believing that by a small outlay the present rugged and uneven path may be converted into one that will afford comfort and ease to the pedestrian.

In January 1861:

As Charles Whitting Esq of Sandcroft House, Uphill, was driving along Locking Road, his carriage came into contact with a heap of mortar which had been very incautiously left by workmen. Fortunately the horse behaved most docile and Mr Whitting almost miraculously escaped personal injury. It being dark, the damage to the vehicle could not be ascertained but it must be considerable and the cost of which the negligent parties will assuredly have to pay.

A few days later:

ACCIDENT AT UPHILL

As the guests from a dinner party were leaving the residence of TT Knyfton Esq, the carriage belonging to the Rev N Wodehouse of Worle came into collision with another with such force as to unseat the driver and do damage estimated to at least £10. One horse was unhurt but the other was injured.

Uphill experienced its first road traffic offence in January 1862 when Hugh Rockett Esq saw George Weedon of Uphill driving his cart without using the reins. As most horses knew their way perfectly well, this caused no problem, but Mr Rockett stopped the cart and ordered Mr Weedon to get down. "He however turned rather saucy, but at length descended by the side of his horse." What George did not know was that Hugh Rockett was also Chairman of the Magistrates. He ended up in court and was fined 5s and costs or 14 days imprisonment in default of payment.

Later that year the *Mercury* praised:

Uphill road widening and other visible improvements made by Mr Charles Whitting of Sandcroft House. The work is pleasing to the eye and adds to the safety of travellers.

The editor blamed a careless rider in December 1867:

As some persons were riding on horseback through Uphill, one of the horses which did not seem to be under proper control knocked down a child of between three and four years of age and severely injured her. The poor little thing was conveyed home bleeding profusely besides receiving a badly bruised face and head, had her arm very much hurt and sustained some internal injury. There were many children in the road, there being no pathway at the spot, having only just been let out of school, and the party rode heedlessly on without enquiring as to the injuries of the child. A passer-by informed the parent of who they were.

In January 1868 there was an:

accident when a pony and trap hit a dangerous curb stone on a dangerous turning near Mr Fear's farm in Uphill. The trap overturned, throwing out the occupants who suffered bruising. The horse was fortunately uninjured, but the shafts were broken off the trap.

In ten years the number of houses in Uphill increased by nearly a quarter and in 1865 more land was scheduled to be laid out for streets. Charles Whitting planned to build on an orchard, Thomas Knyfton on an orchard and two fields. Even the name of Payne returned when the executors of Charles Henry Payne sold a patch of arable land to builders. An advertisement promised:

DWELLINGS FOR THE WORKING CLASSES

In order to meet the pressing wants of several families, and in anticipation of an increased demand for small tenements, consequent upon the enlargement of the works at Brean Down and the River Axe, a gentleman possessed of some very eligible land contemplates erecting a number of comfortable cottages in the village – a class of buildings much required.

New building needed sand but the beach lay under the jurisdiction of two Lords of the Manor, Mr Pigott in Weston and Mr Knyfton in Uphill. The illicit taking of sand from the beach was punished in court by fines or prison. As a magistrate, TT Knyfton sentenced a local man for taking sand, justifying the sentence by reference to his own business interest. This was followed by the announcement:

TT Knyfton Esq, lord of the manor of the manor of Uphill, has arranged to supply builders of this town with sand from the Uphill Backs.

Uphill Road vanished under sand when Mr Pigott removed and sold the eight-foot high sand dunes which had for centuries resisted winds, sand drifts and high tides.

Chapter 27. Mary Hancock's Fire

Job Hancock and his family farmed 40 acres and lived next door to 70-year old Miss Mary Hancock who farmed 30 acres. With Mary lived her sister Elizabeth and her brother (another Job) who farmed 70 acres. In January 1863 the *Mercury* headlined:

DESTRUCTIVE FIRE AT UPHILL

A fire broke out on the farm premises of the Misses Hancock (two elderly maiden ladies) which ended in complete destruction to the house and premises and of the greater part of the furniture. Grave suspicions presented themselves that the fire was the act of an incendiary. The fire was first seen from Weston by JH Smyth Pigott Esq who informed the police with orders to get out the fire-engine.

A Mrs Madge heard a crackling noise outside her door. She saw a baker's cart belonging to a neighbour Mr Groves on fire inside and called to him to put it out. She also heard a noise further down the road and saw the roof of the farmhouse in which the Misses Hancock lived in flames and heard one of the ladies screaming for assistance. Plenty of help was soon obtained but nothing could be done to stop the progress of the flames which had got firm hold of the thatched roof of the building. While numbers present were content to watch the progress of the flames, others, more thoughtful, helped to remove the furniture from under the burning roof and the road was soon strewed with damaged articles. The bedding, boxes of clothing etc were taken to a place of safety comparatively uninjured. When nothing more could be saved, the crowd looked on and seemed rather to enjoy the sight than to commiserate with the poor ladies so ruthlessly turned out of bed and doors with little clothing on a cold winter's night.

Meanwhile Mr JH Carter, Customs House officer, sent a messenger to Weston on horseback to fetch the fire-engine, which arrived at 12.40 drawn by the messenger's horse. In ten minutes the hose was affixed, the engine filled with water, and the pumps manned by coast guardsmen under the superintendence of Mr Matthews. For some time the only result of the pumping was a grumbling noise in the interior of the engine, which obstinately refused to be pumped, and grave apprehensions were entertained that it would not work at all. After another fifteen minutes strenuous application the suckers of the engine began to tell, and the water made its appearance at the end of the hose-pipe.

By this time the flames had extended themselves all along the roof and were seen breaking out at the gable at the east end. A successful endeavour was made to save two barns adjoining, when the roof falling in shut up the fire between the walls and prevented the flames from spreading further. Fortunately the wind was in the south-east; had it blown from the east, some thatched premises on the adjacent property of HS Pigott Esq, the residence of Mr Carter, with the whole of the documents belonging to the Inland Revenue, would have been endangered.

Too much stress cannot be laid on the disgraceful state of the fire-engine and the absence of anything like order in its management. When wanted, the first difficulty was to find who had charge of it; then as to who had the key of the engine house; who could be got to work it; where to get a horse to draw it; and when at the fire it was found so out of order as to be almost useless, and, had the house been a high one, would have been quite useless.

The premises which are a complete wreck, nothing but the bare walls standing, were the property of Mr Burton of Sandford who was not insured; but the furniture was. The estimated loss is from £150 to £200.

Just two days earlier, the fire would have been whipped up by a "very severe storm of wind and rain that hit the coast from the north west, destroying much of Weston's sea wall and many boats".

The fire service came under review by Weston's Board of Health in April when they agreed that the existing fire-engine was too small, the water supply inadequate and the firemen unable to meet the needs of a rapidly growing town. Two and a half years later when Weston's population had topped 10,000, plus summer visitors, the town had a fire escape but the nearest fire-engine was at Bristol. Eventually the Board frugally suggested a Volunteer Fire Brigade. In December 1870 a new fire-engine and hose arrived by rail but it was1879 before a fire brigade, fully uniformed and equipped by local businesses, drove the horse-drawn engine on a ceremonial tour from Weston Town Hall out through Worle, Hutton and Uphill.

A different sort of fire burned in March 1863 to mark the wedding of the future King Edward VII. A bonfire was built on a grid of iron rods across Uphill windmill tower:

A lad, one Oliver Counsell, was borne up a ladder reared up against this side of the pile and set it alight.

A few days later Oliver's cousin William Thomas died in infancy. Oliver, aged 4, was the son of Robert Counsell, Parish Clerk and Assistant Overseer of the Poor. This was a Church appointment, made by a vote of ratepayers at the Easter Vestry meeting. Robert resigned from this job in 1867 and was replaced by Harry Hancock.

Chapter 28. The Gould family

UPHILL WHARF AND WEIGHBRIDGE

J and T Gould in thanking their numerous friends for their liberal patronage, hereby inform them that they have provided a large and well assorted Stock for the ensuing Winter.

IN THE COALYARD are several hundreds of tons of coals carefully selected from the best Welsh and Forest of Dean Collieries. J and T Gould call special attention to their Wall's End, Llantwitt and Newport Red Ash.

IN THE BRICK AND TILE YARD are upward of 200,000 excellent bricks. A quantity of Double, Single, Roman and other Tiles – Flooring Squares – Crease – Drain Pipes – Fire Bricks – Squares &c.

IN THE SALT STORES They have fine Table Salt, Rock do (for Stock); and agricultural ditto.

IN THE LIME KILNS AND QUARRIES will also be found Aberthaw – Pebble Lime – White do. Building – Curbing – Broken Stones and Gravel.

IN THE WOOD YARD Faggots, Fir Poles, Poles &c

Orders given to their Men; sent by Post; left at Messrs GOULD'S, 13 High Street; Mr JB DELAY'S, Weston-super-Mare;

or at Mr WILKINS'S, Banwell, will be promptly attended to.

GOODS DELIVERED WITHIN 12 MILES. Terms Cash – Haulier's Receipt Valid. Vessels arrive every Spring Tide with Welsh and Forest Coals.

James Gould was born in Wiltshire in 1813, his brother Thomas in 1819. With his wife Bridgilina, Thomas served in Jamaica as a Baptist missionary before returning to live in Wheatstone House in Uphill. The brothers bought the Wharf businesses from Arthur Stone in 1866 and advertised for custom. James ran the shipping side of the business and the coalyard where Wharfe Farm now is. His best coal sold for 10d cwt. He recommended housekeepers to try "Llantwitt and Wall's End coal for Parlour and Drawing Room use; Newport mixed for Kitchen purposes and closed Stoves". Coal was traditionally carried and delivered in baskets, but in 1867:

> The London method of delivering coal in sacks is replacing baskets – it avoids waste, is cleaner, and saves labour and time in breaking the lumps.

Uphill villagers collected their coal in barrows or donkey carts but the merchants loaded up their horses and carts every morning and had their carts' contents checked and certified at an official weigh-bridge alongside the Wharf office. On one occasion the *Mercury* told how:

> Mr Gould, Uphill coal merchant, had delivered a load of coal. The horse was turned for the return journey but had not gone above 50 yards when it dropped to the ground and "died in harness". The animal was valued at £12 and had not been overworked. The cause of death was given as "disease of the heart".

After deliveries around Weston, carters collected the previous day's ashes and returned them to a pile near the brickyard. The ashes were screened and sold to builders to make ash-cement building blocks. Such recycling was profitable, but neighbours complained:

> A large heap of lime, coal ashes, and other rubbish has for several weeks stood over the well leading to the parish pumps rendering the water unendurable. This is as likely to cause fever as the rhyne nuisance.

In 1864:

> Mr James Gould of Uphill was at Highbridge station seeing his daughter off to Burnham. Mr Gould had his hand on the door handle. When the train moved off, he walked with it, still talking to his daughter. It was then quite dark and Mr Gould forgot that the line there curves away from the platform. He fell with considerable force against the moving carriages which threw him between the platform and the rails. The carriages passed over and crushed his hat but, strange to say, with the exception of dislocating his shoulder, Mr Gould escaped uninjured. He returned to Weston and sent for Mr Stringfield, surgeon, who reset his shoulder. His daughter was fortunately unaware of what happened until the following day.

James Gould was married for a second time in August 1865, to Miss Anna Day in Bath Baptist Chapel.

His brother Thomas Gould owned the clay pits, brickyard, kilns, tile sheds and a large workshop where today's Beach End Road meets Thornbury Road. His workers made tiles and bricks there by hand from local clay, living with their families round the yard in a cluster of single-storey cottages.

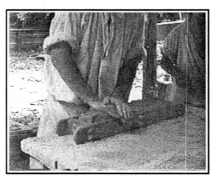

Brick-making   mould

Thomas and James also imported Somerset salt by boat from brine-wells at Dunball on the River Parrett for use in cheese-making. It was stored next to the brickyard in their Salt House and sold in 28lb bars for 6d each.

Alongside the road into the quarry, stone-crackers broke up stone unsuitable for building for use as road-surfacing. On the quarry floor, two lime-kilns burned day and night, one producing brown lime, the other white. Brown lime was made from limestone pebbles brought in by boat with coal from Aberthaw. It was used in cement required to set underwater, as in bridge foundations on the Somerset Levels. White lime

used Uphill limestone. Farmers spread it to improve soil and builders mixed it into white-wash, mortar, plaster and concrete. A narrow-gauge quarry rail-track carried the product from the kiln to the quayside for export in Gould shipping.

Uphill lime kiln

At a time when social life spilled over from overcrowded homes to the street, the kilns provided free 24-hour warmth where those with nowhere else to go could gather to gossip and drink Night-time shadows provided welcome cover for courting couples. Tramps found somewhere warm to sleep near the chimneys: sometimes too near, as the fumes could prove fatal.

The Gould family was closely involved with Uphill Chapel, raising funds to reduce the chapel debt and giving tea parties for Sunday School children:

> The annual tea meeting of Wesleyan Chapel at five o'clock was followed by addresses by the Revs R Sergeant, C Newman, T Gould and Messrs Pond and Rossiter.

The brothers supported nonconformist services at an outdoor "preaching station". On 9th July 1864 the *Mercury*:

> The annual tea meeting of the Uphill Preaching Station was held on board the sloop *Arabella*, a new vessel lying in the River Axe. Considerable interest was felt in this meeting because of its novelty and a large number of persons assembled.

The vessel, which was launched on 2nd June, is of 130 tons and was named after and christened by the only daughter of Mr Thomas Gould who is part owner with his brother and Mr Oliver Camm. It was built by Messrs Evans and Allen of Gloucester, is ketch-rigged, and is designed for the home trade, in connection with Messrs Gould's coal and salt business. Mr Oliver Camm is captain.

The boat was gaily decorated with flags from the mast head, and although very roomy it was not capable of accommodating more than half of those who had taken tickets. Those who arrived late had to wait while those who came first partook of their tea. The number who sat down to tea was about 300, and about 500 were present on board and on the embankment close to the vessel to hear the addresses which followed. There were eight speakers on religious subjects.

One was introduced by Mr Gould as Mr JN Levi, a coloured gentleman who had been some time amongst them and who was now about to return to his native Demerara. He called for three hearty cheers for the success of the vessel adding that after all that had been said by the previous speakers there was little for him to say. He would give his farewell address but would not think of inflicting on them a long speech. He had been three years in England and had received many kindnesses for which he offered his most heartfelt thanks. He was glad to know that his labours had been attended with success and had their approbation. He was about to return to his native country to labour in the Lord's vineyard and he begged that they would remember him in their prayers. The doxology was sung and the meeting terminated.

Mr Levi was probably the first black person to live in the village. While the adults' attention was taken, some children wandered away:

> During this assembly, three children got into a boat at some distance from the vessel by a plank from the water's edge. While the children were in the boat the tide rose and the plank floated. Attempting to return to the shore all three got onto the plank, which slipped, and they all fell into the river. Boats were immediately put off to their rescue, one of the children having fallen in a part of the river which was rather deep. Considerable excitement on board the *Arabella* caused the suspension of the proceedings. Two of the children were able to walk out of the water and the third was fortunately rescued with the aid of a boat, but not until she had received such a lesson as will most likely deter her from again venturing on the water in a similar manner.

Arabella may have been the vessel involved in a coastguard report of "mysterious signals to cutters in the bay" as "Jim Gould sailed out from Uphill in his coal barge." Uphill Customs Tide Waiter Norris spotted kegs alongside the barge which was grounded by the failing tide. As the kegs were full of rum he confiscated them and

the vessel, and charged James with smuggling. The court however accepted Gould's defence that the captain had seen the kegs floating and stopped to salvage them as a public duty.

His brother, Thomas Gould the Baptist minister, also found himself in court in 1866. He lived in Wheatstone House with his wife Bridgilina, their daughter Arabella and two sons, Temple and Thomas Edward. At Weston County Court in November 1866, Thomas Gould faced a claim for:

> £2 9s 6d by the father of Eliza Madge who at the age of 15 went into the service of Mr Thomas Gould as a domestic and there formed an acquaintance with the defendant's son aged 17 between whom an improper intimacy had existed. The amount claimed was for medical attendance in her confinement. The defendant pleaded that a father was in no way responsible for the debts of a minor son.

The Court gave its verdict for Thomas Gould, but two months later:

> Temple Gould of Uphill was summonsed to show cause why he should not contribute to the support of the illegitimate child of Eliza Madge of which he was the reputed father. The prosecutrix called Mr Robert Counsell who deposed having asked the father of the girl if he could not settle the case. There was some little discussion about family affairs and the Bench, not having the evidence before them to make an order, dismissed the case.

Within days the case reached Axbridge Petty Sessions. The court heard that the case had been dismissed at Weston because the father was too humble to employ counsel to represent him. Fuller evidence was given:

> Eliza Madge, aged between 15 and 16 was employed as a domestic servant in the house of Mr Thomas Gould of Uphill. The defendant Temple Gould was his son. On many occasions the young man and girl were left alone in the house and on one occasion "kept house" together for a fortnight. During this time the intimacy commenced and was afterwards continued, resulting in the birth of a child. The defendant was ordered to pay 2s 6d a week maintenance.

Eliza's father William Madge was a labourer born in Devon. It was his wife Frances who had raised the alarm when Mary Hancock's house burned down and his son John who had served ten months for stealing from the White Hart till. Eliza was the oldest of five daughters. Thomas Gould wrote to the *Mercury* firmly denying that the two had ever been left alone, upon which the editor declared the subject closed.

Temple Gould took over his father's business and died aged 59 on 26th September 1906.

Chapter 29. Generous Gentry

When his daughter married in June 1865, farmer John Harse spared no expense in making his mark on the social scene. The *Mercury* reported:

GAY WEDDING

It is not often this little village becomes the scene of so much gaiety and good feeling as on the marriage of Mr Samuel Baber, second son of Mr Benjamin Baber of Hutton and Miss Anne Eliza Ellis eldest daughter of Mr John Harse of Slimridge House, Uphill.

The morning was one of "merry, merry sunshine" and the villagers were early astir, decorating the church, erecting a triumphal arch over the gateway and placing flags on the church tower and other suitable positions in the village.

The wedding party, which was conveyed in carriages and greys, consisted of Mr Harse (father of the bride), the Misses Fanny, Emma, Alice and Georgina Harse (bridesmaids), Mr Joseph Harse, Mr Franz Baber &c. As the party left the sacred building, several of the young girls attending the village Sunday School, in which Miss Harse had been a teacher, strewed flowers in the pathway and merry peals struck out from the church bells.

The bride's mother Elizabeth seems not to have been present; she died aged 58 on 26th February 1868.

A month later, Miss Catharine DD Crotch, 27-year old daughter of the Rev William Crotch, married Mr Nicholls of Bridgnorth at a quieter parish church wedding. The bride wore a moire-antique dress, lace veil and lace shawl. In December her brother William Duppa Crotch was also married at Bridgnorth.

In 1866, Charles Whitting of Sandcroft extended his lands, buying Totterdown Farm for £5,620. He also sent his 19-year old daughter Anne to Germany to complete her education. As a rich landowner, he provided for those less fortunate, his generosity being effusively reported by the *Mercury*. When Anne returned from Germany he invited the village school children to a tea:

Nearly 100 juveniles were present and after being plentifully regaled with plum cake and tea were regaled with several innocent pastimes. Some pretty little pieces were nicely sung by the children in the presence of Mr and Mrs Whitting and family whose kindness will no doubt long be remembered by the youngsters.

Every year at Christmas he gave a supper to his cottage tenants and their wives:

After justice had been done to a good supply of roast beef and plum pudding, each guest was regaled with grog and a truly pleasant social evening was enjoyed.

In 1868, as Commandant of the 6th Somerset Volunteers, Captain Charles Whitting conducted the annual inspection of the unit and then marched them all:

to a sumptuous Christmas repast at Sandcroft House, Uphill. Fifty members joined dignitaries from town and county enjoying beef, mutton, game, poultry, plum puddings and salads, followed by steaming grog.

He entertained his cottage tenantry to the usual "sumptuous repast of roast beef and plum pudding" also at Sandcroft House. Similarly:

The Lord of the Manor, TT Knyfton Esq sent round to most of the villagers a joint of beef while other gentry have likewise contributed to make their poorer neighbours enjoy a happy Christmas.

The Knyftons gave an annual summer treat at Uphill Castle to boys of Colston School in Bristol who:

arrived in Weston by train and marched behind their band to Uphill. Mrs Knyfton is a lineal descendant of the philanthropist Colston who founded the school.

Balancing their deferential reporting of generous charity, the *Mercury* regularly deplored the meanness of the rich:

Another instance of the appreciation of honesty by the upper ten thousand which occurred in Uphill. A young man was on his way to Uphill with a load of beer when he saw something lying by the roadside. He found it to be a rich Paisley shawl evidently dropped not long previously by a lady of position. The young man urged forward his steed to overtake the owner and came up to a lady who was leisurely taking a walk. He asked her if she had lost the shawl. She immediately recognised it as her own much prized Paisley and after many expressions of joy she awarded the finder with the munificent sum of two pence! But such liberal acts as these are by no means confined to the ladies of Uphill as very similar instances have come to our notice in Weston. The wonder is that lost articles are restored to their owners until a definite reward is announced.

Chapter 30. Speedy Sports

Hunting, the *Mercury* thought, was the sport of gentlemen:

It is surprising that while every landlord and tenant seems desirous of encouraging the meet of hounds in the neighbourhood, that there should still be some "duffers" who, possessing a limited number of acres, strive to assume a position they do not enjoy, instead of encouraging that gentlemanly sport which the aristocracy of England WILL cultivate, would disturb and deprive the "Men of England" of their manly and health-giving exercise. Carpenters and tailors are good in their way, but we shall sigh over the day when the clods shall deprive the Squires of the healthy and invigorating pursuits of the chase.

The quarry was the hare, called "pussy" and hunted by greyhounds:

A CAPITAL RUN – The hounds of Wyndham W Lewis Esq met at Uphill Moor. A hare was almost immediately found and away she ran along by the railway cutting, on towards the residence of the Rev W Crotch. She bounded away in the direction of the River Axe, crossing the line and dashing away by the side of the old river which she boldly crossed, making her way by Mr Henry Amesbury's house, hotly pursued by the hounds with the huntsmen well up. Pussy then made away towards Lympsham apparently determined to outstrip her pursuers – made a clever double and retraced her steps for some distance. Instead however of continuing on the level she bore away to Bleadon Hill, the music of the merry pack evidently urging her onward. Clearing the hill she descended by the cutting and recrossed the railway line and was ultimately run into some distance from the spot where she was first found. The chase throughout was a most exciting one, the hounds not being once at fault. The run occupied 1 hour 40 minutes and the distance was quite 16 miles, the worthy squire and one or two other bold riders being in at the death.

Not all went to plan when Mr C Smith's hounds known as the Max Pack saw in the New Year of 1866:

A pretty good mounted field attended. The hounds worked well but ineffectually for a considerable time when it came out that the hare marked for the day's sport had met her death from the gun of some legitimate sportsman who popp'd her off long before Mr Smith arrived.

Determined not to be outdone, a "drag" was obtained which gave both horsemen and pedestrians about an hour's good run. The hounds went at a rattling pace and the mounts followed in capital style, swerving neither right nor left but going straight ahead and taking everything they came to. In the evening a select party accepted the invitation of C Whitting Esq of Sandcroft House to dine with him when all who know that gentleman's character need not be told that the dinner comprised a profusion of good things and that the bottles were marched round in "double quick time".

The following Christmas:

The Burnham Harriers met at the turnpike gate at Uphill. The hounds were thrown out but puss dodged them and was lost. Another hare was soon started and after a clipping run of over an hour and a half which pumped out the steeds and excited the riders she was killed in open.

Indoors after dinner, with a cigar and a decanter of port, billiards became the gentleman's game. The newly invented vulcanised rubber provided quiet cushions for solid wood table-rims and celluloid balls proved an improvement on ivory except when they caught fire.

Shooting was the sport of the ordinary man. Pubs held regular shooting matches, offering prizes for the best haul of pigeons and sparrows. At Christmas 1867, the *Mercury* declared:

Uphill village may be the *entrepot* of the neighbourhood for Pigeon and Sparrow Shooting Matches. Mr Peter Phillips of the Strand House put up a fat pig and several geese, Mr Amesbury of the Dolphin offered a fat sheep, a purse of sovereigns and a large number of geese and Mr Ham of the Flat Roof Inn Bleadon provided some remarkably fine geese. Many took part, enjoying considerable success and satisfaction.

Not all were successful:

A gentleman more acquainted with aquatic diversions than sports on *terra firma* took his first shooting excursion into the country and was fortunate enough to bag some game – a tame magpie. Encouraged, he went hunting on the sands and in a few seconds, game was again in view. The gun was immediately levelled and securing an accurate aim, a report and flash followed. Our gallant sportsman found to his surprise that his game was a young farmer quietly sitting underneath a sand-tot, enjoying the evening breeze and whose hat had been mistaken for a rabbit. Several of the shots struck the supposed game in the face and although one eye has been injured, it is hoped that the sight will not be impaired. We trust this will be a lesson to our Uphill adventurer.

Foot-racing was cheap and popular. Hundreds regularly watched and wagered on running matches known as "pedestrianism" along the Uphill Road. Spectators stood outside the Strand Inn, cheering, laying bets and drinking. In 1867 there were side-stakes of £2 when "Godby of Uphill raced Young of Bleadon but Young won from start to finish". A crowd of up to 2,000 turned out to cheer and bet on races between "Hornett, a well-known Weston professional runner and various amateur challengers".

Some contests were run against the clock, illustrating the quality of individual runners. Stakes of £5 attracted competitors to attempt to cover 150 yards in 16 seconds, an event won by a runner called Tinckling.

In February 1863 the *Mercury* reported:

A match of somewhat singular nature took place at Uphill. The contest was between a man and a horse, the owner of which backed his animal, a grey gelding called "St George", to go sixty yards, starting from the Dolphin Inn, towards Mrs Poole's farm, and to return in less time than it could be performed by a professional gentleman from Bristol who backed himself to eclipse the pace of the steed. The start was well effected by the umpire who is a well-known vet of Weston, the biped taking the lead and maintaining it till about 20 yards from home, when the rider of "St George" cleverly forced his nag and won by about ten feet! The result was hailed by enthusiastic cheers.

Although bare-knuckle prize-fighting had been outlawed by the beginning of 1825, the sport continued illicitly, encouraged by heavy betting. Police stopped the fights when they could but bare-fist fights remained a popular way of settling differences, usually outside a pub with no time limit. In April 1866:

Two young men named Bailey and Norville met near Uphill to test their strength by way of a few rounds. A great many admirers of the "manly art" assembled to witness the sport. After one hour and twenty minutes of hard fighting, in which some good pluck was shown on either side, the sponge was thrown up in favour of Bailey.

In the 1860s, that great social liberator the bicycle arrived, rapidly provoking demands that the magistrates do something about the "Velocipede mania" as bicycles were propelled through the streets at a furious rate to the danger of the public. Another great crowd of:

old and young turned out to witness a race between two Velocipedes on the Uphill Road. Mr Williams' vehicle was the decided favourite, opinion being that the difference in the circumference of the wheels would tell in his favour. The velocipede owned by Messrs Harris and Gough had undergone sundry alterations, handles having been constructed for the hands, thereby relieving the legs when required. The distance was from Gough's Library round Uphill and back – about four miles and a half. The losers should give five shillings toward Weston Hospital. After an absence of about twenty minutes the vehicle propelled by Messrs Gough and Dyer came in sight and in another three minutes won easily, Mr Williams' vehicle being a considerable distance behind.

At Christmas 1869, hundreds of spectators gathered for the West of England Bicycle Races on the Uphill Road starting from Forty Acres Field. The Trial Stakes of two miles went once round Uphill's roads and the Welter Stakes of five miles went twice round the village. The riders were called jockeys and competed under fancy names like Fairy Queen, Juno and Nina. They found it difficult getting over the loose sand at the entrance to field but despite a strong wind and cutting sleet the five-mile race was won in 31 minutes. Spectators took cover in a marquee where:

Host Wiltshire dispensed 'creature comforts' between races.

❏ ❏ ❏ ❏ ❏

Chapter 31. Uphill Benefit Society

The booming insurance business, providing the first security for working people, arrived in January 1860:

UPHILL FRIENDLY BENEFIT SOCIETY

It is in contemplation to establish a Friendly Society at the Dolphin Inn in this village. The principal feature, after providing for sickness and burials, is that the funds will be divided among the members every five years. We understand that several names have already been enrolled and that the laws are to be submitted to Mr Tidd Pratt for his approval. Applications to Mr F Cox, Dolphin Inn .... At a very well attended meeting Mr Gladstone took the chair and Mr B Cox explained the rules. Thirty five members were enrolled.

In May 1861 Uphill absorbed the new movement into its traditional procession behind a band from inn to church and from one source of free food and drink to another:

The picturesque little village of Uphill presented an appearance of unusual gaiety in consequence of the gathering of the members of this excellent society. The members, accompanied by several friends (many of whom we are credibly informed have since joined the "Band of Brotherhood") assembled 9.30 am outside the Dolphin Inn. They marched with the Artillery band to the home of the Rev S Bennett and then with him to the Church. From there they went on to Uphill Castle the residence of TT Knyfton Esq, that gentleman – as is well known – taking a lively interest in everything appertaining to the welfare of the working classes. The worthy Squire behaved in his usual urbane and liberal manner and fully maintained his well known character for Old English hospitality. The establishments of Charles Whitting and WD Crotch Esqrs, Messrs R Poole, T Whitting, Luff and other farmers were next visited, all of whom vied with each other in placing before their unexpected, but nevertheless most welcome guests, "substantials" not forgetting full frothing flagons of "genuine home brew'd" and brimming bumpers of cider to wash down the edibles.

The cavalcade returned to the Dolphin Inn where they partook of dinner, served in such a superior manner as to reflect the highest praise on the culinary powers of the worthy host and hostess, Mr and Mrs Cox. After toasts to the Queen, the Society and its officers, speeches praised the

success of the society which was due to the work of Mr Cox. About 80 guests were present. The exterior of the Dolphin was tastefully decorated with arches, evergreens, flags and floral devices.

A year later, in 1862 for the Society's second anniversary:

At 9 am a procession of members formed at Hobbs' Boat Inn headed by the famed Weare band and proceeded with their blue and white rosettes to the Dolphin Hotel. From there they processed to the parish church led by the band to hear a sermon preached by the Rev S Bennett, the curate, and then to the Rectory. Although absent, the Lord of the Manor TT Knyfton Esq showed his support with a munificent gift to the club. They went on to visit Charles Whitting Esq and then the Rev Crotch. On its return the procession called on Farmer Luff and Slimeridge farm, the residence of Mr Thomas Whitting. Society members sat down to dinner in the Dolphin Inn at 4 o'clock, an excellent and sumptuous repast. After this they adjourned to the large room upstairs for music and dancing in the true old English style. In all, the capabilities of stomach were tested and found able to bear a goodly quantity of cheering lotion without affecting the brain.

By 1865 the event had become a major item on Whit Tuesday in the village calendar, graphically reported by the *Mercury*:

UPHILL CLUB MEETING

This usually quiet little village was all jollity. The Friendly Society held a club feast or what is called a "club walking". Flags floated in mid air, the villagers turned out in all their Sunday best, hawkers were present offering their goods for sale, nut sellers with their "crack 'em and try 'em before you buy 'em" were very busy; a German band was trying to scrape together a few coppers by the strains from their beautiful (!) instruments; a gypsy woman would step up with "Please Sir, would you like to have your fortune told?" How could you refuse? You hand her a small piece of silver and she informs you that there are two young good-looking amiable and loving ladies at enmity with each other because they both love you and know very well that you won't have both – and that you will choose the dark one because she will make the best wife.

Then you run up against another of the same tribe holding a tambourine and she informs you that she has been playing and dancing and now pleads for a copper. A woman sings out from behind a stall "Won't you please have a gingerbread, Sir? They are very nice, Sir. Only a penny apiece, Sir."

"Here they come," sung out a little urchin and out of the Dolphin Hotel came several men bearing poles with emblems and flowers on the top. The procession was formed and, headed by the Weston fife and drum band, wended their way to the church where Divine service was read by the Rev Stephen Bennett. In his sermon he implored them not to let it be said that they went to church in the morning and joined in revelry and drunkenness in the evening. After the service the procession took its walk and returned to the Dolphin about three o'clock where they found an excellent dinner awaiting. The dinner did the host and hostess great credit. Mr and Mrs Stone's healths were drunk and we heard the exclamation, "Us niver had such a good dinner afore, I'm blowed if us 'ave."

Having reported the accounts in good order, the president pointed out that "under 4d per week secures 7s a week and medical attendant if sick. But", he added reprovingly, "not enough gentry are members".

❑ ❑ ❑ ❑ ❑

Chapter 32. "Uphill one large Cesspool"

Rumours rose in November 1861 of a fever epidemic in Weston. As healthy air was advertised as an attraction to summer visitors, the town surgeon rapidly declared that any fever was at a low level but did urge the "removal of miasmatic poison from the neighbourhood of residences, such as undrained pigstyes, manure, dust heaps etc".

The Hutton Jury of Sewers was a statutory committee of men who owned land bordering Uphill Rhyne. Under their foreman Joseph Hancock they perambulated its banks twice a year before adjourning to the Ship "where an excellent dinner was served up in style by Mr and Mrs Every. The wines and dessert were commended for their excellence". After the loyal toast they considered such matters as the need to open a second "eye" or gate at the West Bow to meet flood emergencies. In 1863, they found "all satisfactory except a bridge belonging to TT Knyfton which was in such a dangerous condition that jurymen had to go some distance to cross the rhyne safely." But their only reaction to the pollution dumped by Weston was to note that the "rhyne should be cleansed".

Land-owners took a sterner view. TT Knyfton, Charles Whitting, the Rev Robert William Crotch and the Rev Stephen Bennett began legal action in September 1864 against Weston-super-Mare Board of Health as:

> the Board had negligently and injuriously conducted certain sewerage works, whereby they had fouled the stream of water called the Uphill Rhyne, and caused other injurious effects, by which the parties were severely damaged to the amount of £1000.

This was followed by a scathing *Mercury* report on elections to the Board of Health when only the candidates turned up and voted themselves into office. The new Board proposed a 13-inch brick sewer to Uphill Pill relying on gravity and the ebb tide to discharge the sewage out to sea. Against a background of national concern over the pollution of rivers, Mr Knyfton declared that he would oppose this scheme and any other that did not carry the sewage out to Black Rock. Unable to satisfy anybody, the Board brought in a consultant, Joseph Bazalgette, whose innovatory sewage system for London remains in use in the 21st century. Having inspected Weston's Disinfecting Works and the proposed sewer to the outfall at Uphill, Bazalgette approved the scheme generally adding that an extension to Black Rock would cost more than it was worth.

An alternative popular with those who stood to make money out of it was "irrigation". This process was claimed "to remove the sewage and thus avoid the expense of litigation and the nuisance which invariably arises from the removal of foetid matter". The sewage was spread on agricultural land and left there to purify itself and fertilise the ground. Mr RL Jones, steward of the Pigott estate, told the Board:

> The Lord of the Manor of Weston-super-Mare expresses his willingness as an experiment to take as much of the town sewage as would irrigate five acres of land. He would probably take it all and would get it there by means of wooden shoots (chutes). He would bear the expense of doing it and would prefer the gross to the deodorized sewage.

But the Board preferred Bazalgette to Pigott. And when the case of Knyfton v the Board reached court, the Master of the Rolls desired the Board to:

> do all they could to remove or abate the nuisance. The only alternative was to put the sewage on land but that was owned by the plaintiffs who would not agree to it. The plaintiffs are entitled to say that the river shall be undefiled.

He granted an injunction stopping the use of the rhyne for sewage and gave the Board three months to comply. He added:

> The plaintiffs own the land along the proposed line of the sewer from the town to the River Axe. They must give all reasonable facility to any plan of the defendants, who are ordered to stop the flow of sewage into Uphill Rhyne.

Adopting the Bazalgette scheme as "about the best possible", the Town Commissioners ordered the construction of a sewer from Orchard Street to the Disinfecting Works and onward to Uphill where, as the *Mercury* put it:

> the accumulated filth of the neighbourhood will be discharged into the River Axe near the Black Rock.

The irrigators did not give up, claiming that Weston produced 400,000 gallons of sewage a day which, if utilised on the land would raise £3,500 a year compared with the £11,000 estimated cost of building a sewer. Mr Pigott didn't give up either. Seeing the prospect of a perpetual income from renting out land crossed by the sewer, he proposed a pipeline to Sand Bay, into deeper water and further from the town.

Unexpected opposition from the Brean Down Harbour Company threatened legal action against the Axe plan as it would pollute both river and sea, damaging the commercial prospects of the harbour. Given three months by the Master of the Rolls to stop the flow of sewage, the Board of Health desperately considered reactivating the disinfecting works. In the nick of time the Harbour engineers decided that the Axe sewage would not injure the docks; the Attorney-General intervened to give the Weston Board time to complete the sewage works; and work began on Bazalgette's Uphill sewer. But a great gale swept in from the Atlantic in November 1865 and in heavy rain the sewerage excavations at the mouth of the Axe collapsed into the river. Work recommenced but in January 1866 the *Mercury* trumpeted:

THE SEWAGE QUESTION

Weston cannot afford to trifle with her present great prosperity; and viewed in any light whatever, the contemplated scheme of carrying sewage into the Axe is bound to be suicidal.

Death from fever became so frequent that families hired hackney carriages to carry corpses to the cemetery. Uphill's mortality rate was four times the average:

ALARMING FEVER

Fever is still raging in Uphill. Two adult females in the prime of life (one the mother of a family) have died from its effects. A correspondent suggests the appointment of a medical officer to ascertain from what cause so malignant an affliction arises. Should the fever extend to Weston, the effects would be fatal to that resort of fashion in more ways than one.

The *Mercury* in April 1866:

It would be well if the landed proprietors of Uphill and others connected with the matter lose no time in remedying the state of things brought to light at a Weston Board of Health meeting. Uphill, in common with Weston, is naturally one of the healthiest and sweetest little spots in the West of England; yet by inattention to drainage – and common sanitary law – it is converted into one large cesspool.

This prompted Weston's Board of Health to set up an inspection:

The Surveyor's report on the drainage of Uphill described the state of nearly every residence in the village. Throughout the whole place there was no proper drainage, as the bog-pits (earth closets) overflowed into open ditches which emptied themselves into the rhyne, causing contamination of the water. Such an offensive state of things was highly dangerous to public health.

Mr Stringfield, town surgeon, retorted defensively:

I have attended a case of fever at Uphill and know of two others. One was attended by a non-professional man and that as well as another has died. The house drained into a ditch. My patient is quite well. An open drain came from Mr Whitting's house and the whole of the neighbouring cottages making a deposit in the drain to the depth of six inches. Mr Counsell the overseer of Uphill said it had always been so and they had never received any complaint.

Now it appears that it is our drainage that has caused Uphill to be unhealthy. It is no worse at Uphill than for some years past and we are endeavouring to remedy the nuisance as fast as we can. For some time now we have let nothing go into the rhyne. It is not only the drainage of Uphill that runs into the rhyne, but also that of Oldmixon, Hutton and Locking.

Thomas T Knyfton personally mapped the drains, water pumps and wells of Uphill Castle, adding explanatory notes. Rainwater from the roof and waste from the scullery and brew-house were piped through small drains into the main drain. This ran under the house and was big enough for a man to walk through. Pipes led from it to an open ditch at the south end of the Home Paddock. Sewage was disposed of separately. Water closets emptied into a pit outside the study window. When this was nearly full it drained into a further pit. He refuted the Surveyor's report on his property:

My house has no bog-pit and no sewage from any house of mine drains into the rhyne. The reason for the fever in Uphill last November was that a married couple named Stone came from Weston into the parish. The poor woman was extremely ill from fever from which she died. Some of the neighbours took the infection and imparted it to others. Happily it has now ceased. I have no fear for the future of the parish when we are relieved of the insufferable nuisance which Weston Town Commissioners have illegally inflicted on us.

In reply to that, James Gane, another surgeon, wrote:

I have inspected the rear of many Uphill houses and find that there are bog-pits behind Mr Knyfton's house which receive matter accumulated in water-closets and privies. They become silted up and need to be emptied. They have an offensive smell which produces diseases of the most alarming type. No gentleman would allow such a state of things to be about him but would seek a remedy by drainage to a common sewer as is found in Uphill rhyne or, which I recommend, to construct a covered sewer to the river Axe.

With regard to Mrs Stone, she did have some illness – not the fever – in Weston before going to live at Uphill. I saw her on the day of her death and she had fever then. A person in her weak condition going into a district of a bad sanitary state is likely to become infected with typhus fever or ague.

Eminent medical opinion is that the disease is transferred not by emanations from the body but from evacuations from the patient. I looked at another house where there had been fever. Three or four families lived there and they all shared two privies at the rear of the house. These were choked up solid. Their contents oozed into a nearby ditch and gave off a stench. This was the obvious cause of the fever.

In May the Hutton Jury of Sewers formally inspected their watercourses as far as Uphill before enjoying another splendid Ship Inn dinner.

❏ ❏ ❏ ❏ ❏

Chapter 33. Building Bazalgette's Sewer

More delays followed the collapse of excavations across Joseph Harse's Slimeridge fields where the modern techniques of pile-driving and concreting were found necessary. Summoned in July 1866 to explain the lack of progress to the Master of Rolls Joseph Bazalgette explained that the contractor was a good local builder but did not understand that type of work. He began in October 1865 but unexpectedly ran into soft sand and by December all the work had collapsed. He was employing 120-140 men which was not enough but no more were available because of Government works on Brean Down. As the *Mercury* commented:

> Several times the work has been left in the evening in apparent safety and the morning's dawn has shown a heart rending wreck, the land, notwithstanding the stout piling, having slipped for some yards, snapping the deals and beams and completely smashing and burying the brickwork that had been laid.

Weston Museum took charge of:

> a well preserved skull of an aboriginal British ox found in the trench dug for the new sewer. It dated from the ancient Britons and was the progenitor of our domestic cattle.

Although Uphill farmers John Harse and James Evans claimed compensation for damage caused to their land by the works, New Year 1867 saw the:

OFFICIAL INSPECTION OF NEW SEWER

Weston Board of Health inspected the newly constructed main sewer extending from the River Axe to the tanks in Uphill Drove. The inspection committee first proceeded to the outlet near Black Rock in the Axe Rive when some, bent upon examining the interior of the work, courageously entered the mouth and explored the entire vaulted passage extending over two miles, while the "outsiders" walked over the arched channel to see that all was right above. Fortunately there are "man holes" at different parts of the drain at the first of which our subterranean explorers thankfully lifted their heads to inhale fresh air and imbibe French brandy, the latter elixir being freely dispensed by the *terra firma* pedestrians.

In this way, wading through slush and with no more light than a few "dips" sent forth, did our hidden travellers trudge on their dark and dreary journey, finding no relief, save that now and then afforded by the bottle and the breeze at the widely separated breathing holes. At length the goal was reached....

The report given by the explorers as to the interior workmanship of the structure is most gratifying. The work will be opened next Tuesday when the Board of Health intend celebrating by dining together. A wall will at once be erected to prevent any further flow of sewage into the rhyne and thus dispel all cause of action and prevent further litigation in connection with our sewage.

Within days the legal proceedings terminated. The work, begun on 12th October 1865 had taken two years; no life had been lost; the cost had risen from the initial contract for £9000 to £12000; over 2 million bricks had been used. At the official ceremony, a copy of the Notice of Opening was put in a glass bottle and dropped into the sewer and a half-crown reward offered to the finder. In the village:

> The Board and spectators who had journeyed from Weston by way of the sands – by far the cleanest way – and three or four residents of Uphill watched the penstock valve being raised. Sewage – and the bottle – rushed through. The party walked through muck and mire to the outfall where the force of the sewage passing into the river left no doubt that the drain was capable of cleansing itself.

> The majority of the company then repaired to the Ship Inn at Uphill where Host Every administered to their bodily wants.

The penstock was the two-way valve that let sewage flow out and stopped sea-water flowing in. The Board paid a man 25s a week to operate the penstock and clean the disinfecting engines. In March 1867:

ACCIDENT AT THE PENSTOCK IN UPHILL

On Saturday morning before daylight, Hillman, the man in charge at the outfall, had a narrow escape from being drowned by the sewage and washed out to sea. He was standing on one of the iron girders raising the valve when the spanner slipped off the valve spindle and he fell to the bottom of the chamber. Fortunately the valve was only slightly raised and with the assistance of a coastguard, Hillman was got out more frightened than hurt, his clothes emitting a strong effluvia from his bath in the sewage.

In May, Joseph Harse applied for the penstock job asking for 15s a week. The Board gave him 39s a year and made him responsible for the cost of any failure up to £100. He was soon in trouble. Not understanding that iron gearing had to be kept oiled he found he couldn't raise and lower the penstock at every tide. As a result, sea-water flooded back to the disinfecting works. He was warned that if he failed to do his job, sewage would not clear, causing foul gases to build up inside the sewer.

Thomas Knyfton soon complained about the smell from ventilating shafts and John Quick wrote from Uphill Drove:

> The drainage scheme is so badly done as to prove still a great nuisance. Before the present work was carried out, my family suffered greatly in their health; some of them having breakings-out like boils or carbuncles on various parts of the body; whilst other were laid up with slow fevers. My medical man assured me this arose from the impure water which had been poisoned through the drainage matter mixing with it. To the same cause was attributed the deaths of several of my cattle and sheep. The completed work brought no better success.
>
> My wife was suddenly taken very ill and confined to her bed. When she recovered enough to go to a physician, he said the cause of her illness was inhaling impure air. Within a few yards of my house is a man-hole cover of the new drain and when the wind is in a certain direction, the effluvia which surrounds my dwelling is most horrible, disgusting and sickening. I suffer from the effects, my limbs being considerably swollen and paining most severely. The probability is that my family, which is not a small one, may again get ill in turns.
>
> I am not a wealthy man and ill-prepared to meet the heavy doctor's bills which I have to pay. Under these circumstances, some compensation is due to me from the Board of Health.

Fearing "a law suit a year", the Board proposed first to close all venting manholes. Advised that this would cause "gas to go back into houses and engender fever" it filled the vents with charcoal and hoped that a good draught through the drain would help: "If there is not enough, small fires in the shaft would help". In February 1868, while they considered building a 40-foot ventilation shaft beside the penstock, the sewer exploded:

> The valve at the penstock chamber had been removed to be repaired, and replaced by a wooden self-acting trap at the outfall.
>
> From the indentations, a heavy stone must have been hurled at it, breaking it off its hinges. The flood tide was unusually high and flowed up the drain, meeting the sewage. There being no ventilation as the manholes were recently closed, the

drain burst. One breach was in   Uphill Brick Yard, another in Uphill Drove, the crown of the drain being blown off for 3 or 4 feet. The liquid ascended into the air like the streams of a fountain. The sewage was turned off at the disinfecting works while the mouth of the drain was boarded up to keep out the tide.

> A reward will be issued for information on who damaged the trap door.

Engineers pointed out that the sewer carried storm water for which it was not designed and recommended replacing the wooden valve with one of cast iron as it had to hold a pressure of at least ten tons, with a spare valve in case of accidents. Ever economical, Weston Town Commissioners repaired the old valve and put it back. At the same time they put up a board with instructions to Joseph Harse painted on it. But when their Surveyor found the valve shut and enough static sewage to show that it had not been opened for at least 24 hours, Joseph Harse was given three months notice for neglect of duty. Hillman was reinstated and paid 25s per week with a cottage and garden rent free. Thomas Knyfton owned the land around the penstock and now demanded compensation to allow any person, including Hillman, to cross it.

James Evans took legal action claiming that construction of the sewer had caused structural damage to his house and that "noxious fumes and excreta damaged the health of his wife Mary Ann":

Extract from James Evans' legal action   [SRO]

Chapter 34. On the Farm

The average local weekly wage for a farm labourer was eight shillings – worth about £18 in 2006 – and life was dominated by the need to earn enough for the family to live on. Harvesting brought in an extra two shillings a week. Other seasonal piece-work such as turnip hoeing, mangold pulling, hedging and draining was back-breaking and the regular daily tasks still had to be done. Children picked vegetables or fruit and cleared stones from the fields, all for trifling wages. Boys aged 7-10 regularly drove horse-drawn ploughs and carts. Women worked in the fields. As they had a child every two years throughout their child-bearing life, older sisters looked after babies while mothers worked.

Some farmers sold produce cheaply to their workers but it was of such poor quality that it would not sell at market. Part of the wage was "free" cider, often so bad that it undermined health. The wife drank tea and the children had "tea-kettle broth" which was hot water flavoured with a few hedgerow herbs or ends of bacon, or sometimes just the warm water. Food consisted mostly of bread and cheese, or bread dipped in cider and a bit of bacon for the husband after work.

Weekly shopping costs for a labourer's family averaged 6s on bread, 8d on ½ lb of butter, 6d on 1 lb cheese, 8d on 1 lb bacon, 2d on ½ lb sugar, 4d on 2 oz tea and a pennyworth of pepper and salt. They also needed candles costing 3½d and two shillingsworth of coal to augment the free firewood they were allowed to collect from the bottom of hedges.

Although clothes could be mended and handed down, father's boots had to be kept in repair – another 7d for the cobbler. Sick Club insurance cost 6d and any child that went to school had to pay 3d. Soap, washing soda, starch and blue-bag cost 3d a week.

Their cottage came with the job and the rent of 1s 6d was deducted from wages. Although good landlords kept workers' houses in repair, many families lived in two or three rooms with no sanitation.

While children laboured in the fields, animals had protection from the law. James Palmer was fined 5s 6d for allowing 5 donkeys to stray on the highway at Uphill as was Peter Phillips of Halfway House. Weston Petty Sessions heard that William Jones had allowed three donkeys to stray in Middle Lane, Uphill. He pleaded they had got out without his knowledge but was fined 1s for each donkey.

A letter to the *Mercury* in July 1868 expressed disgust at seeing in Uphill "some persons breaking in a young mare preparatory to shoeing. After being beaten and worried until quite exhausted, the animal died the following morning." This drew a fast and firm response from Robert Fear of Uphill Farm:

> The owner and others were endeavouring to shoe the colt previous to breaking in. She was a young mare near thoroughbred and consequently high spirited. All the energies of as clever, experienced and humane a smith as this district can boast of were unavailing. The animal died from the injuries sustained through falling on her head and not from being "beaten and worried".

The same Robert Fear sued the Bristol & Exeter Railway Company for £10 in February 1869 for an injury to one of his cows which had reduced its value from £20 to only £8. The animal was in Three Acre Field rented from Mr Knyfton. The field was separated from the railway by a quickset hedge, a rail fence, a ditch and a bank. James Wolff, the servant of Capt Avery, saw the cow lying in the ditch and told Robert Fear. He found the sinews in the leg were severed and called the cow-doctor. When asked in court why he took two months to complain, he explained that he hoped the cow would get better. Asked why he had never complained about the fence he said that nobody knew who had built it, although the railway company had repaired it since the accident.

James Exon, a former railway ganger or labourer, gave evidence that all the fences along the line had been put up by the Company and when he retired there was a fence at Three Acre Field. Local farrier Henry Brock said that a piece of glass or iron could have caused the injury. Farmer John Harse confirmed the valuation on the animal and told the court that there were fences all along the line. Another farmer, James Evans, said the company had fenced all the fields when the line was built. In his opinion fences were needed, as a ditch was an adequate barrier if full of water, but not if dry. The Company's defence was that it did not fence ditches unless asked by the farmer and then only as a favour not an obligation.

James Evans himself appeared in another court case charged with refusing to pay 11s 4d wages due to William Lewis, his "servant in husbandry". Evans claimed that Lewis had left and gone to work for someone else without asking for his money. Mrs Evans, however, said she had given Lewis a week's notice but refused to pay him as he left the next day without working out his time. The court struck a balance by ordering James Evans to pay 11s to William Lewis who then had to pay the court costs out of it.

Another of Robert Fear's supporters, John Harse, advertised:

> STRAYED, from UPHILL,
> a yellow and white COW, in milk.
>
> Any person restoring the cow to the owner, Mr HARSE, Uphill, Weston-super-Mare, shall receive £1 reward.

Great Christmas displays of meat on butchers' open counters had precise identification of origin:

> Choice heifers, South Down sheep and a beautiful fat lamb grazed by Mr Joseph Harse of Uphill.
> Weston Christmas Meat and Poultry Show
> – in our butchers' shops –
> Mr J Harse, Uphill: 5 Porlock sheep.
> Mr Jno Harse a fine lamb.
> Mr W Fear, Uphill: 5 Down sheep, 5 Southdown sheep.

One of John Harse's sons left Slimeridge to join the 19th century exodus of ambitious young men to the colonies, his deeds being reported in the *Mercury*:

> James Harse, a sergeant in the armed police of Akaroa, New Zealand, has been commended for dealing with a violent prisoner.

Newspapers frequently ran advertisements encouraging emigration:

> **QUEENSLAND – All adults paying full fare to the Colony will receive a £30 land order equivalent to 30 acres to be selected by themselves.**
>
> **(Adults are all passengers aged over 12. Two children are charged as 1 adult.)**
>
> **Free and assisted passages are also available.**

Like the Harse family, the Pooles were long-established farmers. When Richard Poole died in 1862 he was mourned as a "yeoman of Uphill, well known and highly respected".

He had only recently celebrated gathering in his corn crops with a Harvest Home for his labourers and neighbours. They enjoyed:

> … an excellent supper, consisting of prime ox joints and gigantic puddings, nor was there any absence of the etceteras necessary to feast the stomachs of the 33 guests.

Edward Luff owned Manor Farm on Uphill Batch, the road up to Bleadon. Now Uphill Road South, it became known locally as Luff's Hill. Mr Luff's son, another Edward, continued farming there into the 20th century.

Edward Luff 1935   *[RBC]*

As the village's oldest inhabitant in 1951 Edward Luff described his family as:

> farmers and always have been. They were great cheese-makers, and attracted dealers from Taunton who would come periodically and buy up all the cheese that they could lay their hands on.
>
> When I was a boy there was a lot of unemployment and after the morning's work on the farm had been done, men would straggle off to the village street corners to while away the time. Between 10s and 12s 6d a week was a common wage for a labourer.

In June 1863 his father took a worker named Chandler to court:

> to recover 4s 9d, three days wages. Chandler had asked Mr Luff for time off work to look for a missing uncle and permission to use one of the farm horses to help the search. He agreed, but Chandler stayed away longer than he should. When he returned three days later, the bridle was broken to pieces. He thus forfeited his wages but Chandler claimed it was all done with permission. Both men refused to settle out of court which ordered in favour of Luff.

Another of his workers,

> Joseph James, labourer of Uphill, was charged with unlawfully absenting himself from the service of his master Mr Edward Luff with whom he had agreed to serve twelve months for £9 10s until Lady Day 1867. The defendant said he left his work because the master threatened to "put the pick into him". This accusation was strongly denied by Mr Luff's solicitor. James then claimed he had only a monthly agreement to work but, following evidence by Mr Luff's son, he was ordered to pay back half his wages and costs.

A similar court summons involved John Delay in his role as market gardener. The dispute was with John Harris a "servant in husbandry" over wages and notice. Magistrates again struck a balance by ordering Delay to pay the wage due and Harris to pay the costs. Shortly afterwards, John Biss Delay died from asthma and dropsy, being remembered as a "respected inhabitant, the village postmaster for nearly forty years".

Uphill poultry did well. Edward Luff's goose hatched ten goslings and then three weeks later she laid eight eggs and was sitting on them. George Vowles, a workman employed by Ferdinand Cox the coachmaker, kept hens in his yard:

> A hen of the Barton breed, belonging to George laid two eggs, weighing seven ounces each. One of the eggs when opened was found to contain five yolks.

Another:

> common Barton fowl belonging to Mr G Hill of the Castle Lodge laid the largest egg ever seen, measuring 11½ inches round the ends, 9¼ inches in girth and weighing 12 ounces. The shell was perfectly smooth and did not appear to have given the hen any extraordinary effort in laying.

Farmer Evans' son, also James, lived in Wyndham Lodge, Uphill. He rejoiced in:

> A Prolific Duck – which in the last twelve months has produced an extraordinary number of broods, in all 47. The birds are all living and the mother has commenced laying within six days from hatching the last brood.

The excellent hay harvest of June 1865 produced about 30 cwt per acre. James Counsell's crop of fine apricots was stolen but "some fine melons and grapes were cut in the gardens of Uphill Castle". Thomas Knyfton extended his estates in 1865, buying Oldmixon Farm for £1,400.

An idea for fun on the farm appeared in a magazine:

Scientific farming amusements.

> Cover a barrel with stiff stout paper, tied round the edge. Place a board to give rats access to the top of the barrel. Sprinkle cheese on the paper for a few days until the rats believe they have a right to it. Find a rock measuring about six inches high and put it in the barrel. Then fill with water, leaving only enough space on the rock for one rat to stand. Cut a cross in the centre of the paper. The first rat falls through into the water and climbs on the rock. The paper closes and the next rat does the same. They fight for the place on the rock. The noise attracts other rats which all fall in and share the same fate.

Then, in 1865, the "Cattle Disease" arrived:

> This terrible visitation has carried off several cows and other animals belonging to yeomen in this neighbourhood. The greatest care should be taken not to mix flocks which come from different fairs and markets, as the disease spreads with great rapidity; and is so contagious that a flock of sheep being driven along a road so taint the atmosphere as to affect those animals which may pass the same way within a few hours afterwards.

William Fear of Uphill and six other Weston farmers signed a letter to the *Bristol Post* denying that deaths in their herds were caused by the "cattle plague". The *Mercury* claimed that there was no "Russian cattle plague or murrain" in the Weston area, but cited several cows carried off by the newly named foot and mouth disease: nine had died at three farms in thirty days. At a meeting in Bristol farmers were told of:

> Russian plague or rinderpest, known for time immemorial in Russia, where it sweeps off myriads of oxen every year. It is not known elsewhere in the world except by importation. It needs instant slaughter and destruction of all waste. Import controls and trained inspectors are needed.

Poultry farmers urged people to eat poultry instead of meat and an enterprising Mr W Beak offered an alternative solution:

> This disease is brought on by foul gases in our atmosphere. It can certainly be cured by Tipper's Mystery, a celebrated and sure antidote for disorders in horses and cattle.

In October, prayers were said in all churches to allay both cattle disease and cholera. By January 1866, the Cattle Plague was confirmed in markets at Bristol, Clevedon and Taunton. Weston and Uphill farmers met to consider vaccination against the disease. The government issued Orders in Council forbidding the movement of live beasts and also specified parts of carcases. Eventually, on 5th January 1867, Somerset was declared "clear of cattle plague there having been no case in the county since 4th November".

Chapter 35. Lines on Uphill Church

By 1864, the old hilltop church had fallen into disrepair, prompting RVW Silcock to compose "Lines on Uphill Church":

Roofless! Save to the canopy of heaven!

> Food to the stormy blast – a standing wreck;
> Centuries have rolled on, by thee they've passed
> And turned a smile, but thou art here,
> Remembrancer of days gone by. Oh, man!
> Cast a stray glance at the work of time,
> Thy ancestors sleep aye, perhaps
> In this baseless fabric's domain. Hark!
> To the hollow-sounding wind it echoes,
> Through yonder ruinous tower – it whistle;
> The cry of spirits answer, unheard by man!
> How oft the bells have pealed their merry notes
> On marriage days; the funeral dirge
> Has alike been thy inmate, ancient tower;
> Thy gravestones stand on God's allotted acre,
> Monuments of Time's great combat with man.

Later that year, Thomas Tutton Knyfton funded the restoration. Old Cornish roofing slabs were removed from the porch and used to repair the chancel roof. The belfry was restored, the rood screen removed and the chancel:

> thoroughly repaired and converted into a mortuary chapel. The walls of the roofless nave and porch were repaired and the porch door was bricked up. The arch between the nave and the tower was built up and a large North window introduced to let in more light.

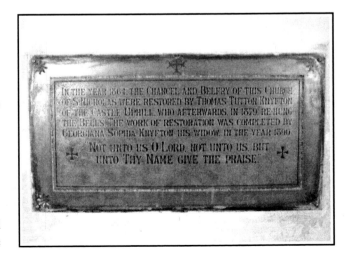

Repairing old St Nicholas Church   *[UVS]*

❑ ❑ ❑ ❑ ❑

Chapter 36. Rector Stephen Bennett

Victorian progress brought a new spirit of enquiry which probed the traditionally unquestioned sources of authority. Village clergy were not immune from this. In November 1862 a letter to the *Mercury* posed:

A Point of Law

Some curious proceedings have taken place in Uphill with regard to the making of a church-rate. At a vestry meeting where there were only three persons, a rate was made of 3½d in the pound instead of the usual one of 1d. This needed a fourth party who was soon found and in consideration of "largess" bestowed upon him in the shape of several articles of wearing apparel by a clerical functionary, affixed his sign-manual to the order empowering the rate. We hear that great opposition will be made to payment of the rate. Is the rate made by such underhand work legal?

This question was rapidly rejected by the churchwardens on behalf of the new Rector Stephen Bennett. The living,

value £307 p.a. with a parsonage house was in the patronage of J Fisher Esq. It became vacant by the death of the Rev Frederick Trevor.

Stephen Bennett, an unmarried 34-year old, had been the curate. He served the parish from 1862 to 1890, considerably improving and enlarging the Rectory and outbuildings. An enthusiastic gardener, he added trees and extended the lawns, shrubberies and flower beds. His successor the Rev AJ Burr acknowledged Stephen Bennett's work:

It would take the pen of a Cowper to present an adequate picture in summer of this charming spot. In the garden is an immense standard rose tree – Souvenir de la Malmaison which was planted in 1877 – probably the largest rose tree in England. Its diameter is 12 feet, from ground to bloom is 3 feet, from the ground to its point 8 feet. It yields a large amount of blooms in June and September.

The rector spent his own money on the church building, prompting a letter to the *Mercury* in November 1864:

Uphill Parish Church has been much improved of late years and we are indebted to the Rector for this good work; but how is it that with a number of wealthy inhabitants they cannot give

the poor old parishioners a little fire-place in the church during winter months. The music is very good, and better than in some larger churches; but if Mr Crotch and some of the parishioners would give us an organ it would be better than the little harmonium.

Soon after this appeal there was an:

AMATEUR CONCERT AT UPHILL

The Uphill Church choir gave a concert at the parish school in aid of the church organ fund. The event (for a concert in a country parish is an event) created quite a pleasurable degree of excitement through the village, and just as the treat was talked about several days before it came off, so will the success of those who were engaged in it be chatted over during those long summer evenings and by the fireside during the next winter. The audience flocked betimes to the school-room which fair and dextrous hands had made gay with sweet-smelling and eye-bewitching flowers. The concert was directed by Mr Edwards, organist of the church.

Queen Victoria's Church of England offered the broadest range of services from something near Methodist simplicity to something not far from Rome. In a querulous article on 22nd September 1866, the *Mercury* combined references to roads, sewage and Satan with a commentary on the direction of the stewardship of the Rev Bennett:

The road to Uphill is now pretty well as level as a bowling green making it a pleasant walk which would be pleasanter if the Board of Health would look to it. The Uphill congregation far exceeds that of any ordinary little country parish. It is the nearest approach to High Church in the neighbourhood, all of Weston being strictly Evangelical. This attracts visitors with soft hats and straight collars who like long coats and short sermons, having the prayers chanted, and the East the cardinal point for the Creed ... where they use Hymns Ancient and Modern, sing the closing Amen after each and the clergyman preaches in his surplice. Decorative colouring warms up the interior of Uphill new church.

The author then described the walk to old St Nicholas, telling the legend of how the builders of the original church had started it at the foot of the hill but the devil carried the stones every night to the top of the hill. In the end they gave up and built it where it still stands. This excursion into legend allowed a reference to the state of Uphill rhyne:

> .... judging from the poisonous odours that rose from a small "Phlegathonic rill" which Westonians used as a public drain, the evil savours of the original builder still lingered round the spot.... This awful open sewer was quite sufficient to give a foundation for the strange legend. Notices forbade entrance to the old churchyard and the walls bristled with broken glass.

The final remark sniffs at the Wesleyans:

> Next to the new church is a small ivy covered chapel. When his own service is complete, the minister locks the chapel, walks a few yards and goes into the Anglican service.

Stephen Bennett may not have read the article as ill-health kept him from the parish for twelve months. In September 1868:

> Uphill Church is closed for decoration and cleansing, chiefly at the expense of the Rector, the Rev S Bennett. The church has received a gift of a handsome lectern and Bible from parishioners Mr and Mrs H Brittain of Ellenborough Park. Mr T Edwards has recently improved the choir.

When the church re-opens, weekday services will be in the evening instead of the morning to allow working men to attend and candles have been placed in the church to give necessary light. This has offended some parishioners who have left the church and joined the Methodists. In February 1857 the Privy Council ruled that candles may be placed on the altar provided they were used for lighting. This led to controversy and disputes.

A year later, the Curate, the Rev CF Hawkins, conducted Uphill's Harvest thanksgiving in a church lavishly decorated in the traditional manner with farming produce. Through his own "kind liberality" he rewarded the church choir with outings to Wells.

But there was discord in the village. At Christmas 1869 villagers paid one penny admission to a "Miscellaneous Entertainment":

> The parochial hall, the schoolroom, filled with a large company. Several highly respectable people sat in the front row but otherwise the audience was disorderly and ill-behaved. After a pianoforte duet by the Misses A and MG Whitting there were readings by Rev CF Hawkins, Messrs Whitting, R Minifie and O Poole. Three of the performers filled the time between pieces by attending to their knitting.

Font decorated for harvest   *[UVS]*

Regrettably the audience applauded by rattling tongs, pokers and shovels against the fireplace. The concert raised 15s to pay for tallow candles to illuminate the holy altar at Christmas. Some villagers however saw these as "symbols of Romanism".

❑ ❑ ❑ ❑ ❑

Chapter 37. Victorian Christmas

Long before any problems over ritual and candles, villagers celebrated Christmas simply with a church service and a few home-made toys for children tucked into one of father's knitted socks with an orange, an apple and some nuts. Dinner was cooked over the fire or perhaps in the village baker's oven for a few pennies. Some snared rabbits on the moor; some fattened their own geese in the backyard; most looked for a present of meat from their employer. Boxes of presents were handed out to servants in the big house on Christmas Day and opened at home the next day: "Boxing Day".

As prosperity grew, those employers displayed their growing wealth in a new form of Christmas which was literally Victorian being copied directly from the royal family. The Christmas tree, six branches tall, was decorated by the family's young ladies who spent hours making:

> garlands, snowflakes and stars, sewing little pouches for secret gifts and paper baskets with sugared almonds in them. Small bead decorations, fine drawn out silver tinsel came from Germany together with beautiful angels to sit at the top of the tree. Burning candles were placed in wooden hoops for safety.

Mass-produced toys included dolls' houses, miniature furniture, tiny musical instruments, guns and swords. The trees and other decorations were removed on Twelfth Night, January 5th, to avoid bad luck.

Family and guests worked up Christmas appetites with vigorous dances: a quadrille, a waltz, a polka, a gallop and a march. Their Christmas dinners started with oysters, going on to goose, followed by beef and mutton with port jelly. Turkey became increasingly popular. After a great plum pudding flickering blue with flaming brandy, came mince pies, nuts and fruit. It was all cooked out of sight in the basement kitchens and spirited up, apparently effortlessly, to the table.

Daughters and wives also decorated the church, although not always to everyone's full satisfaction. A "Frequent Attender of Uphill Church" commented:

> On entering, the first sight was a text "unto us a child is born, unto us a child is given" which was very badly presented. Otherwise, the font was very prettily decorated and reflected much credit on the artist. The screen in front of the communion was also trimmed in a very creditable manner. The walls were hung around with triangles covered with moss and the windows with sprays from the churchyard yew.

The choir visited houses, singing new popular carols such as O Come All Ye Faithful, Once In Royal David's City, See Amid The Winter's Snow, O Little Town Of Bethlehem and Away In A Manger.

❑ ❑ ❑ ❑ ❑

Chapter 38. The Rifle Volunteers

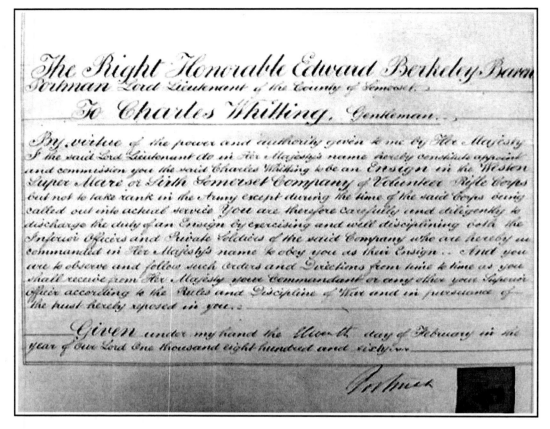

Charles Whitting's Commission
[Permission kindly given by SRO to use the image from file A\AKH\29\1]

Through the 1850s, Uphill villagers read in the *Mercury* of the Somerset Light Infantry's actions in the Crimean War at Sevastopol, and in the Indian Mutiny where Somerset soldiers won two VCs. Nearer home, French posturing led to the formation of Volunteer units, which recruited from "those classes who do not enter either the Regular Army or the Militia". This usefully gave local gentry a new social cachet as Volunteer officers.

The first three officers of Weston's Rifle Company in March 1860 included a 14-year old Ensign, Charles Edward Whitting from Uphill: Whittings were to serve with the unit for over half a century. The *Mercury* reported:

THE RIFLE CORPS VOLUNTEERS

Yesterday the Weston-super-Mare or Sixth Company of the Somerset Volunteer Rifle Corps made their first appearance and attracted a vast deal of attention. The members of the corps assembled on Flagstaff Hill and having been put through various evolutions by Sergeant-Major

Slattery, they marched four abreast through most of the public streets of the town, accompanied by Capt Law, Lt Baker, Ensign Whitting and Surgeon Hitchens, to the Town Hall to take their Oath of Allegiance. The weather was beautifully fine, the church-bells rang merrily, guns were fired, flags were waving from a number of house-tops and the streets were crowded with spectators.

In October 1861:

The 6th Somerset (Weston-super-Mare) Volunteer Rifles marched to Uphill where there is a range for firing upwards of 900 yards on a level but which is quite open and exposed to westerly winds.

The Somersets were also titled "Prince Albert's Regiment" and when Prince Albert died just before Christmas 1861, Ensign Whitting turned out in his smart uniform to a ceremonial parade. With black sleeve-bands and reversed arms, the Rifle Corps slow-marched through Weston's streets to funereal music from their band. Shops closed for three hours, curtains were drawn and flags flew at half-mast. The *Mercury* announced the arrangements on pages edged in black. It was a sombre display of the deference that underpinned Victorian society from bottom to top.

A few weeks later "The Rifle Corps marched through Uphill and took of refreshment at the residence of Ensign Whitting" who was shortly promoted to Lieutenant.

Patriotic Prose. A recruiting poster of 1864.

Recruiting poster

In 1864, the American Civil War reached the English Channel when the Federal ship *Kearsage* and the Confederate *Alabama* fought a sea battle off Cherbourg. The gunfire was so intense that it was heard 120 miles away on Uphill hill, 144 feet above sea level. Below the hill in Uphill Butts, the Weston Rifles were firing in the monthly competition for the Knyfton Cup, valued at £10, donated by Mr Knyfton to encourage efficiency of marksmanship. The location was lyrically described by the *Mercury* as:

> pleasantly situated at Uphill, beneath the rocky ledges that stretch some distance along the road and close to the picturesque old Norman church and ancient burial ground. Backed by the little

church and the rocky hillside, the view from the range is diversified by the sight of the spreading waters of the Channel and the opposite coast; while, looking backwards, the vision is enchanted by the sight of Weston and the verdant woods which constitute such a pretty background to the place.

During the summer:

> Mr Cox of the Dolphin House has a booth on the ground for the supply of refreshments which the heat of the day rendered all but imperative.

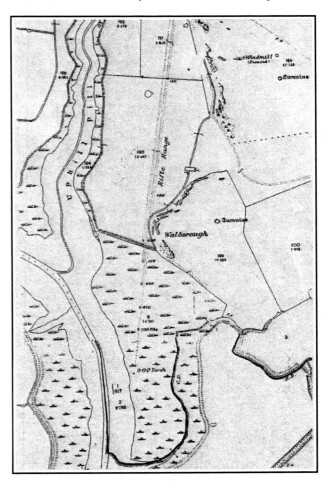

Uphill Butts　　　　　　　　　　　　*[UVS]*

In September 1867, TT Knyfton extended his patriotic support for the Rifles by entertaining them at Uphill Castle. Fifty men headed by Major Law, Lt Whitting and Ensign Davies marched behind their band covering the two miles from Weston at Light Infantry pace in half an hour. Mr Knyfton and a group of Somerset and local worthies received them in:

> a splendid marquee on the beautiful lawn in front of the castle. The table was heavily laden with delicacies of the season: lamb, chickens, veal,

roast and boiled beef, meat pies, plum puddings, pastry, salads and cucumbers. To drink they had beer, cider, sherry, claret, cognac, gin, ginger beer etc.

With such support from Uphill, the Rifles established themselves as a social institution as well as a military force. That meant dressing appropriately. Headgear on formal parades was the shako hat. Otherwise the Volunteers wore flat peaked caps, with plumes when marching with the band or in public, without plumes for musketry drill, firing on the range and indoor training.

The shako hat

This finery was provided and paid for by members but in 1868 the Lord Lieutenant ordered them to change to government pattern clothing and accoutrements – still paid for by the men. The cost for the unit amounted to about £200 and local people set up a fund to meet this.

Somerset cap badge

In December 1868 the annual inspection of Weston's 6th Company of the Somerset Volunteers was taken by Charles Whitting now Captain Commandant of the unit. Afterwards he invited the Company to a "sumptuous repast at Sandcroft House, Uphill" also attended by county and local

dignitaries. The party of fifty feasted on beef, mutton, game, poultry, plum puddings and salads, followed by "steaming grog".

Militia bullets from Hillside Cottage garden

New weapons followed the new uniforms and in 1870 breech-loading Snider rifles replaced old Enfields accompanied by the order "Hand in old ones and all kit, clean". The company trained at summer camps every year, sometimes on Salisbury Plain, sometimes locally in a field alongside what is still Camp Road on the edge of Wells with firing on a range near Priddy, now Yoxter Camp.

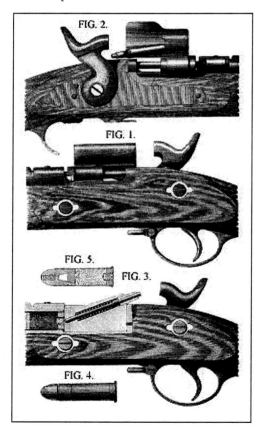

Snider rifle breech

Volunteer Review 18ᵗʰ June 1861   *[Weston-super-Mare   Review]*

❑   ❑   ❑   ❑   ❑

Chapter 39. Uphill Gun Battery

TT Knyfton Esq, Deputy Lieutenant of Somerset and R Kinglake Esq swore in the first recruits to the Weston-super-Mare Battery of the 2nd Somerset Volunteer Artillery Corps. That was in August 1860 and by December some of the men had already been struck off the roll for "abuse to officers". The officers themselves quarrelled bitterly and publicly over the relationship between rank and social position, even their wives using their husband's rank on visiting cards: "Mrs Captain ……" After a series of resignations and scandals that led to street rioting, Captain Hugh Rockett found himself in command of 100 men and two 32-pounder guns.

32-pounder gun

These arrived by rail from Woolwich Arsenal and were temporarily parked in front of Rogers' Hotel until an emplacement could be built on Uphill beach at the end of Cold Harbour Road:

VOLUNTEER ARTILLERY CORPS

A battery and earthworks are to be erected near the Strand House on the Uphill Road upon some ground belonging to TT Knyfton Esq. Corporal Barton of the Royal Engineers will superintend the works and as he will see to the proper completion of bastions, redoubts etc, we may be sure of a first-rate erection.

Corporal Barton rapidly issued his specification and invited estimates:

Being about to commence the erection of a two-gun Battery on the Beach between Halfway House and Uphill, I enclose a Sketch of the Battery by which you will find the whole of the Parapet is 12 feet thick at the Base. The interior Sodded Slope 45 feet. The height in the Interior to be 7 feet. The Sods are to be about a foot wide and are to be laid one on each other for the revetment ...

Samuel Clarke, a member of the Corps, bid £26 4s 2d which was accepted by the committee on 12th January 1861 with a contract signed on the spot. Not unnaturally Samuel Clarke complained bitterly when he found "somebody else whose bid was unsuccessful has now started the work". But on 2nd February:

THE BATTTERY

The Battery between Halfway House and Slimeridge House is approaching completion. The embrasures are formed ... epaulments are also complete ... and the quick and efficient manner in which everything has been done reflects considerable credit on Mr John Davis, the contractor. Ere another week the Battery will be finished and the guns placed in position.

By 16th February:

THE BATTERY

The earthworks and platforms of the artillery battery being constructed on the Uphill Road have been completed and work is proceeding on the magazine. It is anticipated that the guns will shortly be placed in position. The construction of the battery follows representations that were made about the lack of coastal defences in the Bristol Channel area.

On 20th April:

FIXING OF THE WESTON-SUPER-MARE ARTILLERY GUNS

Volunteers from Bristol and Clevedon arrived by train at excursion rates and paraded with the Weston unit, all with their bands. The Weston band is old-established and composed almost entirely of Germans, long-resident in the town. They escorted the cannon on a trolley pulled by six powerful horses along the road alongside the beach to Uphill. There Mr Cox had hung flags from the Dolphin and fired a number of miniature cannon in celebration. Once on the beach, the trolley stuck in the sand and the guns had to be separately dragged by Volunteers to the battery where they were eventually mounted.

On 13th July:

The Artillery Corps proceeded to their battery for the first time for ball practice since the fixing of their guns. The target which consisted of a hogs-head barrel was placed at a distance of 1,140 yards. There were four rounds fired:

No 1 good elevation, two yards to the right.

No 2 good elevation, two feet to the right.

No 3 good elevation, two feet over.

No 4 good elevation, two feet short.

There were upward of one thousand spectators present.

After the firing, the Corps, preceded by their band, marched to Uphill where they were entertained by Capt Rockett.

In September 1861, however, Capt Rockett resigned because of ill-health. Remembering earlier bitter feuding, the men of the Volunteers met to vote on a successor. They elected Capt Gore Booth and on their behalf Sergeant Major Gregory recommended his appointment. The Lord Lieutenant cautiously questioned Capt Booth about rumours of scandals but Booth firmly denied them and was confirmed in command. Still suspicious, the Lord Lieutenant tentatively suggested amalgamating the Artillery and Rifle Corps but this was firmly rejected by the Rifles.

At first all went well. Weston's Volunteer gunners marched to the battery on the beach for a weekly live firing practice which must have enlivened the tourists as well as the fishermen. But within a year parades turned into protest meetings about Capt Booth. Many of the men refused to obey when called out under the Riot Act. NCOs and men claimed that the captain collected their subscriptions but never published accounts and that he never involved others in decisions. Capt Booth disdained any answer, simply publishing an order calling in all weapons.

The *Mercury* provided an outlet where the disgruntled gunners stated their case with letters and a long sarcastic poem, supporting them in a leading article branding Capt Booth as "obstinate and wrong-headed". The unpopular captain uttered no public word but closed the unit, shipped the guns to Pembroke and retired from service. The Uphill gun battery ceased fire and quietly subsided into the dunes. In 1869 the old Artillery uniforms were found stored in the Town Hall, "rotted and moth-eaten", and were disposed of.

In contrast, the moorland behind the battery, today's golf course, provided a venue in 1865 for a "grand display" by the 2nd Gloucestershire Engineer Volunteer Corps from Bristol and the 26th Somersetshire Rifle Corps from Bridgwater.

But Volunteer service was not all squabbling and showmanship. The Irish nationalists known as Fenians subjected the country to a wave of terrorist atrocities, explosions and killings. Many of their members were veterans of the American Civil War who had fled the Irish Famine and who now returned with American support. The *Mercury* quoted:

> intelligence reports that two American ships with Fenian crews are carrying arms and ammunition to the Bristol Channel. Royal Artillery detachments have been sent to garrison the Severn forts including the construction works at Brean Down. Local stocks of gunpowder have been made secure and Volunteers have been ordered to keep their rifles ready at home.

Chapter 40. Brean Down

Victorian industry boosted the speed and power of war with mass production of weapons and fast movement by rail:

> The most prominent and interesting classes of London's Great Exhibition in 1862 were devoted to Armstrong and Whitworth guns, rifles of all sorts, models of iron-clad frigates and similar warlike devices.

By then the first purely steam-powered ironclad warship the French 5,600-ton *La Gloire* was in service. Making 13 knots and carrying 36 breech-loading 66-pounder guns, she presented a direct challenge to British naval supremacy. Patriotism and fear led the government to consider how to defend the Bristol Channel and its vital commercial sea-lanes. High-tech Admiralty thinkers proposed a fleet of fast gunboats using the new telegraph to deploy it as needed, but the Commons preferred a traditional system:

> A heavy gun battery on the extreme western point of Brean Down, batteries on each side of the Steep Holmes, similar batteries on both sides of the Flat Holmes and a fort mounting heavy ordnance at Lavernock Point just below Penarth Roads. Their interlocking fire would require no greater range than 2,000 yards.

They allocated £3,000 immediately for this, but it was a further two years before the *Mercury* announced:

> The tender of Mr Pollard of Taunton for erecting the Brean Down fortifications has been accepted by the War Office. The erection of huts, forges &c will be commenced shortly, and the Spring will, we hope, see the works connected with Brean Down Harbour in full progress.

A small army of labourers camped on the Down and began their work in harsh conditions with little concern for safety:

> Accident at Brean Down fortifications – A mason was moving a stone along a narrow plank when he fell some 15 feet receiving some contusions about the head and other injuries. He was taken to Uphill and is favourably progressing.

A few years later:

STEEP HOLMES ARTILLERY MEN

> We hear on most reliable authority that an order has been given for beds and bedding, to be delivered at the Steep Holmes, for the use of the Artillery who will soon take charge of the fortification of the island.

This concern over the defence of the Bristol Channel reflected the commercial value of its unbroken flow of shipping. The sight of potentially profitable trade sailing by was too much for Victorian entrepreneurs and on 18th February 1860 the *Mercury* reported plans for extensive docks at the mouth of the River Axe. Marine engineers arrived to survey Brean Down. The scheme was to build a great breakwater enclosing a deep-water harbour, with adjacent docks and a railway along the Down. This would create a port directly accessible from the open sea at all stages of the tide. Direct rail links with London would cut a day from the journey to New York compared with travelling via Liverpool. Support came from Trinity House and the General Post Office whose consultant reported that:

> there is no part of the Kingdom so well suited for a packet station as Brean Down.

By 1861, the Brean Down Harbour Company had raised its capital and hired its contractors. In the Dolphin and the Ship, Uphill's boatmen knew all about the turbulent waters that swirled round Howe Rock, but the experts thought they knew better. Long detailed letters in the *Mercury* explained how these new developments would combine Channel defence with a great international port and rail links with London. One recommended that Brean Down could also be the terminus of a new Atlantic cable, the whole project to be cheaply built by convicts housed on the Holms. Commander E Hardy RN drew on his nautical experience to declare "the Holms comparable with Gibraltar".

On Guy Fawkes' Day 1864, the iron-hulled paddle steamer *Wye* steamed out of Knightstone and across the bay to the site of the proposed harbour. The Town Band played and Lieutenant Whitting's Volunteer Rifles fired a celebratory fusillade as a foundation stone was lowered to the sea-bed under a marker buoy. Uphill villagers watched from the hill or their boats but the wind blew away the stirring words of the official address:

> Here we find a vast promontory extending far out into the sea, well sheltered from gales … and with capabilities for a deep-water harbour at comparatively trifling cost … capable of accommodating the largest vessels and being the emporium of commerce from every quarter of the globe.

Laying the foundation stone 1860   *[UVS]*

That night the marker buoy broke loose and drifted off, fetching up on Steep Holm. The foundation stone vanished without trace. While villagers in the Dolphin and the Ship may have seen this as an omen, the company went ahead with their Harbour Foundation Stone Festivities. With true Victorian philanthropy they entertained 640 "poor women" to tea in Weston's new Town Hall. The party consumed 80 2lb loaves of bread, 15 lbs of butter, 3 cwt of cake and 2 tins of biscuits, washed down with 25 lbs of tea, 10 gallons of milk, and 40 lbs of sugar. And with true Victorian confidence the company announced that the buoy and flag had not actually been lost and had been rapidly replaced.

Company publicists were delighted by a poem in the *Mercury* on the "Proposed Harbour at Brean Down" conjuring up the thoughts of the helmsman of a big ship, perhaps Brunel's famous *Great Eastern*, on entering the port after battling through a gale in the Irish Channel:

Before us lies safety – Brean Down –
Hard to port, man, and go round the pier;
See ahead quite a flourishing town
Young Brighton, call'd Weston-sur-Mer!

No rocks and no sand banks are near,
The water's full deep all around,
From three to ten fathoms all clear
Within a good anchoring ground.

Keep your eye fixed on Uphill old church,
Long a land-mark to sailors of yore;
Like an eagle in stone on its perch,
It guided their crews safe to shore.

Doing its best to promote local interests, the *Mercury* expressed fears that contractors would find access to Brean Down difficult and suggested building a bridge over the Axe.

Plan for Axe bridge   *[Permission kindly given by SRO to use the image from file Q/RUP/243]*

But as this would have cost a further £20,000 it remained a suggestion. The paper confidently described progress on the works during 1865:

Brawny navvies divested of coat and waistcoat wield spade and pickaxe with zeal … removing tons and tons of soil and stone to the water's edge as the basis of the railway.

Life for the navvies was harsh. They lived near their work on the barren moor in a squalid settlement of huts with no running water, no sanitation and no relaxation but alcohol. Local benefactors did, however, pay for a Scripture reader and a temporary school for workers wanting to be educated. In January 1866:

Mr Stevens the hard working missionary of the Brean Down Harbour and Fortification Works was returning home last week when he was overtaken by a tremendous storm. The wind became so boisterous and the night so dark that he became benighted and was consequently unable to cross the river. He was given shelter for the night by Mr and Mrs Chapman, sincere supporters of the mission.

22-year old labourer Solomon Boley seized the chance to make money by hauling stone from Uphill quarry to the harbour works. His wife Eliza joined him in a cottage on the Down where their daughter Alice was born. At a Bristol Industrial Exhibition, Charles Phillips of Weston's Royal Potteries displayed a model of Brean Down Harbour made out of Weston clay:

The massive piece of rock about to be cut away for the railway to the harbour, the pier, the railway tunnel, the lighthouse, the ships lying at anchor in the harbour, and even the tiny figures of the coastguardsmen on the look-out on shore, are portrayed with a minuteness of detail. The vessels, with their masts, spars, and rigging (all formed of clay) are lying out in the harbour, while on shore workmen are depicted in various attitudes.

William Drewitt, agent for the Harbour contractor, moved into Uphill in 1866. By the end of the year, the Bristol & Exeter Railway Company announced that it was ready to start constructing both broad and narrow gauge lines which would carry supplies to the fortifications as well as the harbour. The *Mercury* noted with some satisfaction that the work would require "a temporary wooden foot-bridge over the Axe to overcome the delays and dangers of the ferry" adding for the benefit of holidaymakers that this "would be appreciated by all who are fond of rambling".

After repairing winter storm damage, 16 masons and about 60 labourers completed the first part of the contract by September 1867. As the constant sound of rock-blasting reverberated round Uphill, potential tradesmen for the next phase arrived to see what Victorian engineers and navvies had achieved.

At the rocky foot of the Down's cliffs, a solid masonry wall projected 150 feet into the sea, 10 feet thick at its base and 5 feet wide at the top, backed by thousands of tons of shingle and stone to make it "an impregnable structure". The next step was to create the harbour itself enclosed within two 500 foot solid stone breakwaters out in the bay and linked to the Down by a bridge 60 feet long. "All problems of tidal flow", claimed the promoters, "have been overcome". All they needed was the "co-operation of landowners" … and more capital investment. Thomas Knyfton owned much of the land where the docks would be built and would doubtless have co-operated eagerly once the capital was in place to pay for it.

But, within a few days, a heavy gale of wind and rain swept up the Bristol Channel and Uphill people could see spray flying high as waves smashed into the Brean Down breakwater. It was another month before work resumed but the site engineer promised that storm damage would be speedily repaired. Over forty men worked through the winter and, spared more gales, the *Mercury* reported in April 1868 that:

> despite unfavourable predictions about this great

undertaking, the Brean Down Harbour is making rapid progress.

Always with an optimistic eye on local enterprise, the *Mercury* looked ahead to when Brean Down Harbour:

> will transform the long bare promontory, for many centuries or thousands of years, so lone and desolate, into a scene of bustling animation, and the whistle of the railway train will take the place of the scream of the wild bird, leviathan vessels will be safely havened in the dock, not far from where the little fishing smack was wont with difficulty to hold its own in the stormy gale.

Uphill will then be merged into Weston and its individuality lost. The old Castle, now so many years occupied by that "good old English gentleman" (his lady will excuse us calling him old) the Lord of the Manor, Mr Knyfton, may have to come under some Parliamentary Act of Demolition and make way for a railway station or for offices of some monstrous Newport and Llantwit Coal Company.

The future of the Carthage of the West is certain.

❑ ❑ ❑ ❑ ❑

"The Carthage of the West"   *[Permission kindly given by SRO to use the image from Martha Coates file DD\X\NWT\3]*

Chapter 41. Fishing Rights

Watching all this from the bay were Uphill's fishermen. They had just discovered the benefits of insurance, through which they insured a single net and then claimed that any damage or loss had been to that one. But the insurance business caught up with them, establishing a Boatmen's and Fisherman's Association, a Friendly Society which insisted that all insured nets had to be officially marked. But, finding that Uphill men took more care of their nets than those who fished off Birnbeck, it lowered their premiums.

Uphill's fishermen made their living from sprats and shrimps. They rowed from the Axe along the deep channel through the mud-flats, marked with tree-branches lashed to poles visible above high water. Lines of stakes supported nets that filled with fish as the tide swept in its constant clockwise course round the bay. Fishing rights off the Down were ancient and valuable. In the 15th century one boat's catch of sprats was measured in cartloads and a catch of cod and whiting was counted in hundreds. In June 1865:

TAKING FISH UNLAWFULLY

Abraham Pople and William Pople at Uphill were charged with unlawfully taking a quantity of fish valued at about 1s in certain water at a place called Bar Hang in Uphill Bay, the private property of JH Smyth-Pygott Esq the lawful owner. Mr Phitlott appeared to prosecute on behalf of Mr Pigott; the defendants were undefended.

William Pople said the charge against him was a false one; Abraham Pople (his son) admitted putting down nets to take some fish. Mr Phitlott produced the original lease which was dated 1788 and gave Mr Pigott the right of fishing in the place described, and said in 1853 Mr J Watts rented the fishery from the prosecutor for a period now expired.

A witness named Day said some years ago he had worked the fishery for Mr Watts and knew where the stakes were placed and the nets laid down at Bar Hang near Black Rock. On April 18th witness and Dyer went out to Black Rock and saw several nets hanging on the stakes. They pulled up the nets and Pople senior came up and said the nets were his and he admitted having put them there. Those nets were in the same position as Watts's stakes used to be. The defendants were together on that day and the elder said he would hang the nets there and the younger Pople placed the nets there in different places. On 19th April witness and William Dyer saw the younger Pople take fish out of the nets

near the stakes and put them in a basket. William Pople was on the bank and went down to meet his son. Witness did not see the elder Pople take fish at any time but he claimed the stakes that were in the water.

William Pople: Did I tell you the nets were mine or I had anything to do with the fishery?
Day: No but you were in the boats and you claimed the stakes.
Pople: I did not put the stakes down this year but when Mr Watts had possession of the fishery he gave me liberty to fish there. That was three years ago. I have not been there fishing at all this year.

William Dyer said on 18th April he saw the elder Pople at the fishing ground. He asked what they were doing there and he said pulling up Mr Pigott's stakes. Pople said the stakes belonged to him and not Mr Pigott and they could try it out and he would see the stakes were put down again the next day for although they were pulled up ten times he would put them down afresh. On April 19th he saw the younger Pople take out the nets.

The younger defendant said rather than any bother he would rent the fishing.

The elder defendant said, "What really passed was this. Charlie Day said to me, What do you think of it? I replied, It's very cold. There was nothing said about the nets".

Mr Pigott, who was only present to watch the proceedings, did not press the charge. Mr Kinglake the magistrate fined Pople junior 10s and costs, warning him that if he was charged with a similar offence he would have to pay the full penalty of £5. The senior defendant was dismissed.

The biggest sprat catches came during November fogs. As they said on Uphill Wharf, "A clear sky keeps away the small fry." There were good hauls in 1865 and roads echoed to the cry "Sprats O!"

George Bailey, James Parish and William Coles were taken to court charged with stealing a bag containing 4 lbs of sprats from Mr Harse of Slimeridge Farm but only Bailey turned up. As he was the least guilty of the three and of previous good character, Mr Harse did not press the charge.

In 1867 when tons of sprats were landed, the price dropped from 2½d lb to 1d lb and then to 3 lb for 1d. This was no use to the fishermen but was welcomed by the working classes who cured the sprats and stored them for use in the winter. They thus avoided paying the exorbitant prices of butchers in Weston who were charging 8d or 9d lb for beef and mutton.

Chapter 42. Flora and Fauna

All this was small fry compared with sea-life further out in the channel. In November 1860 two bottlenose whales were spotted in Sand Bay. One was shot and killed, provoking a local argument over, not conservation, but proper scientific designation: whether this was a *Hyperoodon Butzkoff* or *Hyperoodon Rostratus*. In July 1863 fishermen shot and caught another whale out of a shoal of a dozen in the bay.

Bottlenose   whale

Workmen on the Brean Down Harbour scheme in summer 1865 spotted a big fish stranded by the tide in shallow water. They landed it with difficulty and cut off a steak to cook and eat. But when a workmate told them the fish was a shark they threw it all into the sea. In February 1868 two Birnbeck fishermen found a stranded seal, four feet long, healthy with fine fins and two formidable rows of teeth. They killed it and sold it to Weston museum.

Wild life was primarily seen as a challenge for the sportsman, with the cooking pot or the glass case as suitable destinations. In March 1864 fishermen got out their guns when "at least two thousand wild ducks settled in Weston Bay, the water being quite black with them". James Gould proudly shot "a fine specimen" of a Peregrine Falcon at Uphill in January 1861, selling it to collector Augustus Stone of Hopkins Street, who was "happy to show him to interested parties". The *Mercury* commented:

> We may say that the bird has haunted Weston and the neighbouring towns and villages for some years past and has committed great havoc among the poor pigeons. Rewards have long been offered for his head.

Like the peregrine, ravens were considered threats to farm stock. In March 1866:

> As some sheep and lambs were feeding on Brean Down they were suddenly attacked by two large ravens. One lamb was killed and partially devoured on the spot whilst a second had its eyes pecked out. It is most unusual for our district to be visited by these birds and should they return they will not be so fortunate in getting off a second time.

A few days later:

> One of the Brean Down ravens has been shot by one of the works staff and given to the owner of lambs. Its wing span measured a full 4 feet 6

inches. Another pair of ravens has since visited the Down.

Rarity of a species only added to the attraction. In 1862, "Two rare hoopoes were shot locally" and in September 1866:

RARE BIRDS

Two specimens of the Grey Phalarope (*Phalaropus lobatus*) were shot by two gentlemen in the vicinity of the River Axe at Uphill. This phalarope is very rare in England. Any specimen which does find its way here must be regarded as a stray bird, beaten from the line of its migration by the violence of the winds. This bird is chiefly American but is only at home in the summer in the extreme north and there is no bird perhaps which approaches nearer to the poles.

In 1868, the first cuckoo was heard in Uphill on 23rd April, St George's Day. The cuckoo was a bird of superstition. Hearing the first cuckoo brought bad luck, averted by turning over money. Those not lucky enough to have any money had to run straight ahead as fast as possible. And anyone who hadn't heard a cuckoo by Midsummer Day could expect to be dead before the next Midsummer's Day.

The same year, a mild winter kept swallows swooping over the hill as late as December. In winter 1868 a Fulmar Petrel came south from the Arctic to Birnbeck Island only to be shot by a Weston ornithologist. Perhaps it was the same man who shot a Little Gull on Birnbeck, billed as the "smallest gull, a rare visitor".

After some severe storms at New Year, spring came early, celebrated by an Uphill collector who took an egg from a newly made hedge sparrow's nest, describing it as a "great novelty". By then other birds had nested and laid, one starling brood having already hatched and flown. There was no frost that winter and flowers including red roses bloomed over into the new year. In February, Uphill orchards filled with blossom, a peach tree was in full bloom and hyacinths, carnations and primroses flowered luxuriantly, attracting butterflies and wasps. And "a beautiful specimen of the male peregrine falcon was shot between Weston and Kewstoke".

As a reminder of earlier life, Uphill quarrymen opened another cave 60 feet up on the rock face in August 1863. Archaeologist Dr Pooley investigated, finding stalagmites rising from a floor of loam containing the bones of wolf, fox, wild boar, otter and stag, plus a human thigh bone and part of a human skull. He took the entire collection back with him to Oxford.

Chapter 43. Uphill Harbour

In his hundredth year, the village's oldest inhabitant Edward Luff spoke of his boyhood in the 1860s when Uphill was:

> ... quite a thriving little port. Boats would nose their way into Uphill Creek, each bearing about 120 tons of coal or salt, and unload almost within the shadow of the 200-foot high outcrop of rock, which towers above the river. The cargoes were hauled to places as far apart as Weston, Winscombe and Banwell – a tidy step in those days.

Despite the sheltering bulk of Brean Down, the village still felt the force of Atlantic storms. During a violent gale in January 1841, the French brigantine *Conception*, sailing in ballast for Cardiff to take on a cargo of coal, failed to reach the shelter of the Axe and was stranded on the foreshore between Uphill and Weston. Apart from a split rudder she survived and was refloated on the evening tide. Uphill endured a summer storm in May 1863 when:

> ... some fine old elm trees surrounding Mrs Poole's orchard were blown down and one of them fell on a new iron gate, destroying it. Trees of large size were felled on grounds belonging to TT Knyfton Esq. A smack called *Sally* moored off Burnham, dragged her anchors. Those on board made direct for Uphill river, which they reached in safety.

But even the Axe was not always safe. In February 1863, the *Mercury* reported:

A MAN DROWNED

A labouring man of Bleadon, George Crandon, who had been "working out" a coal sloop the *Ranger* in the River Axe near the railway bridge, accidentally fell off the landing plank into the river and was drowned. The body was picked up after the tide had receded. The deceased was a quiet, hard-working man and has left a widow, far advanced in pregnancy, and five young children to bewail their loss. Crandon was a member of the Uphill Friendly Society but had not been enrolled sufficiently long to entitle his widow to the burial fees etc. A subscription will be made among members on behalf of the family. The inquest was held at the Ship Inn when a verdict of Accidental Death was returned.

Another inquest was held a year later:

at the Dolphin Inn on the body of a man dressed in seaman's attire, washed ashore near the River Axe. The body (which had been deposited in the belfry of the old church) was much decomposed, the features and other unprotected parts of the body being quite gone, the effect of having remained some time in the water. He was comfortably clad and had on knitted stockings, one of which had a white top but the other had not. He wore a black silk necktie and had a new silk handkerchief in this pocket. A knife and two or three small coins were also found on him. A verdict was returned of "Found Drowned".

After the inquest the wife of the man, whose name it appears was William Henry Tuckfield, visited the village and recognised the clothing as that worn by her husband, who met his death by falling out of a boat at Cardiff three weeks since.

1865 began with a slight earthquake shock and ended with another great gale which:

> damaged boats at Knightstone including the sloop *Despatch* of Mr Thomas Every, Uphill, a coal vessel. She was driven stern foremost with tremendous force against the wall suffering considerable damage to her stern and sides. With her rudder carried away and her keel broken, she was washed up onto the beach.

When the storm subsided, Thomas Every found the *Despatch* less badly damaged than reported. He had a trench dug from the boat towards the sea and she was safely refloated.

Back in Uphill:

> The body of a man apparently a foreigner was found floating in the river Axe by Coastguard James Pasker. The body was taken to The Ship where an inquest jury chose Thomas Whitting as its foreman. Their verdict was "Found Drowned in the River Axe". The body was 5 feet 4 inches in length, wearing two blue serges and two pairs of trousers. It was interred in Uphill churchyard.

Victorian progress brought more than profit. Although a thriving coastal resort, Weston had virtually no harbour; Knightstone was open for just an hour or so at high tide and the Anchor Head slip was suitable only for small boats. But on 5th June 1867 the deep water round Birnbeck island was crossed by an iron bridge, extended for 250 feet to the north-east to accommodate steamers. Over on Brean Down a worker was injured and the Axe ferryman brought a call to Uphill for urgent assistance. A steamer from the village recovered the injured man and took him to Birnbeck Pier. From there he was carried to the hospital opened in Weston in October 1864.

The Uphill steamer was a Government-surplus steam tug owned by Mr Bissicks of Bristol, aptly renamed *Steamer Industry* and moored in the Axe ready for business. There was nobody on board in February 1868 when the highest tide for years dragged *Steamer Industry* from her moorings. She drifted out across the bay onto a shoal of rocks near the Birnbeck shrimp stakes. The strong tide dragged the hull eastward into the channel between Birnbeck and the mainland destroying eight columns of the pier, ripping off the ship's funnel and masts and leaving the vessel a total wreck. Although Birnbeck Pier had to be closed, the "handsome structure" was still safe as it was designed to remain standing even if every alternate column failed. After repairs costing £150 the pier re-opened. The same high tide flooded Regent Street and washed the sloop *Affo* and the yacht *Mystery* onto the road above Knightstone.

From the new Birnbeck Pier, tradesmen set up a regular steamer service carrying supplies out to the hundred navvies working on Steep Holm. But when a week-end storm in August 1868 stopped the steamer, the men ran out of food. They lit a beacon that shone brilliantly through the storm across the bay, but no one on the mainland knew what it meant. The gale damaged boats in the bay and parts of Weston's new sea-front while in Uphill several fine trees came down on the Knyfton estate.

That gale was surpassed in September 1869 by the "worst storm in living memory". The sloop *Fanny Kemble* carrying a cargo of salt from Bristol to Bridgwater was overwhelmed in the bay with no chance of rescue. Her struggling crew got her into the lee of the Down and eventually into the Axe where they abandoned ship and reached the shore as she foundered. Her hull was swept out to sea but other local boats which sank at their moorings were recovered from the sea-bed when the tide went out.

Weather permitting, boatmen still found leisure for sport. In August 1862 Mr Kington Leir of Uphill sailed his yacht *Fenella* from the Pill to umpire a rowing regatta from Knightstone pier. By 1865 boat clubs were organising frequent races in the bay from Knightstone to the end of Brean Down and back, rowing about 3 miles

❑ ❑ ❑ ❑ ❑

Part 5:   Village Voices 1870 - 1880

Chapter 44.   Uphill in 1870

Uphill panorama by TT Knyfton   *[Tony Lee]*

Population 482: 229 male + 253 female

Rector: Rev Stephen Bennett MA

Curate: Rev CF Hawkins; 1871 Rev Frederick Emmanuel Gutteres BA
Curate-in-charge: 1877 Rev ACC Spalding
Parish Clerk and Sexton: Robert Counsell;
Organist: T Edwards; Henry Frith
Rector's Churchwarden: John Harse; 1878 CE Whitting
Parish Churchwarden, Waywarden and Guardian: Obed Poole

Rate collector: Henry Hancock — rateable value £3,990
Schoolmaster: John James Lovell; Henry Frith
Post Office Receiver: Mrs Mary Minifie

Lord of the Manor: Thomas Tutton Knyfton JP MA of Uphill Castle

The 1871 Census defined Uphill Parish as including Slimeridge Farm, the Sanatorium, Uphill Drove, Windwhistle Cottage, Uphill Hill, Totterdown Farm and Flat Roof Farm. The population had gone up by 40 but there were only four more houses. Familiar village surnames were the Knyftons and Whittings as principal landowners; the Counsells and Goulds; and farmers Evans, Fear, Poole, Hancock, Harse, Luff and Joseph. Mrs Sarah Luff (89), Mrs Rachel Tilley (88) and Miss Penelope Brice were octogenarians.

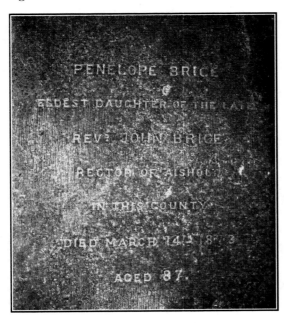

Penelope Brice, Old Church

Adult males shared 24 names, the most popular being William (18) and John (13). Of 123 employed males, 49 (40%) worked as labourers, 32 (26%) were in skilled trades, 10 (8%) in service jobs, 8 (6%) maritime, 7 (6%) farmers, 5 (4%) professionals and 7 (5%) domestic service. The statistics don't include boys who jobbed from house to house, cleaning cutlery and boots.

Adult females shared 11 names, favouring variants of Mary (21), Ann (17) and Elizabeth (18). Of 58 female workers, 30 (51%) were in domestic service, 21 (36%) service jobs, 3 (5%) professional, 3 (5%) agriculture. And one, the redoubtable sub-postmistress Mrs Mary Minifie now a 53-year old widow living in Walnut Cottage, also worked as wheelwright, blacksmith and whitesmith. Remnants of her smithy remain in the garden. Mrs Minifie sold penny stamps for letters weighing up to an ounce and 1½d for 2 ounces. A post-card cost ½d and there were special rates for posting newspapers and

books. From 1871 she had to make more daily deliveries: not easy as few houses had letter boxes in the doors.

Penny Black stamp

In the midst of a snowfall in 1874, 20-year old William Shallish started work at Uphill Castle as gardener and carpenter for Thomas Knyfton, working there until he died. William was a good athlete, winning five cups including the Uphill Manor Plate in public races held in "Mr Harvey's field" where Weston railway station now stands. With his wife Laura from Guernsey and a growing family he lived in one of the four-roomed Sandford Cottages, later moving with six daughters and two sons to the Knyfton property Park Cottage, Old Church Road. Park Cottage was demolished in the 1950s.

Tailor John Lloyd asked 12s 6d to 28s for a gentleman's overcoat, depending on the quality of the woollen fabric. A boy's coat cost from 5s 11d to 10s 6d, a Gent's tweed suit 30s.

Grocers sold tea from 1s 8d lb, coffee from 1s lb, Bird's custard powder in 6d and 1s boxes, sardines 1s large tin and flour 2s peck. Butter cost 10d lb, marmalade 7d for a 1 lb pot, bacon 5d lb and potatoes 3s for 60 lb. Mutton, lamb and pork cost about 9d lb. Smarter shops in Weston purveyed tinned salmon at 9d lb, lobster 8d lb, oysters 6d lb, sweet cured hams 10d lb. A bottle of champagne cost 2s 6d, white wine 1s 6d, claret 1s, port 4s, sherry 1s 6d, brandy 2s and ale 1s gallon.

Finest Cheddar cheese "as supplied to Queen Victoria" went for 11d lb, Melton Mowbray pork pies were10d for the 1 lb size and pork sausages cost 10d lb. A gentleman could smoke a Havana cigar for a penny or for as much as sixpence.A new interest in domestic gardens created a new line of business:

The Minifies also saw the value of advertising their work in the *Mercury*:

Digging clay in Uphill Brickyard left a large flooded pit:

Kate Radford and Frederick Day, both about 4, were playing at Uphill brick pits, floating pieces of wood on the water when Radford fell in and Day, trying to rescue her, also fell in. Frank Harvey, working in the brickyard, saw a hat floating on the water and pulled them out unconscious. Day recovered, but not Radford despite the efforts of their parents and coastguards who lived near. Mr Furnivall, surgeon, of Hutton was called but the girl was dead. She was daughter of Simon Radford, foreman of the brickyard.

Gypsies came and went, settling in tents and horse-drawn caravans for seasonal work. They aroused interest as "children of the forest" but suffered no hostility.

❏ ❏ ❏ ❏ ❏

Chapter 45. Village Weddings

The decade opened with two April weddings in 1870:

> Marriage of Charles Edward Whitting Esq, eldest son of Charles Whitting Esq of Sandcroft House, to Miss Maria Elizabeth Jewell (only child of Henry Jewell Esq) of the Grove, Mylor, Cornwall, at Truro.

After an "elegant wedding breakfast", the couple left Truro for a honeymoon in Paris:

> The father of the bridegroom was not unmindful of his poor neighbours, the whole of the male cottagers of Uphill being regaled with refreshments at Sandcroft House whilst each of their "better halves" had half a pound of tea and one pound of sugar and the children some monster buns. In the evening the tenantry and farmers of the parish were invited to an excellent dinner at the Ship Inn.

Their son Edward Jewell was born in 1872 and Charles Edward and Maria moved into Totterdown House, today's Broadway Lodge. They took out a huge mortgage of £2,359 and virtually rebuilt the place in 1877. Maria died there in 1879 and Charles Edward left the house. He travelled extensively, leaving Edward Jewell with his grandparents in Sandcroft House.

A few days after the Whitting wedding:

> Frances Eliza, third daughter of Mr John Harse of Slimeridge Farm married Mr James Hewlett of Loxton. Her brother Mr Joseph Harse was best man; her sisters Emma, Alice and Georgina were bridesmaids with Miss Corfield and the Misses Hellier; the groomsmen were Mr Joseph Harse and Mr John Harse jun and Master Castle Hewlett.

The sumptuous breakfast at Slimeridge Farm was supplied by Mr Collis of Weston-super-Mare. Church bells rang merrily throughout the day.

Sadly the bride's brother and best man Joseph died in June 1872. After spending the evening in a Weston hotel, Joseph rode his horse home along the beach where he was found drowned the following morning. He was liable to fits and was assumed to have suffered an attack and fallen. The bride's youngest sister Georgina married Robert, eldest son of Mr William Fear of Mark, in April 1873: the curate, Rev Frederick Gutteres, conducted the ceremony in St Nicholas.

The following month at:

> one of the most fashionable weddings in Cheltenham, the Rev Stephen Bennett MA, rector, married Emily, elder daughter of Henry Brown Esq, late Judge in India, at Cheltenham. Uphill was gaily decorated with flags and bells rang on their return from honeymoon.

Flags and bells were not the prerogative of the rich. In February 1874, the groom Richard Jones was a 40-year old unmarried labourer living in Windwhistle Cottage. His bride Jane Wills was an unmarried 34-year old laundress living with her mother Charlotte Wills. Her father had been a sea captain but her widowed mother, now 70, was a pauper receiving £7 a year from parochial relief. Joseph Boley was a labourer and Miss Taylor the daughter of another labourer. But:

> The usually quiet village took on a festive appearance on the marriage of two of our worthy parishioners, Mr Richard Jones with Miss Wills. Mr Joseph Boley gave the bride away and Miss Taylor was bridesmaid. The bride, who is

Slimeridge   Farm   *[UVS]*

the daughter of the late Capt Wills, wore a blue shot silk dress trimmed with white, and a white tulle bonnet. The wedding party passed through a triumphal arch across the roadway. After a wedding breakfast at the residence of the bride villagers enjoyed dancing until late in the evening. Flags were flying and bells ringing throughout the day.

At another Whitting wedding in St Nicholas church in January 1877:

Mr Friedrich Karl August Stahl of Bordeaux married Miss Mary Gwenllen Whitting, youngest daughter of Capt Whitting of Sandcroft House. Her brother Mr EM Whitting was best man and her nephew Master E Jewell Whitting one of the groomsmen. The couple left by train for a honeymoon in Germany.

The following Thursday, the village enjoyed another wedding which linked well-known local families:

Mr George Fear, youngest son of Mr W Fear of Mark, late of Uphill, married Miss Alice Poole of Uphill Farm, only daughter of the late Mr Richard Poole. The bride was given away by Mr Obed Poole her brother. Mr Gould was best man. The bridesmaids were her cousin Miss A Hancock and Miss Eve Fear, sister of the bridegroom. Among gifts displayed at the wedding breakfast at Uphill Farm was a handsome souvenir from TT Knyfton Esq of The Castle. The bells of the old church rang merry peals all day. The wedding celebrations ended with a ball at the farm.

One Uphill marriage did meet problems:

MAN AND WIFE

A lady of the village, in the prolonged absence of her spouse, went in search of him and discovered the "sweet William" comfortably seated with a blooming damsel of about nineteen summers on his knee. At this unexpected sight, she allowed her passions to rise and made an immediate rush at the damsel who had her arms entwined affectionately around William's neck. Venus was not much alarmed at the discovery, but quickly disengaging herself from the faithless one, she gave blow for blow with such good effect that the ill-used wife was quickly obliged to cry for quarters.

The object of their "united affections" sat quietly in his chair during the set-to, watching with sleepy interest and was only aroused by a slight feeling of pain caused by his better half quickly passing her fingers over his face and leaving the outlines of her delicate nails as a mark of her undying love.

❑ ❑ ❑ ❑ ❑

Chapter 46. New Village School

Although State education in England and Wales began in 1870, it was neither compulsory nor universal until 1880 and not free until 1891. Furthermore, buildings and staff had to be financed locally. Up the road in booming Weston, citizens demanded compulsory education to remove gangs of unruly boys from the streets. But Lord of the Manor Thomas Knyfton generously demonstrated his involvement with the village in April 1872:

THE NEW SCHOOL

The new and tasteful buildings erected at the expense and on land owned by TT Knyfton Esq of The Castle were formally opened. There was a good attendance of scholars of both sexes. The buildings were designed by Messrs Wilson and Willcox, architects of Bath, and constructed by Mr John Perry, builder of Weston-super-Mare. The schoolroom is 52 feet by 18 feet, well ventilated, lighted by four windows on the east side and a large Gothic window at the north end. Adjoining is a spacious classroom 16 feet by 16 feet 6 inches and at the south end is a pleasant cottage residence for the master and mistress, containing three bedrooms, sitting rooms, kitchen and offices. Nothing that can possibly add to the comfort of the scholars or their tutors has been overlooked.

The Knyfton family crest remains carved into the stonework on the Master's House. A bell rang daily from a freestone belfry summoning scholars to classes. The school could accommodate 150 children. Named Uphill National School, it was managed by a Committee and supported by voluntary contributions. The first inspection praised schoolmaster John J Lovell for "good results in Drawing examinations, where there were 36 entries".

In 1875, the North Somerset Teachers Association met at Uphill, "the Bristol and Exeter Railway Co having offered cheap fares there". Chaired by Mr John J Lovell they discussed "The best methods of overcoming difficulties of teaching Arithmetic to the lower standards". They criticised the Diocesan Prize Scheme as it selected and named a "best school". This was misleading, as a school could win points simply by cramming its best pupils.

A year later, Her Majesty's Inspector reported:

The school is under good control, carefully taught, and making satisfactory progress especially in Writing and Arithmetic. The Drawing examination also shows a creditable result for candidates G Binding, G Quick, K Manley, K Viney, E Adams, D Binding, H Tucker, S Fear, E Popham, A Quick, W Badman, G Taylor, W Boley, G Pople, W Pople, G Masters, F Henderson, W Courtney, F Courtney, G Vowles, H Henderson, W Popham, W Radford, Pupil Teacher OR Counsell.

The Pupil Teacher was Parish Clerk Robert Counsell's son Oliver.

As a Church School it was subject to inspections by diocesan as well as government inspectors. The Diocesan Inspector checked the school's coverage of religion:

The school is very quietly and reverently conducted and the teaching is evidently given with care so as to interest the children in their work. The character of the school which has stood well for many years is quite maintained. Very good repetition of collects and private prayer. The religious knowledge is very good as is the discipline and tone.

Uphill's new school   [UVS]

Chapter 47. Railway, Roads and Houses

The new railway brought its excitements and engine-drivers often had to be resourceful. In April 1870:

> Between Weston Junction and Devil's Bridge, a truck of empty resin casks on the down goods train was seen to be on fire. The driver stopped within a mile, uncoupled the burning truck and left it to burn out which took three hours. The driver uncoupled the engine and drove on to Burnham to give the warning by telegraphic messages to other trains. He returned, threw the remains off the line, coupled up the rest of the train and continued the journey.

The telegraphic messages went by Morse Code. Although he had died in 1863, the name of "Devil" Payne returned to haunt the Bristol & Exeter Railway. The company had to negotiate with his estate which owned some of the land required in 1874 for a loop line into Weston. Damage to the Lympsham road caused by the building of "Devil" Payne's private station was only now repaired thirty years later.

Uphill's own public station was opened in 1871 and renamed Bleadon & Uphill the following year, remaining in use until 5th October 1963. New Uphill houses featured patterns of red and black bricks, made fashionable by decorations on railway buildings and made possible by cheap transportation of bricks across the country. In 1876, the Great Western Railway absorbed the Bristol & Exeter.

A correspondent complained to the *Mercury* about:

> the very bad state of the side-path of the Uphill Road. On a fine day it is a most pleasant promenade and many more would take advantage if the walking was only decent but it is really painful to walk on. Several inhabitants now go to the pretty chapel in the Sanatorium and how ladies get there in bad weather I do not know. The problem is the protruding stones which could be broken and flattened with a sledge-hammer.

There were accidents:

> As Mr John Adams was returning from Weston-super-Mare in his horse and cart with Mr J Quick and families, the horse shied and overturned tipping the occupants into a ditch. They fortunately suffered only slight injury.

and

> Mr T Buller was out riding on horseback with Miss Jones when her horse became restive. It threw out its hind legs and broke Mr Buller's leg.

The new Highway Board remedied the steepness of the road between Uphill and Bleadon known as Uphill Batch by digging out the crown of the road to a depth of up to 5 feet. As the *Mercury* put it:

> This will lessen what all pedestrians, equestrians or drivers know as a 'good pull'.

At the top of Uphill Batch, the Rev William Crotch left Uphill House which was advertised in 1871 as:

> To Be Let Furnished UPHILL MANOR HOUSE, near Weston-super-Mare, with coach-house, stables, &c, &c. Rent £200 per annum.

John Calland JP (31) lived there for a year with his wife Harriet Ann (40) and their family of five daughters and two sons. The children were cared for by a governess, a nurse and two nursemaids, while Mrs Calland's life was further eased by a cook, a kitchen maid and a pageboy. The house went up for sale in 1872:

> FOR SALE – A Residential Estate, comprising a Gentleman's Residence, in a beautiful position, seated on an eminence and commanding very lovely and extensive views; large drawing, dining and billiard rooms, domestic offices, stables, coach house, harness room, cart house, conservatory and about 46 acres of land. The house is approached by a wooded drive and surrounded by ornamental grounds, flower garden, shrubberies, large croquet lawn, with excellent kitchen garden and orchard. The house is well sheltered by trees on three sides, and is open to the south. Five minutes walk from Uphill Station, half a mile from the sea, ten minutes walk from the church and two miles from Weston-super-Mare.
>
> Messrs Gordon and Nicholls, Solicitors, Bridgnorth, Salop.

John Davies Treherne Esq bought it and put it up for auction in 1875 as Uphill Park Estate. Bidding reached £12,000, but not the reserve price of £12,500:

> … a delightfully situated residential property. 48 acres of highly cultivated land, with fine residence, laid out grounds, carriage drives etc … handsome and costly furniture in the mansion combine to make it a property second to none in the kingdom …

Farmer James Evans now lived in Wyndham Lodge, put up for auction in 1872:

> UPHILL. Public Auction Sale of Freehold Property.
>
> Lot 1 Detached and comfortably arranged VILLA RESIDENCE in its own grounds, with garden, coach house and stable and all other convenient

offices. Two sitting and four bed rooms with kitchen and other offices. Southern aspect.
Also a pretty GOTHIC COTTAGE recently erected in part of the same grounds of about 1 ¼ acre. For many years occupied by Mr William Burdwood.
Lot 2. ¾ acre Building Land adjoining the Ship Inn abutting the high road with an extensive frontage.
Lot 3. Excellent Close of Meadow or Pasture Land on the opposite side of the road to Lot 1, called The Warth or Home Ground, and Harp Acre. About 4 ½ acres.
Lot 4. Dwelling House, Shop, Offices, Garden and Premises adjoining Lot 1, formerly occupied by Mr Gaskell but now his tenant Mr Harris; together with a Close of capital Orchard Land behind the same and adjoining Lot 1. About 1 ½ acre.
Lots 1, 2, 3, and orchard part of 5 are in possession of Mr James Evans, proprietor.

The "Gothic Cottage" was Frogmore Cottages where retired Customs officer William Burdwood lived in No 2. Henry Harris had the grocer's shop in Lot 4.

Sarah Whitting died in January 1882, leaving Wheatstone House to be auctioned at the Ship:

. . . .
1 Wheatstone House,
occupied by Mr Down as tenant, a 7-room Dwelling House with Pantry, Kitchen, Scullery, Pony and Carriage Shed, Yard and Outside Offices.
2 Wheatstone House,
a 7-room Dwelling House with Kitchen, Scullery, Yard and Outside Offices, also with Mr Down as tenant.
Flower Gardens in front and flourishing Fruit and Kitchen Gardens at rear and a good supply of Hard and Soft Water.
. . . .

On the death of landlady Mrs Mary Every in 1873, the licence for the Ship was transferred to John Billinger with John Parffrey as landlord. Within days he had an inquest on his hands:

John Matthews, 47, labourer, had lodged at the Ship for three months. One evening he had a fit. He was sick and then fell asleep on the floor where the landlord left him to recover. Next morning he was found to be dead. A witness Lewis Blackmore, labourer, also lodging at the Ship, said the dead man was drunk. The inquest jury brought in a verdict "Died in a fit of drunkenness".

Innkeepers had to apply for special licences for special occasions. The Ship had the licence to provide a canteen when the Volunteers fired at Uphill Butts and landlord Parffrey now applied for a similar licence to serve fishermen who needed to sell their catch fresh:

Fishermen often brought their fish from Brean Down to the Ship for sale during the night and during prohibited hours on Sunday. Purchasers came long distances and the inn keeper applied to be allowed to serve refreshments to them. The justices decided he could not serve

The Ship Inn   [UVS]

fishermen as they did not live more than three miles away, but he could serve purchasers who came more than three miles.

The landlord changed but traditions continued. In 1877:

According to annual custom, Host Yeo of the Ship Inn entertained his customers to a sprat supper when upwards of 50 guests partook of the delicacies. The "local whitebait" was served in every style that the culinary art could devise, and we need scarcely say that the delicious morsels were devoured with considerable relish by the piscivorous assembly, who were loud in their praises of the liberality of their entertainer.

Along the road, Albert Amesbury had the Dolphin from 1872. In 1875, W Manley took over for two years when the licence was transferred to his widow Mrs Manley.

Meals in the inn "dining rooms" cost:

DINNERS (Hot Joint and Vegetables) ... 1s
TEA (with Shrimps or Cake) 9d
COLD LUNCHEON 9d

Chapter 48.   Crime & Punishment

Although liberal Victorians worked to abolish flogging and hanging, William Bennett had been before the magistrates a score of times and twice whipped before he was 12. In March 1872, he was charged with stealing a Persian cat value 10 guineas from Dr Miles Jackson of Uphill. When the cat was missed, a servant remembered that the boy had been there begging and the police found the cat at the boy's house. Although he claimed that an unidentified lady had given it to him, he was sentenced to one month's hard labour followed by five years in a reformatory school.

Another boy, Frederick Poole of Weston-super-Mare, stole apples from Mr Treherne's orchard at Uphill House, knocking down a servant, Alice Vowles, when she told him to go away. He was fined 10s plus 13s 6d costs or 14 days imprisonment in default. Market gardener Charles Saunders took on James Ponsford as a labourer but soon began missing vegetables. He weighed out and marked quantities of seed potatoes which later disappeared from the store. Police found them hidden in a cupboard at Ponsford's house. Because of Ponsford's previous good character, punishment was mitigated to six weeks' hard labour.

Gamekeepers zealously guarded their employers' land. Joseph Wilson, gamekeeper to Mr Bisdee, saw Robert Amesbury, a Bleadon farmer, with his gun and a spaniel dog on Mr Bisdee's land. He heard a shot and saw the dog searching the ground. Charged with trespassing, the defendant "a respectable farmer with a game certificate" said he had shot a partridge over his own land and was looking where it had fallen.   The case was dismissed.

Anyone with access to the rhyne kept ducks there, but they were an attractive prize for thieves. When John Adams, a carter from Uphill Drove, reported the loss of five ducks worth 12s 6d, a police constable remembered asking 38-year old John Baker why he was in that neighbourhood at 2 in the morning. Baker told him he had got drunk at Uphill and fallen asleep beside the road on his way home. The policeman went to Baker's house and found him plucking the ducks. Baker told the police that William Trego, a 25-year old labourer, had been with him and had twisted the ducks' necks. Baker got six months imprisonment. Although Trego was discharged for want of

evidence he was still cautioned.

Obed Poole kept his ducks in the rhyne between Mr Knyfton's orchard and Mr Luff's field. He saw Gabriel Wilson, a local gardener, standing in the orchard, pelting the ducks with apples. Having isolated one duck from the rest, Wilson pulled a gun from the hedge and shot it. He crossed the rhyne, picked up the duck and put it into his pocket. Questioned in court, he said he had mistaken the duck for a moorhen. Although Obed Poole didn't want to press the case, the Bench sent Wilson to prison with hard labour for one month. They also fined him 50s for using a gun without a licence but recommended mitigation of this. George Bawden, "an old offender", came over from Burnham to steal six ducks value 15s from Solomon Boley who lived next to Uphill Farm. He denied it, saying he "took some wild ducks on Hutton Moor". On inspection, these turned out to include two ducklings meeting the description of those lost.

The Boley family themselves kept the court busy. Solomon was fined five shillings for plying for hire without a town licence and then ten shillings for leaving a horse unattended in Weston High Street. One evening, William Boley assaulted his brother Solomon in the Dolphin. Solomon told the court that William had been drunk and tried to provoke him into a fight and he now wanted protection from him. Others in the pub at the time, William Webber, William and George Cole, said they thought it was just fun. William Boley said the same and denied that he was drunk, but he was fined 10s and bound over to keep the peace for six months. In another case concerning the Dolphin, landlord William Manley charged the village tailor John Lloyd with abusive language and refusing to leave the inn, while Lloyd counter-charged Manley with using threatening language. The bench dismissed both summonses.

Shoemaker John Williams gave evidence when George Palmer was fined 10s and costs for being "drunk in charge of a horse and cart at Uphill". William Watts pleaded guilty to the same offence and was also fined 10s. James Radford was fined 2s for allowing two donkeys to stray on the highway at Uphill and two other Radfords, Walter and Ann, were fined 1s for "unlawfully releasing two donkeys from the common pound at Uphill".

Late one night, Samuel Cross was driving his donkey and cart from Uphill to stay with friends at Lympsham. He passed John Hewish and his family walking to Bleadon. They asked for a lift and as there was only room on the cart for the wife and child, the man walked alongside. When Mr Cross unloaded his cart, a pair of trousers value 20 shillings was missing from his bundle of clothes. Constable Smith searched the Hewish house and found the trousers there. Mrs Hewish told the officer he had bought them but Hewish said he had picked them up at the roadside. He went to prison but when labourer John Madge was charged with stealing a hammer worth 1s 6d from Samuel Knight the magistrates found there was "no felonious intent" and dismissed the case.

William Travis was driving a trap from Uphill when he heard the report of a gun and saw four men, William Whitman, Charles Henry Godbeer, Edward Radford and George Radford, with rifles in their hands. George Haydon said he saw all fire their guns except Godbeer. The police were called and found Godbeer's gun "cold with the snap cap on". All four, members of 1st Somerset Volunteer Engineers, were charged with discharging their rifles on the highway. Whitman and Godbeer were dismissed. The Radfords pleaded guilty, were fined 10s and ordered not to be guilty of such conduct in future.

Some outraged citizens took the law into their own hands:

A gentleman returned to his home on Upper Moor Road (Moorland Road). He found the key gone from the back door although he was sure he had left it in the lock on the outside. He suspected a burglar was still in there and called two neighbours to help. They arrived armed to the teeth and he placed them on guard, with instructions to shoot anyone who attempted to escape. He then broke down his front door with an axe and searched the house. Everything was in order and he later found the key in his pocket.

In one case a magistrate was called rather than the police. Henry Tucker, Frank Harvey and Sarah Binding were sitting on a bench on Uphill Road late at night in January 1873. The two boys "put the girl's feet up onto the bench and lifted her clothes to the waist". Capt Townshend, chairman of Weston magistrates, was informed and came to the scene.

The girl was quite drunk and helpless and the boys claimed they were taking her home as she was ill. Tucker first said he lived at Halfway House but then admitted he lived in Uphill. Blacksmith Richard Minifie arrived and recognised the boys as Henry Tucker and Frank Harvey. The girl, Sarah Binding, was too drunk to walk or speak and the boys helped her with Mr Minifie following to see them home. They fell over four times and then, walking down a narrow footpath in Uphill, all three ran away. They were caught near Mr Whitting's premises but when they reached the high road, they ran away again. At the police station, Captain Townshend himself charged them with drunk and indecent behaviour. He also chaired the court hearing, giving evidence of what he had witnessed, before finding them guilty and fining them £1 each plus costs, with seven days in prison if they did not pay.

There was less fuss and publicity when respectable farmer Edward Luff's son, Walter, was called to court to "show cause why he should not pay for the upkeep of the illegitimate child of Sarah Bailey". The case was speedily dismissed.

❑ ❑ ❑ ❑ ❑

Chapter 49. Village Entertainment

Some entertainments were commercial, put on by travelling performers who booked Uphill's nearest approach to a hall:

SCHOOL ROOM, UPHILL

On Monday January 31st, a Grand MAGICAL and MUSICAL ENTERTAINMENT.

The Celebrated Amateur Conjurer,
PROFESSOR CLAREMONT
(Pupil of HOUDINI and ANDERSON),
has kindly consented to give a
MYSTICAL AND MAGICAL PERFORMANCE
at the above rooms.

DO NOT MISS SO GREAT A TREAT

The First Part of the Performance will consist of
MUSIC: INSTRUMENTAL and VOCAL.

Reserved Seats, 2s; Second Seats, 1s; Back ditto, 6d
Doors will be opened at 7.30.
Entertainment to commence at 8.

Other shows were put on by well-meaning local performers, sometimes in aid of charity. In a "Miscellaneous Entertainment at Uphill" to raise money for Weston-super-Mare Hospital, villagers read from poems and novels, groups sang glees, soloists played the piano. Their performances attracted large audiences but the behaviour of some was described by respectable people as "disgusting" or "disgraceful".

Rowdiness was an entertainment in itself. Families moving from the village were often seen off by a "tin pot band of pots and kettles" to sound farewell. One nervous man got up early and left secretly at dawn to avoid the treatment. Impromptu bands struck up at skimmity rides, when a rowdy rabble dragged effigies of suspected offenders round the village inns to a final bonfire. At Uphill Fete and Gala:

> A "Rough band" marshalled into some kind of marching order headed by an individual mounted on a horse caparisoned as King Solomon's charger. The steed's coat had been striped on one side and spotted on the other, while his ears, mane and tail had so many tints as to cause a North American Indian to be jealous. The gathering marched towards Bleadon being joined by many others on the way. These ran away and hid their instruments in a ditch when two policemen were seen but the Uphill men marched home.

On the third day of the festivities despite many protestations "against vice and immorality" the people met in a field near Uphill railway station lent by Mr W Lawry.

The local band was augmented by the Rhine Band of Weston-super-Mare and some 800 persons gathered to enjoy displays of fireworks at intervals.

The climax of the occasion was the mock trial and condemnation of two effigies clad in male and female attire. After hearing evidence solemnly given, both were found guilty by a jury of villagers and sentenced to death. The judge then admonished the court on the prevailing sins and passions of the world. The prisoners were hanged on a scaffold and then burned on a great bonfire.

The gathering dispersed in orderly manner.

They presumably remained orderly at free feasts such as the "excellent dinner at the Castle" for tenants on the Knyfton estate after their half-yearly audit. At New Year 1878:

> The Rev Stephen Bennett presented each poor family in his parish with a useful joint of meat varying from 3lb to 5lb each according to the number in the family.

> The Parish bell-ringers were treated to a sumptuous supper by T Buller Esq – who has recently come to live in the parish – at the Ship Inn, served in first class style by Host Yeo. The donor presided and Mr Churchwarden Poole was vice-chair. Guests included Messrs Robert Counsell, R Fear, J Gould, A Miller and other friends. After a most pleasant evening of song, toast and sentiment the ringers adjourned to the belfry on the hill, ringing several merry peals.

Thomas Buller's dinner for the bell-ringers became a fine annual event. For Christmas 1879 he:

> bought a 12cwt Hereford ox to be distributed among the poor of Uphill at Christmas. It is to be paraded through the village to whet appetites.

When a project to build a Literary Institute for Uphill collapsed:

> Mr T Buller of The Retreat purchased a central site for £575 and building the Institute will begin soon.

Villagers paid a fee to compete at regular Pigeon Shooting Matches in which birds were netted and released by hand or from a trap in a field alongside the Dolphin to be shot in flight by local marksmen. Prizes went to those who shot most. On New Year's Day 1870, things went wrong:

> a young man named Tristram was accidentally shot in the head and one of his arms while waiting with others to shoot the birds which chanced to escape beyond the bounds. The gun was loaded with large duck-shot which was removed by a surgeon from Weston-super-Mare. The victim is said to be doing well.

Hare hunting was popular. Burnham Harriers with a "merry little pack" of hounds met at Uphill Gate – the old toll-gate. The Highbridge Foot Harriers gathered at Uphill Railway Station where things went wrong again:

> Upwards of 20 sportsmen met. A hare was soon found on Mr Amesbury's hill. She gave a capital run to Lympsham and there doubled back. Unfortunately the Woodspring Hunt met on the same day at the Anchor Inn, Bleadon, but found nothing and were at a standstill when the voices of the Harriers' beagles were heard. Needless to say, the packs at once united, to the annoyance of the pedestrian sportsmen, and went away in pursuit of poor puss at a clipping pace, running the game as far as White House where a double was made and puss made for the starting point where she succumbed. Both hunts were there but the hare was demanded by Capt Shackle on behalf of the beagles and he gave it to the owner of the field.

The smart set, however, rode with the Banwell Hounds who hunted stag. They had their own way of ensuring that they had something to chase:

> At Crook Peak the stag was caught by the hounds. Its antlers were cut off and the animal was carted back to be used another day as quarry.

Two weeks later:

> The same stag was released at Flat Roof Farm Bleadon. The hunt attracted over a thousand spectators, a hundred of them on horseback. The stag set off for Bleadon Church, crossed fields to Hobbs Boat Inn and on to Mark where it was caught after 2 hours and 20 miles.

Again at Flat Roof Farm, Banwell Hounds:

> released a stag at Mr C Boone's Flat Roof Farm. There were over a hundred guests, many in scarlet coats on horseback while ladies followed in carriages. The stag was caught exhausted but uninjured at Batch and taken in a cart to recuperate.

Charles Saunders of Rose Cottage fancied himself as a swimmer as well as a market gardener. During the Boatmen's Annual Regatta, he entered a swimming match for £1 a side. They raced from the committee boat *Mystery* round a small boat and back, covering 200 yards, but he lost to Tito Burge by 40 yards. There was a good view from Uphill Hill of Henry Garrett when he swam from Birnbeck jetty to Steep Holm:

> a distance of 8 or 9 miles in 2 hours 16 minutes, a feat never before achieved. When he landed, blankets and coffee were provided by Host Harris of the Island Hotel.

Team sports were developing. Gentlemen brought cricket to the village from their public schools: Uphill's captain was Charles Edward Whitting and the president was Thomas Tutton Knyfton. In a match between Bleadon & Uphill and Worle Cricket Clubs:

> Worle won with 7 wickets to fall. Mr Temple Gould batted and bowled well and F Young bowled well for Bleadon & Uphill. The match was followed by an ample repast in the Ship Inn.

The bowler, FG Young, owner of Bleadon quarries and lime works, also had enough land at Uphill for Uphill Hill to become known as Young's Hill. He worked for the hunt as a "slipper", ensuring that the quarry was fit to be pursued before releasing the hounds. By 1871, Uphill had its own cricket ground, beating the Institute CC there by 30 runs after Temple Gould had scored 40 not out for Uphill. Needless to say the club held an annual dinner in the Dolphin.

Although the Football Association had established Rules ten years earlier, village footballers still handled the ball and retained their own scoring. A report of a match with Bleadon recorded "three goals, two tries, two touch downs, and three rouges, to one touch-down and a try".

Village football

Chapter 50.　　The Peasantry

During the Seventies, 80% of Britain was owned by 7,000 men of the aristocracy or the gentry. Uphill's pasturage covered 1,077 acres mostly owned by two men, Thomas Knyfton and Charles Whitting. It was rented out to seven farmers and provided work for about 50 men, women and boys. They worked from 6 am to 6 pm in winter and 5 am to 9 pm in summer. Weekly wages ranged from 8s to (occasionally) 12s with free cider. They couldn't buy surplus milk from the farm because owners preferred to fatten the pigs with it. By contrast, employers paid £1,000 a year to run a four-wheel carriage with two horses and £700 for a single-horse carriage.

As Members of Parliament were land-owners, little was done about their workers' wages, although the Agricultural Children's Act of 1873 required a farmer to see a certificate of school attendance before employing a juvenile. This followed a case of a 9-year old boy working as a full-time bird scarer. Most boys did this by loudly rattling a pair of dried rib-bones between their fingers, but some shook wooden clackers.

In April 1872, the *Mercury* reported agricultural conditions in Banwell which were typical of the area:

The farm worker's place looked like a pig sty. It had a sort of door but one had to stoop very low to enter. The miserable hut measured 7 yards by 3 yards. The highest point of the thatched roof was 10 feet but the height of the walls was less than 6 feet. From the top of the walls, the thatch went up to a point with no transverse beams to support it.

The one tiny compartment of the dwelling was divided in two parts, each about 3 yards square, one as bedroom, one as sitting-room. The ground was irregularly paved with large stones with earth between them. The occupant said "It don't heave much" meaning not much moisture rose between the stones. Festoons of spiders' webs and sprays of ivy hung inside from the roof. The walls were made of hardened mud.

The previous owner and his wife and six children all slept in the bedroom. The present occupant was aged 60. He earned 5s a week and paid £2 10s rent a year for the dwelling, a further 10s for the privilege of keeping his pig and some fowls on his master's land and he also rented one-eighth of an acre of potato ground for 15s a year. He wore wretched patched clothes, but seemed contented. He said that when rain came through the roof, his master repaired it. There had been no door, but the master provided a new one when asked.

Although general labourers went on strike at Hutton for an extra 1s per week, farm-workers did not complain, for fear of losing even such miserable homes. Some, however, followed the article with letters to the *Mercury*. Although the paper described them in an editorial as "peasantry", they showed an impressive level of articulate literacy when arguing that, as their wages were too low to keep out of debt, they should get regular overtime and be paid like other workers in coin not cider. The "free food" one pointed out, "is often old hard cheese and sour cider, overvalued by the farmers to make up part of the wage". Their children had to go out to work when very young and therefore remained uneducated. The whole family wore ragged clothes and depended on help from coal and clothing clubs paid for by generous sympathisers. Farm-workers needed a trade union with their own journal to present their views.

Heartfelt letters from emigrants to Canada used phrases like "free of bondage and the tyranny of farm renters in England" and being "without the incubus of Church and State". The *Mercury* advertised "Emigration from Liverpool to the USA or Canada - £3 steerage, children half, infants 10s 6d". Even better were the free schemes offered by governments of empty lands across Victoria's empire to snap up the most ambitious of these hard-working men:

> FREE EMIGRATION TO NEW ZEALAND
> FREE PASSAGES
> Are granted by the
> GOVERNMENT OF NEW ZEALAND
> As under:
> To Married and Single Agricultural Labourers, Navvies, Ploughmen, Shepherds, Mechanics, &c;
> Also to Single Female Domestic Servants, as Cooks,
> Housemaids, Nurses, General Servants, Dairy Maids, &c.
> For terms and conditions apply personally, or by letter, to the Agent General for New Zealand
> 7, Westminster Chambers, London SW.

While losing labour, farmers also lost stock. In 1870, foot and mouth spread across Somerset to Uphill. James Gould was fined for scab in his sheep despite protesting his innocence in a letter. John Quick was charged with "having 23 ewe sheep affected with scab and neglecting to notify the police". He pleaded ignorance of the requirements but was fined 10s and costs. He got home from court to find "the mangled remains of a valuable sheep killed by dogs. The ewe, valued at £3, left two orphan lambs". When John Harse found a cow dead in a Slimeridge field, the "discolouration of flesh showed it had been struck by lightning".

Tenant farmers also came under pressure from their landlords. William Fear rented a field from Edward Saunders of Huntspill Court but was given notice to quit because "he allowed the grass to grow for a long period without depasturing, he cut and carried away a large crop of grass, he neglected the fences, hedges and ditches". The action was based on conditions dating back to a previous owner. Both parties were represented by barristers and solicitors, suggesting that farmers were not too hard up. The dispute was settled out of court with a payment from Fear.

Obed Poole kept bees and was Hon Sec of the West of England Aparian Society. In 1878 the Society added a competition category of "honey secured without killing bees". Thomas Buller sent an egg to the *Mercury* "laid by his black Spanish fowl, measuring 3½ inches long and 7 inches in circumference, containing three perfect yolks".

Prices of produce went up and down. Under the 1871 headline "Milk Oh! Fourpence Quart", a *Mercury* correspondent complained "Milk rose to this price last year during drought but has not come down again this year when very wet. Other areas charge 2d quart for better milk." But there were no complaints from shoppers when quicker and cheaper shipping brought fresh American beef onto the market, forcing down prices of local beef to 8½d per pound.

Nevertheless, bread remained the largest food item, supplying half of people's energy needs. Average consumption was 6½lb per person each week. It was almost the only food eaten by women and children, as men, paradoxically called the "breadwinners", were given what little meat was available.

By 1880, all bread was white, which pleased the socially pretentious and made more profit for the miller and the baker who whitened the flour with alum salts. This bread was easier to digest by those too poor to afford butter but it also worsened malnutrition in the working classes. Although adulteration of flour was stopped by the Sale of Food and Drugs Act in 1875 with checks by Public Analysts, imported cheap American grain, processed industrially, produced even more profit, as well as white flour of little food value.

A popular Victorian image of haymaking was already being romanticised by those who didn't have to do it:

"JOLLY HAYMAKERS"

As an instance of the healthful and bracing air of this village, Mr and Mrs Charles Harrill two old and highly respected residents – their united ages being 164 years – helped Mr Robert Counsell gather his hay crop. So well did this octogenarian couple labour amongst the "pitchers and rakers" under a "broiling Midsummer sky" until the work was complete, their exertions stimulated their juniors to exertions which in these modern days had been almost lost sight of.

Haymaking – Sandcroft House in background   [UVS]

Chapter 51.   Water and Weather

Marine life was so abundant that anything of interest was promptly killed and put on show. A "beautiful specimen of Glaucous Gull or Burgomaster" was shot off Birnbeck. A bottle-nosed basking shark and its pilot fish were netted in a herring-net by the yacht *Mystery* in the Bristol Channel. Measuring 5 feet long and weighing nearly 1cwt, it bared a triple row of teeth. It was brought ashore and exhibited in Weston-super-Mare where "a cast is to be made for the new Museum". Down the Channel at Steart Bay fishermen caught a sturgeon weighing 160lbs.

> A Swordfish was captured at Brean Down fisheries in one of Messrs T Padden and Palmer's sprat nets, by Edward Pople and George Davis. Its length including the sword was 8 feet 9 inches and its largest circumference 3 feet 8 inches. The sword was 2½ inches wide and 3 feet 8 inches long with three grooves on each side. The fish resembles a huge mackerel. It has been preserved and is on display.

Sailors' families paid into insurance schemes. In 1870:

> Sophia Collins, a widow without family of Uphill, received £4 from the Shipwrecked Mariners' and Royal Benevolent Societies. Her husband Thomas Collins had been second mate of the steamer *Greek* lost on 3rd December 1869, he having been a subscriber to the Society.

Some Benefit Societies developed from simple insurance schemes into more formal social organisations:

Members of the Loyal Star in the West Lodge of the Oddfellows followed the remains of their deceased Brother James Probert Smart to his grave in Uphill churchyard where the Rev T Gutteres and rector Rev S Bennett conducted the funeral service. James Probert Smart was captain of the *Pioneer* steam barge trading between Bristol and Cardiff.

> He lost his life a week ago, getting on board his vessel at Redcliff Bank.

T Pearcey, "eldest son of the coastguard", fell from the bridge fifty yards from his home in Coastguard Cottages:

> Standing on the bow of the river, he lost his balance and fell into several feet of water. A youth, James Morgan, apprenticed to Mr Charles Young, jumped in and although unable to swim, rescued Pearcey. He was insensible, but brought back to consciousness by being rubbed by Messrs A Stone, C Young and others.

Off Brean Down:

> Ten English sailors took possession of the American ship *Vicksburg* in the Bristol Channel. They secured the first and second mates below decks under guard and then brought the ship into Cardiff where they were charged with mutiny.

1870 opened with an icy thunderstorm, "leaving the roads white with banked hailstones like snow". In October:

> An unusually fine aurora borealis was visible to the north from Uphill hill. For twenty minutes

Coastguard Cottages   *[UVS]*

the whole horizon was lit with masses of colour. The sky filled with streamers of white, suddenly changing to pink and carmine, with a deep purple corona. Eventually the colours merged into a pillar of pale light.

In a summer of "tropical heat" in August 1871, "a snake 27 inches long was seen in the road before being killed by boys" but a claim that "a cat caught a locust" brought assertions that the locust was probably no more than a large grasshopper. Another display of the aurora in 1873 was followed by storms as forecast. by folklore

Disputes over fishery rights reached the court again, the prosecution claiming that:

> John Bathe and William Lucas, fisherman of Weston took fish from Bar Hang in Uphill Bay. This was leased to Samuel Harvey by John Hugh Smyth-Piggott who had owned the water for 200 years. Harvey paid rent of £17 per annum for the fishery including the right of bathing. This permitted summer fishing from Black Rock to Mulpit Stone in Sand Bay.

The defence quoted:

> a case in 1829 when the Poples were fined for erecting a "hang" where one was already erected, but this was a different type of offence. The present defendants had fished the bay for fifteen years without permission or consent or interruption. Their method was to stick two poles in the sand 100 yards apart with their boat attached to one of them. Between them was their net, the upper floating on corks and the bottom weighted with lead. The net filled on the ebb tide. This was 500 yards out from the land. Other fishermen had done the same for 40 years.

The case was dismissed "for want of jurisdiction". The men were fishing for sprats in a season which began well in 1875 with good catches going to Bristol and London markets. The *Mercury* reported:

> The fishing stakes under Brean Down are not usually fished at night but good catches attracted boats out on a calm sea under a slightly clouded moon. The fishermen emptied their nets and loaded their boats. The owners of stakes nearest Uphill landed safely in the river.

> Those fishing from the tip of the Down went ashore for refreshment, returning to use the flood tide to bring them in. They were nearly in the Axe when a sudden gale struck and the men could not pull against the raging sea. One man stood in the mud for two hours holding his boat.

Two men who failed to return were found next morning stranded on rocks below the Down. Two others were still lost and during the day parts of their boat and some clothing were seen in the water. After a search of the Down the following evening, the men were found safe at the gun battery.

A French schooner *Modiste et Marianne* carrying coal from Newport to Bordeaux "struck the Holmes rock in thick weather" and foundered in ten minutes. The crew escaped in their own boat, rowing to Cardiff. In the Bay:

> An elderly man named Bossance rowed the surgeon from Brean Down coastal defence batteries to Weston Pier. Returning to Uphill, he found the current was too strong for him. He anchored his boat and tried to walk ashore but sank in the treacherous mud. He had sunk three feet when fortunately he was seen by Mr WC Dyer from his home in Claremont Crescent. Mr Dyer, with a Mr Coles, rescued him with a flat-bottomed boat just as the rising tide reached up to his neck.

Fisherman William Pople agreed to rent Uphill ferry from John Lloyd for £1 per quarter-year. In 1876, he was taken to Weston County Court for refusing to pay, claiming that Lloyd had no right to charge as the Axe was tidal and not owned by him. The court found in favour of Lloyd "as there had been an agreement to pay".

In January 1877, floods inundated 70,000 acres of Somerset, destroying labourers' cottages and leaving them homeless as well as workless. The floods resulted from improved drainage of high ground while ignoring the onward drainage across the levels. In February, "a great westerly gale" struck the Uphill area. And in October came the "worst storm perhaps of the century" when sixty tiles blew off the Sanatorium roof and some of its windows caved in:

> Thirty fine trees came down in the Castle grounds. Their extent could cover over 200 people. The storm damaged trees in the farms of James Gould, Edward Luff and Robert Counsell. The entire head of Mr Harrill's laburnum tree was twisted round. Tiles blew off at Mr Lloyd's. The whole tile-house was destroyed at Mr T Gould's pottery and its contents of 1200 tiles destroyed. Roofs came off cart-houses. Ricks were damaged and the crown of one of Mr Boley's ricks blown away entirely. Tiles came off roofs from the Dolphin along to the Oldmixon turning. Part of the pinnacle on the west side of the old church was dislodged and the roof of the new St Nicholas damaged.

❑ ❑ ❑ ❑ ❑

Chapter 52.   Brean Down Battery

Growing international military and commercial rivalry prompted Sir J E Eardley Wilmot to write to th *Mercury* from London:

Work at Brean Down Harbour has been suspended for nearly two years through an unhappy accident but the harbour, fort and railway are all needed more than ever owing to the outbreak of the Franco-Prussian War. This essential work should be subsidised by government.

And again:

There is an urgent need to complete Brean Down Harbour and Fort in case of war. We should compel the Bristol & Exeter Railway to complete the railway line to Brean Down and thus provide a link with the English Channel defences. This would enable us to transport coal speedily from South Wales via Brean Down to all our naval ports. I have inspected the fort and found the battery to be very efficient with excellent accommodation and storage, but it has no guns. We need a Tunnel through the eastern end of Brean Down towards Bleadon. In war we would also need a gunboat in the harbour. No other harbour exists from Lands End to Bristol which is in a tidal river. I urge action.

Leading articles in the *Mercury* and *Daily Telegraph* supported his appeal:

The fort should have seven guns capable of firing 21 rounds per minute, with an effective range of 7 miles. Its fire would then overlap that of the Steep and Flat Holm batteries. The new harbour is on a direct route to New York without any need for ships to tack. It also provides a short route for cattle from Ireland to reach markets in London.

The topic went quiet until March 1872:

The Brean Down Harbour scheme has been at a standstill since the death of the contractor Mr Chaplin. There has also been difficulty owing to lack of funds. Recently the wealthy Marquis of Bute with some experienced coastguardsmen surveyed the parish and bay of Uphill and decided to run steam packets twice a week from Cardiff to Uphill. They intend using the Uphill railway, trading in Welsh coal in one direction and Somerset fruit the other.

And after yet another four years, a *Mercury* leader asked:

Why is Brean Down harbour speculation not taken up again? The Great Western Railway is investing in other harbour schemes and is involved in rail, docks, coalfields.

The fort fared better. In September 1872:

Flat Holme Battery now has a Royal Artillery garrison of 51 men. They operate four batteries of the "terrible" Moncrieff guns. As on Steep Holme, the soldiers live partly under canvas. Another 57 men form the Steep garrison where the Batteries are enfiladed with those on Flat Holme and Brean Down.

Moncrieffe   gun

Brean Down Fort covered 4 acres and was accessible only on the landward side, through an iron gate across a bridge over a dry moat. Fifty men lived in the barrack block to the left with officers in the HQ block to the right. They manned seven 7-inch muzzle-loading guns each weighing 7 tons, firing 112lb Palliser shells able to penetrate 8-inch steel armour plate at half a mile range.

The garrison was augmented by a Brigade of Artillery Volunteers formed in June 1874 from local units who joined the Regulars at Brean Down Fort as needed. The Volunteers trained at summer camp on the Down, working the 7-ton guns in the fort as well as their own 40-pounder Armstrong breech-loading rifled guns.

Armstrong   40-pounder

380 Volunteers sailed across the Bay from Portishead Pier on the steamer *Taff* and anchored off the Down. Inside half an hour they had disembarked in boats. They then climbed the cliffs without scaling ladders and hoisted their kit up a human chain from the boats. They formed up on top and marched along a path cut half way down the slope to their camp-site near the fort where they erected 64 bell tents as living quarters. Quartermasters issued 600 blankets and 300 waterproof groundsheets for bedding, but it was to be hard lying as there were no palliasses, the cotton covers which men stuffed with straw or heather as mattresses. Two marquees housed Headquarters. The men ate in a large dining tent which held 150 to 200 men and in a barrack room in the fort where 100 could eat.

Their cooks used British Army Soyer Stoves designed during the Crimean War – and which were still in operational use 150 years later in the Second World War:

SOYER'S FIELD KITCHEN OR CAMP STOVES.

Each apparatus contains a cauldron holding 12½ gallons. Two of the apparatus easily cook for a company of 100, and even more, if required, and both stoves can be carried by one mule, and loaded inside with sufficient dry wood for two days' consumption for a full company, whereas an additional quantity of fuel for one day's further consumption may be carried outside between the apparatus on the animal's back. The weight would then be 60lb under the

full charge of a mule. The cauldron is made of such a material as not to require tinning, and the saving of fuel is remarkable, being above eight-ninths under the old system, the allowance to each man being 4½lb of wood during the spring and summer months, which were formerly consumed for cooking only. These stoves will also burn any kind of fuel, and are entirely free from smoke.

Soyer Camp Stove

Field training was just as efficient, save that:

> One Armstrong shot fired on Brean beach hit a rock and ricocheted over the Down to land in Weston Bay.

Chapter 53.   Health

Weston had a public dispensary and a hospital had been built in Alfred Street in 1865 but most Uphill people still depended on patent medicines, persuasively advertised:

TILLEY'S FAMILY PILLS,
As prepared by the late
LEONARD TILLEY, Uphill.

The efficacy of this Medicine has been experienced for some years in the neighbourhood where the Proprietor lived; they have been, and still are, highly valued for the many cures and benefits derived from the use of them. Many persons, after having been given over by the Physician or Surgeon and who have been discharged from the Infirmaries as incurable, have received lasting benefit from the use of them, joined with other remedies prescribed by the Proprietor.

They will be found highly serviceable in the following diseases: Bilious Complaints; Blotches on the Skin; Headache; Indigestion; Pain in the Stomach; Piles; Rheumatism; Scrofula or the King's Evil; Gravel; Worms; Ulcers; Scorbutic Complaints, &c.

The Public will be pleased to notice that
CHARLES GRIFFITH
CHEMIST, 35 HIGH STREET, Weston-super-Mare
has purchased the whole and sole right and interest in the Medicines known as
TILLEY'S PILLS AND OINTMENT
by whom the above-named articles will be faithfully prepared. These Pills are entirely free from all Mercury, and may be taken at any time with perfect safety.
Sold in boxes at 7½d, and 1s 1½d.

Some ailments needed professional attention. A tumour identified as *naevus maternus* or a "mother's mark" was removed from the head of the 18-month old child of Mr John Riden in Uphill: the surgeon, Mr J Gane from Lympsham, used the newly available chloroform in the operation. Some gentry enjoyed after-dinner sniffing of chloroform, but it was not yet considered necessary for women during childbirth, as pain was seen by male medical professionals as part of God's beneficent plan.

When Queen Victoria was prescribed chloroform for Prince Leopold's birth, however, it became acceptable for those who could afford it.

Tetanus was a constant peril for agricultural and quarry workers. Rabies, carried by packs of stray dogs, became almost an ordinary disease. The cost of the compulsory dog licence was nevertheless reduced from 9s to 5s a year and muzzling orders were seldom made. A rabid stray bit a girl in Weston before being chased onto the beach and killed. The wound was cauterised by a doctor but the outcome is not known.

Death often came without explanation:

> Inquest at the Ship on Robert Boley, 5 months, son of Solomon Boley, labourer, of Uphill, found dead in bed by mother. Verdict: "Found dead in bed".

Robert was one of Solomon and Eliza Boley's ten children; another Robert was born two years later.

> Inquest at the Dolphin on Mrs Sophia Rattle, 50, nurse to Mrs Harris who died after suffering violent pains in the head. Verdict: "Died by the visitation of God".

Her death notice read "Sophia Rattle age 62, relict of the late Mr Samuel Rattle of Worle".

The pursuit of prosperity and profit encouraged the adulteration of food. Mark Minifie had a milk retailing business "Weston Pure Milk Supply" selling milk for 2½d a pint at the doorstep from churns pushed round the streets in hand-carts. Receiving complaints from customers, he went with Solomon Boley, now a milk wholesaler, to check their suppliers in dairy farms.

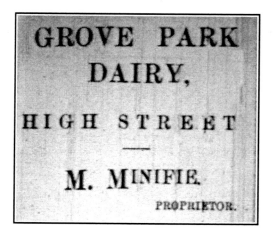

GROVE PARK DAIRY,
HIGH STREET
—
M. MINIFIE.
PROPRIETOR.

In the farmers' presence they collected specimens in corked, sealed and labelled bottles. The public analyst in Axbridge found that the milk from farmer James Evans was 50% water and injurious to health. Mr Evans was fined £5 and all costs. Solomon Boley's brother William, Uphill's dairyman, was also fined £5 and costs – or 3 months in prison – for selling milk that was 30% water. One of Mark Minifie's delivery boys, William Templeman, did his own milk-thinning on the way round and received the same sentence.

A *Mercury* leader in January 1871 claimed Weston to be among the healthiest of fashionable watering places in the country. Thanks to its good drainage and healthy air, rich Bristolians had found refuge in the resort during their cholera epidemic. The Board of Uphill Sanatorium reinforced the claim by insisting that they never admitted anyone with an infectious disease. Patients convalescing after typhoid were released only after 21 days' quarantine.

But fears remained of infection. Free lime was handed out to poor families in Weston's "back-slums" as disinfectant and wealthier householders began ventilating bedrooms in all weathers as a safeguard against "sewer gas" which they believed seeped insidiously back up drains into their homes infecting the occupants.

At a time when an etiquette book advised that it was "unmannerly to kill a bed bug or other insect when in company", all classes needed:

Chapter 54.   Parish Churches

With a typically 19ᵗʰ century display of erudition, the *Mercury* reported the state of Uphill's old church on 1ˢᵗ November 1873:

A Walk to Uphill

...clear against the sky, on the height, bare and treeless, the ancient parish church of St Nicholas – a slanting path through a field led to three projecting stones doing duty for a stile in its compound's enclosure wall. These having been surmounted, a drop of five feet placed your correspondent within the consecrated burying ground of great antiquity, and now from paucity of numbers in the parish – the population is less than the enumerated components of the cavalry charge at Balaklava – from the salubrity of the neighbourhood and other reasons, rarely resorted to for interment, a few old ruinate lichen-covered tombs and mounds of grass were visible. Only one perpendicular gravestone of modern elevation, which, solidly fixed, with lettering deeply carved (from the workshop of Hare, of Weston) recorded:-

Sacred to the Memory

Of

JOHN BISS DELAY

Who Died 17ᵗʰ April, 1868,

Aged 64 Years

———

Also SARAH, his wife

Died 16ᵗʰ April 1869, Aged 65 Years.

———

JANE DELAY,

Mother of the above-named John Bliss Delay,

Died 4ᵗʰ May, 1866, aged 86 Years.

And the names of a son and two daughters of the above also are thereon engraved. On the immediate left is a stone to "John Biss, of this Parish, Mariner, who died 29ᵗʰ September 1792, aged 58 years" and on the immediate right, one to some of the Biss family.

The name of Delay appears to exist no longer in tranquil Uphill. Mr JB Delay was a painter and glazier – and likewise held the highly confidential appointment of receiver at the post office of Uphill and was much respected as a tradesman and parishioner by all. ...

The Rev F Trevor, the former and revered rector, and the Rev George Cuff, the curate, have ceased to follow their sacred calling and though changes are comparatively slow to occur in Uphill, yet the last fourteen years have made their mark.

Your correspondent climbed another part of the precinct wall and descended direct to the door of the Dolphin Hotel and thence past the provision store of HH Harris and soon afterwards the new school buildings and then the post office, at the back premises of which was Minifie's, the wheelwright and smith – all sufficing for the wants of the peaceful, healthful, retired locality.

Nothing was done and in 1877 Parish Churchwarden Obed Poole complained about the disgraceful state of the old churchyard. He proposed using church offertory collections to improve it, but said he could do nothing as long as sheep were allowed to be pastured in the old burial ground. He also pointed out the dilapidated state of the wheels in the belfry of the old church but a resolution to repair them foundered as it would cost £20. The Lord of the Manor came to the rescue yet again in 1879:

For some weeks now, TT Knyfton has been entertaining a circle of distinguished guests at Uphill Castle, including the Lord Bishop of Winchester who was welcomed with a peal of bells from the old church. These bells had been so out of repair as to make ringing dangerous. TT Knyfton paid for them to be re-hung and fitted with new supports by wheelwright Mr John Barstable of East Brent and this was their first peal.

The Seventies opened with the Rev Stephen Bennett MA as rector, the Rev CF Hawkins as his curate and Mr Robert Counsell as the Clerk and Sexton. Mr T Edwards retired as organist in January 1871 after many years. The Rector's father, Thomas Bennett Esq, was now Patron of the living. The *Mercury* described a picture of happy simplicity:

Uphill village schoolchildren were kindly invited by the Rev S Bennett, rector, to tea on the rectory lawn, where upwards of 90 partook of an abundance of good things, after which games &c were indulged in and a most enjoyable evening was spent. The worthy rector was loudly cheered for his hospitality.

But, in April 1870, the paper reported a "somewhat lengthy sermon" in which the Rev CF Hawkins referred to Purgatory. It claimed that the majority of the congregation – "Protestants of the village" – were amazed at the "Romish" word. In the same issue the paper published what it called a "somewhat amusing letter signed A Moderate Churchman but in the handwriting of a lady":

The Late Curate's love for his Flock

Why do the Weston people dislike the clergyman of Uphill if the people of the parish do not complain? Why do the Weston people interfere and why do they ridicule the late curate of Uphill? Perhaps they do not know the good he has done while in the parish; how he visited the poor, the sick and the needy; how he helped them both in their temporal and spiritual wants. Oh! Where shall we find another such minister who will work with the people both night and day? How he loved the people whose souls he had to give an account for. What a loss to Uphill. I hope our good rector, Mr Bennett, will get another such curate who will do as he has done, for he was beloved by all who knew him.

In February 1872, the *Mercury* reinforced a strong leader against Popery with:

EVENSONG with sermon was announced for St Nicholas at Uphill at 6.30 but no more than a score were present in the dimly illuminated edifice. Just before seven the congregation increased to about seventy, the greater part children and young persons. Six surpliced lads emanated from the vestry followed by the Rev CF Hawkins and Rev HP Denison, singing the processional hymn Onward Christian Soldiers. Prayers were read – or rather stumbled over and jumbled together – by the last named gentleman, certain members of the congregation crossing themselves and otherwise behaving ridiculously.

The lessons were read by Mr Hawkins who said, "There will be no sermon as the priest who was to have preached is not here. I would also mention that a newspaper has stated that I have been suspended. This is not true."

The choristers preceded the clergy and promenaded the aisles to the amusement of the rural part of the congregation, the juveniles looking on with distended eyes and mouths, not knowing whether to laugh or cry. The clergy made low obeisance on passing the altar. The lookers-on who crowded the doorway appeared to relish the joke and while laughter could be heard on the outside, a general titter was audible inside the building.

The reference to "suspension" is not explained, but the 1871 Census named the 49-year old Rev Frederick Emmanuel Gutteres BA as curate. Ordained in 1846, Mr Gutteres joined the Royal Navy, serving in the Crimea at the bombardment of Sevastopol and then in the Black Sea, being awarded the Crimea and Turkish Medals. He lived in The Gables, Uphill, with his wife Agnes Eliza and three daughters until 1873 when he left for Devon, dying there in 1899.

In 1877, the Rev ACC Spalding worked as curate-in-charge of the parish. The Rev CF Hawkins remained living in the village until 1878 when he left for Wiltshire. He died in 1884, being remembered in St Nicholas as a "popular preacher who attracted large congregations".

Church routine continued with Tithe Dinners at the Dolphin for "those privileged to pay tithes". At Harvest, Easter and Christmas the church was lavishly decorated by the tithe-payers' womenfolk:

Christmas decorations in St Nicholas church.

Mrs Bennett did the pulpit, tracing the panels with evergreen and tinsel. A gold cross surmounted with a gold crown filled the centre panel, and the initials alpha and omega in holly berries appeared in the side panels. The lectern was decorated with silver tinsel and evergreen, with IHS in letters of green and gold.

Miss Whitting did the font, richly adorning it with hothouse flowers and a cross of pure white blooms floating in the water. The windows were decorated by Mrs Gutteres with green and gold words on the sills reading: *This day is born a Saviour which is Christ the Lord*. Holly and sacred symbols hung on the walls.

In 1879 Charles Edward Whitting gave the church a Bible and a brass eagle lectern. Years of local fund-raising produced £210 for a new organ, a two-manual instrument in a case of varnished pitch pine made by Mr W Sweetland of Bath. It had "over 500 pipes, two octaves of pedals and a list of stops". Choir master Mr Frith played at a service of thanksgiving followed by tea in marquees on the rectory lawn. The local Yeomanry joined parishioners in the evening at supper in the rectory. They assembled in a "reception tent warmed by an American stove" and the evening ended with "dancing to the Rhine Band".

Chapter 55.   Chapel Vandalised

Religious prejudice erupted in Uphill when vandals smashed windows in the Wesleyan Chapel. Although some culprits confessed and paid for the damage, more followed and *Mercury* headlines told the shocking story on 5th December 1874:

THE UPHILL CHURCHWARDEN CHARGED WITH BREAKING THE WINDOWS OF THE WESLEYAN CHAPEL

Obed Poole, Churchwarden, appeared in court charged with breaking windows to the value of 30s, the property of Benjamin Brice, George Evans and others, trustees of the Uphill Wesleyan Chapel.

The evidence was all circumstantial. The defendant lived in Uphill and was churchwarden and guardian of the parish. Some Uphill men were at an entertainment in the London Inn. The others left earlier and John Parffrey, landlord of the Ship, offered to accompany Obed Poole back to Uphill. Defendant declined and left at 1am.

The attacker walked through Church Path at the rear of Capt Whitting's premises and entered through a door into his lawn. He took an iron trident that was supporting a rose tree and carried it through the fence on the north side of the chapel premises. He used the trident to break the windows. The culprit had to be at least 5ft 11in tall to reach the windows, even with the trident, which was found there by the police. The noise of the smash was heard by Mr and Mrs Saunders living nearby at just the time Obed Poole would have been there.

Witness Robert Minifie, keeper of the Wesleyan Chapel stated that all was in order when he had locked up as usual at night. On opening up next morning he found considerable damage was done to the windows and sash. He had since repaired it.

Witness Richard Minifie, his brother, the village smith and postman, said he remembered the defendant saying in November after other damage to the chapel, "All the d- lot will be smashed before the winter is out." He was sure the defendant had said it seriously. At the time he told Thomas Gould who remembered it. He had lived 21 years in Uphill and knew the defendant all that time. The defendant was Mr Knyfton's prime tenant and also waywarden, churchwarden and guardian of parish. He was also secretary of the Weston-super-Mare branch of the English Church Union. The witness was a member of the Church of England, not a Wesleyan. He respected the defendant as he had supported the witness's trade in Uphill.

The Police Sergeant presented a map showing the culprit's presumed route along the church path at the rear of Capt Whitting's property (Sandcroft). It showed how the doorway in the wall gave access to the garden and then an old hole in the fence led to the north side of the chapel.

Witness Charles Saunders lived 10 yards from chapel. He and his wife heard the glass break at about 3 am just before the milk cart passed. At the time he thought it was cats on his greenhouses.

Witness William B Frampton left the London Inn with the defendant at 1 am. The defendant was sober.

Witness Lot Staples said he had been employed by S olomon Boley. On 6th November he was working in his cider house when the defendant came in and said "All the d- lot will be smashed before the winter is out."

The Prosecution pointed out that the defendant had refused Parffrey's offer of company which showed he planned to commit the offence. He was a strong Church of England man who disliked non-conformists. He was moved by zealotry made worse by the effect of drink.

The Defence had testimonials to the defendant's good character from Archdeacon Denison, Rev S Bennett, Rev F Hawkins, Rev F Gutteres and Capt Whitting but these were not read out. The defendant's remarks on breaking windows were meant as a joke. If he had meant it, he would not have said it. If the listeners had believed him, they would have warned the trustees.

After a discussion on the propriety of a devout churchman using the word "damned" even in a joking way, the Bench divided 2 and 2 on its verdict and gave the defendant the benefit of the doubt. Against the legal advice of the clerk, the magistrates then bound Obed Poole over to be of good behaviour for six months in his own surety of £100 and two other sureties of £50 each.

Meanwhile, the Wesleyans grew in strength. They opened a Sunday School and farmer Edward Luff gave a donation towards a Christmas tea-party for about 50 children. Visiting preachers the Revs TJ Pattenden and WT Nelson attracted large congregations with hymn singing accompanied by Miss E Snodgrass on the harmonium. Messrs Hillman and Beeston came in from Weston-super-Mare to preach and Messrs Luff, P Amos, W Rendall, Minifie, Hillman, Walters and Bezzant gave readings and led singing. Missionaries gave lectures and "ladies Luff, Slocombe, Podger, Counsell, Tilley provided refreshments at tea meetings". In September 1879, a large congregation heard of the growing success of Uphill Wesleyan Sabbath School with Mr Edward Pavey and Mr Harse as superintendents. They were told that the village population was 500 "but the church holds only 250, which means work for the Wesleyans in Uphill".

❏ ❏ ❏ ❏ ❏

Chapter 56.   Voice of the People

After a century of violent popular revolution in America and Europe, Victorian Britain was changing and "Liberty" became the watchword. The qualification to be a magistrate was reduced from ownership of freehold property to the occupation of a dwelling house rated at £100 pa:

> This makes a new class eligible to join the magistracy and represents a great social change.

Women were not yet part of this "new class". Feminists in London demanded equal rights and education based on equal intelligence but their humbler sisters in Weston struggled for even such basic rights as a seat while working. Rural widows were still evicted on the death of husbands who had been tenan farmers. And when, in January 1875, a woman stabbed another at Lympsham, the magistrates listened seriously to her defence that she was "hag-ridden by a witch with the evil eye who came by night to terrify her. The only protection was to draw blood from her."

Voting in Parliamentary elections was made secret; Karl Marx was active in London; Trades Unions were organising national strikes. In Weston building labourers set up a Labourers' Union in 1873 and carpenters went on strike, rejecting an offer from master builders to increase their weekly wage to 3s 4½d. By 1878 employers faced intimidation from gangs of trade unionists trying to impose pay rises.

But in 1875, the public affairs of Uphill remained in the hands of a few villagers appointed each year at Church Vestry Meetings of parish ratepayers. Ratepayers were landowners and businessmen whose property exceeded a certain value. The Rector chaired the procedure of electing parish officers. This was by nomination with any voting restricted to those present. The Rector first nominated his own Churchwarden and the meeting chose another to represent the parish. Then came the Parish Clerk who organised church services, helped by the Sexton who was caretaker and grave-digger and looked after church security. Overseers organised relief of the poor and a Waywarden looked after such public works as road maintenance. The same men were generally re-appointed each year.

The Easter Vestry Meeting in 1875 was typical. Farmer John Harse, 68-year old widower of Slimeridge Farm, was re-nominated as the Rector's Churchwarden with Obed Poole – despite his recent appearance in court – again the Parish Churchwarden and Waywarden. Obed Poole, born 1851, was the stepson of William Fear of Uphill Farm. Robert Counsell, 50-year old builder, of Myrtle Cottage and Abel Young of Flat Roof Farm just over Devil's Bridge became Overseers. Having declared the parish accounts in order, the meeting resolved to build a wall along the rhyne at Coastguard Cottages to protect the public and to widen the road and lay a drain in the ditch at Totterdown.

In 1877, however, the Lady Day Vestry heard long arguments over qualifications for voting. Some wanted each ratepayer to have one vote, but the chairman ruled that each man's number of votes depended on the rateable value of his property. After Obed Poole was re-elected Waywarden on the proposal of Capt Whitting, a new voice was heard, that of Robert Minifie, 41-year old wheelwright of Sandcroft Cottages. He stood up and referred to a recent sudden death in the parish, saying accusingly that there should have been an inquest but the "powers that be", including the press, had failed in their public duty. The chairman firmly ruled the issue out of order and closed the meeting.

The following year, 1878, the Rector was absent from the March Vestry meeting and Thomas Buller, the wealthy Wesleyan, moved that Parish Churchwarden Obed Poole should preside. Capt Charles Whitting preferred to invite the curate to take the chair but Poole pointed out that the curate was not a ratepayer and therefore not qualified to take part in their business. The meeting promptly voted 28-year old Mr Poole into the chair. Thomas Buller proposed the re-election of Obed Poole as Waywarden saying he had discharged his duties so ably that "no other road in the Axbridge Union was in so good a state of repair as those of Uphill". This was seconded by Samuel Travis of Albion Villa in the new Moorland Road which needed a lot of work doing on its road surface. But Edward Morgan Whitting, Capt Whitting's second son, seconded by James Gould, countered by moving the election of Edward Luff as Waywarden. Samuel Travis told the meeting that Mr Luff had not been asked if he would stand and would certainly refuse. At this Obed Poole was elected and, the *Mercury* reported, "the bells of the parish rang forth merry peals".

Whether the peal was normal procedure after a meeting, or a comment on the democratic process is not clear, but there was certainly considerable public interest in the meeting of the Axbridge Board of Guardians a few days later. This Board was the governing body of Axbridge workhouse and included a representative from each community it served. There were two candidates for Uphill, the sitting member Obed Poole and Charles Edward Whitting, the Captain's elder son. The Board decided to deliver voting papers round the village where placards and exploding fireworks made it a lively election before CE Whitting was elected by 67 votes to 36.

A week later, there was so large an attendance – 60 ratepayers – at the Easter Vestry meeting in April that it was adjourned to the old schoolroom. In the absence of the Rector, Capt Whitting proposed and Obed Poole seconded Thomas Tutton Knyfton as chairman. The parish accounts showed a deficit of £18 13s 11d and Charles Edward Whitting remarked that the bills were not receipted and questioned if the accounts should be passed by the meeting. In his role as Parish Churchwarden Mr Poole explained that they were not receipted as he had no money to pay them; if they were not paid it must be the fault of the rector. Coastguard boatman Thomas Davey then asked if the Rector was not bound by Act of Parliament to attend the Easter vestry. The chairman replied that he was not legally bound to attend, but ought to. He added that there was £26 5s 3d to the credit of the parish and he thought they should approve the accounts as appearing satisfactory.

> Thomas Buller objected: Until Mr Poole produces receipted accounts he cannot retire from office. When the rector sends his cheque, the c hurchwardens can get rid of their liabilities and retire but it would not be fair to tax their successors with the amount due.
> The Chairman: The deficiency is not large.
> Mr Buller: But let us do things straight. The meeting must be adjourned until all the accounts are paid.
> The Chairman: Under the old law, deficits were carried forward. Now that there is a parish rate and no church rates, things may be different.
> Obed Poole: The churchwardens are not bound to submit the accounts to the vestry meeting. It is a matter between them and the rector.
> Robert Minifie: It is a matter of right that parishioners know how their money is expended.
> Capt Whitting: The books do not show that last year's deficit was paid.
> Obed Poole: I received a cheque for £14 from the rector and £1 8s 9d is still due to me on that account. It was three months after the last Easter vestry that I got the £14.

Matters did move on but hit a new stumbling block when John Harse declined re-election as Rector's Churchwarden complaining that he had "not much inclination to attend church as the services had so degenerated", a reference to the Rector's unpopular High Church "Ritualism". At this, Samuel Travis proposed and Mr Morris seconded Methodist Thomas Buller as Churchwarden while John Treherne of Uphill House supported the old régime by proposing Charles Edward Whitting.

Showing an astute grasp of committee procedures, 29-year old blacksmith Richard Minifie challenged the system by seconding CE Whitting as Churchwarden "on condition that he removed the cross placed on the communion table contrary to law". His brother Robert added to the pressure by asking if Mr Whitting would "see that the Ten Commandments were replaced in the chancel from which they had long been removed". Charles Edward Whitting showed his form by promising that he would do his duty if elected but could not promise to change "what had been there for years".

After "an animated public dispute over the wearing of surplices and forms of worship" another Minifie brother, William, joined in, asking Mr Whitting to state exactly what he would do if elected. William said he opposed one gentleman filling all the public offices in one parish and he also thought Mr Buller being a Wesleyan should not stand for Churchwarden. He and his brothers had been:

> kicked out of the parish church by the lawbreaking of its officers and when I appealed to my respected landlord Capt Whitting, what did he do as churchwarden? He retired from the job (laughter) and allowed the rector, curate and churchwardens to do as they wished (applause). Mr Poole had always done his duty to the church party and when there was any conjuring to be done, he was always ready to put on his wooden leg (laughter).

Unmoved, Mr Whitting would not promise anything. Mr Morris asked who was most likely to remove Ritualism from the church, Mr Buller a Non-conformist and follower of John Wesley, or a man who took part in the present services. The meeting voted 33 for Buller and 23 for Whitting but James Counsell demanded a poll of the whole parish. When he added that he would be pleased to pay Mr Whitting's share of the expenses, William Minifie commented that it was a change for Mr Counsell to put his hand in his pocket. Amidst derisive laughter the chairman thankfully declared the meeting closed.

Coloured placards around the village urged "No Popery; vote for Buller the Protestant candidate". A majority of ratepayers supported Buller, but, because voting was weighted in favour of those who paid more rates, CE Whitting was elected.

The Rev S Bennett presided at the Easter Vestry in 1879 and many ratepayers attended. They agreed to increase church insurance from £2,000 to £3,000 and then the elections and disputes began. When the Rector nominated John Harse to continue as the Rector's Churchwarden, Thomas Tutton Knyfton commented that this office used to be unwanted but was now considered an honour. Adding that one man should not hold more than one office, he proposed Mr Henry Brown as Parish Churchwarden and Capt Whitting seconded.

> But Robert Minifie objected: Does Mr Brown understand his duties?
> Henry Brown: I don't understand what *you* want.
> Robert Minifie: You are already Overseer, and Squire has just said honours should be divided.

He went on to attack "illegal ornaments and services" in the church and after ten minutes of bitter argument the Rector closed the meeting.

As the people's voice became louder at vestry meetings, the *Mercury* continued to provide an outlet for those who for good reasons preferred to remain anonymous. Signed "A Yearly Tenant" a letter in March 1871 pointed out:

> The Sanatorium has paid 500 guineas to Capt Charles Whitting for a piece of sandy soil for which they also pay £10 per annum. I don't blame him as the value of land has risen in the last 20 years from 30s to £3 per acre. But I hope he, as a Poor Law Guardian will give some back, thus obtaining the gratitude of the sick poor and the respect of upper classes.

That "piece of sandy soil" was chosen as the site of the Sanatorium because "its good record has proved the area to be the healthiest in town". Consequently, "25 Villa Residences" were authorised to be built on Upper Moor Road, now to become Moorland Road. They were soon sold to the aspiring middle class. :

Sale
Moorland House, Upper Moor Road, Uphill.

This 10-room detached residence is a well built Villa with a carriage road at the side, Fruit and Kitchen gardens at the rear, and with extensive land and sea views. Adjoining Building land or walled garden with 92 feet frontage on Upper Moor Road and 97 feet on Middle Road, occupied by Mr S Brown, florist.

And profitably resold six months later:

Moorland House, Uphill to let unfurnished or for sale: Detached, drawing, dining, breakfast and 5 bedrooms, with kitchens and offices. Large kitchen garden, carriage entrance, good views.

There were problems. In April 1879, a letter went to the Chairman of the Local Board, Weston-super-Mare:

> The undersigned inhabitants of Uphill and Moorland Roads beg to call your attention to the bad state of the Side walk from Lea Hurst Villa Uphill Road to Weston-super-Mare, and venture to hope you will have the same put in good repair

Robert Were	Brean Down Villa
Thos Gould	Fairview
Charles Whitting	Sandcroft, Uphill
John Gale	Moorland Road
Theo B Gould	Cyprus Villa
H Brown	Plevna
M Augusta Kelly	Moorland House
Mariane Soacly	Claremont Villa
OLW Poole	Stanley Villa
Charles Binning	Rutland Villa
MK Thomas	Belgrave Villa
W Cook	Cressley Villa
Samuel Travis	Albion Villa
James Rossiter	Albion Villa
FJ Brown	Lower Moor Road (Southend Road)
Samuel Rowsell	Lower Moor Road
Thomas Lye	2 Fair View
BT Banks	Paull Villa
Robt Collins	Ashley Villa
JP Daunton	Ravenhill Villa

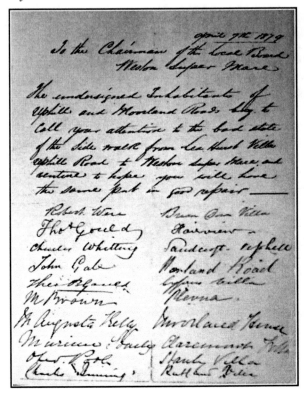

The Moorland Road petition, page 1.

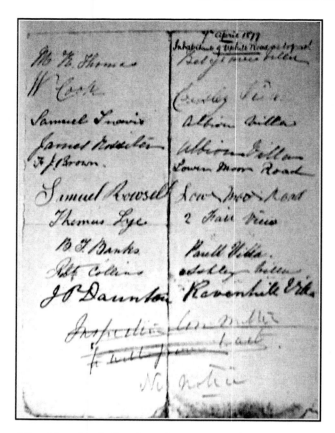

The Moorland Road petition, page 2.

Although the Town Commissioners bought Weston Water Works in 1878, Moorland Road still had no public water supply or drains a year later. Its articulate rate-paying householders duly complained. The Town Commissioners wriggled, claiming that the road was not in Weston but in Uphill and therefore part of Axbridge Rural Sanitary Authority. Their Clerk pointed out that the purchase of the Water Works included powers to supply Uphill with water and that one water-pipe would be big enough for both areas. The Bazalgette drainage scheme, however, was for Weston only, not Uphill. If Uphill residents wanted to discharge into the sewer, they would have to pay. Not wishing to be involved in this unending debate, Axbridge Rural Sanitary Authority declared that Uphill would be better dealing with Weston than with them. When the Uphill representative — Overseer Obed Poole — urged prompt action to safeguard public health, the Axbridge chairman recommended Uphill to establish a properly constituted Parish Committee to handle the matter.

For the first time in their history the people of Uphill would be given a constitutional voice.

In the meantime, the 1879 Lady Day Vestry meeting attracted another big attendance. Ratepayers voted Churchwarden Harse into the chair and the names of Temple Gould, Henry Brown, Thomas Buller and Abel Young were

proposed for the selection of Overseers. The Assistant Overseer personally knocked on doors to collect the rates and his salary provoked "a warm debate with excitement and personal feeling." James Gould proposed the re-election of James Evans of Wyndham Lodge at the same salary of £30 a year, but Henry Brown proposed cutting it to £25. This was seconded by Richard Minifie, countered by his older brother William who pointed out that the job covered a bigger area now that Moorland Road was built on and that smaller houses made collection difficult. He proposed £35 pa and after a noisy debate the meeting voted for £35. At this stage James Evans said he only wanted £30 but Robert Minifie, oldest of the three brothers, insisted that, as they had voted for £35, he had to have it.

Roads were the next issue and Obed Poole was re-elected Waywarden. The expense of repairing Windwhistle Lane was avoided by declaring it private property. They noted the "bad state of the road near the parsonage" and heard from "Mr R Minifie that the road from Mr Knyfton's to the Sanatorium was being encroached on and the surface scraped away as it was saleable as manure." On that note the meeting closed with no progress on roads, drains or democracy.

Richer rate-payers had no doubts about who would actually foot the bill for improvements. Charles Edward Whitting quoted Thomas Tutton Knyfton as objecting to the cost of Moorland Road's drainage and water being charged to the rest of Uphill which had had no problems with water or drainage since the new sewer some sixteen years earlier. But, in July 1879, the *Mercury* reported:

… excitement in the parish of Uphill which has seen a rash of posters in different colours announcing a ratepayers' meeting at The Ship to discuss the drainage of Moorland Road. Some read "Vote for Buller" or "Buller and Economy". In spite of this, not many attended the meeting. They voted Mr Buller into the chair and he explained how the scheme could work but interruptions turned it into something more like a tap-room squabble than a ratepayers' meeting. Although the scheme would cost several thousand pounds, he would contribute £1,000 if three others would do the same and this would avoid having charges on the villagers. This produced loud applause. Mr Obed Poole and others ridiculed the chairman, but at the end Mr Buller and Mr Poole shook hands and declared friendship. Mr Buller said that if Uphill ever had its own MP, Mr Poole would be up among the great radical parliamentarians.

A few days later, a Vestry meeting was called to establish a Parochial Committee as required by the Axbridge Board. Their purpose was "to consider the drainage of Moorland Road into the common sewer". So many attended that the meeting was adjourned to the new schoolroom. The Rector was voted into the chair and Overseer Temple Gould nominated "the Rev S Bennett, and Messrs TT Knyfton, C Whitting, H Lovibond, T Buller (Guardian), O Poole (Waywarden), H Brown and T Gould (Overseers), John Harse (Churchwarden) to be declared the Parochial Committee of Uphill". Some disputed the procedure and would have preferred an open village meeting, but the nominees were approved and voted in as the Parochial Committee.

On 9th August 1879, the new Parochial Committee met in the schoolroom where Thomas Knyfton, Charles Whitting, R Lovibond, Thomas Buller, Obed Poole, John Harse and Temple Gould discussed Moorland Road's drains and water supply. On 30th August, their report reached the Axbridge Rural Sanitary Authority:

Moorland Road – In 1872 the Freehold Land Society's Estate sold 20 acres in 300 lots for building one house on each lot. It is a good road, half mile long, 30 feet wide, with a footpath on each side. There are now 36 houses scattered through the area. Uphill Parochial Committee visited each one and questioned the owners.

They drank the water to test it and found the water generally good. Bog-pits were imperfectly constructed and so close to the wells that pollution is unavoidable in the light sandy soil. A ditch runs all along the backs of the houses. Some owners have stopped it up causing gardens to flood after rain. We saw no offensive matter likely to cause an epidemic. There has been only one death there since building began. If the ditches were cleaned and the bog-pits moved, there would be no need for further action for this number of houses. Uphill has had a parish pump for many years past and it has been very useful. We recommend a similar public pump to supply water for Moorland Road.

Exactly a month later in Uphill, "Mr T Buller of The Retreat provided a handsome trough of pennant stone for the parochial hydraulic engine" as the *Mercury* described the pump. The trough had hitherto been two boards in a V-shape.

Axbridge responded defensively:

every new house in Moorland Road is provided by the builder with a well and a bog-pit.

Cleaning the ditch and care of the bog-pits is the responsibility of the owners and subject to enforcement by the Sanitary Officer. At the present rate of building there is no need to do anything for another quarter century. If anything is done, therefore, Uphill will have to pay for it through its own rates.

It concluded that there was no need for the Axbridge Board to do anything. In December, therefore, the residents of Upper Moor Road went over the heads of Uphill Parochial Council and the Axbridge Board, commissioning their own engineer's report and submitting it to the Local Government Board in London:

The road is 1320 feet long with 23 villas. Their wells are sunk in sea-sand. They fill with surface water, as there are no springs. Cess pools overflow especially as rainwater cisterns run when full into the bog-pits. Weston-super-Mare used to have the same problems but the town built a waterworks which pumped water from an unlimited pure spring at Milton. It also built a sewer running into the River Axe. During the wet winter months, the area from Uphill Castle Lodge to Whitecross Estate, known as "The Forty Acres", is always flooded. This is because the land between the Sanatorium and Uphill Drove is flat. The engineer recommends draining the houses into the main sewer which is 12 feet below ground level and also providing water from the Water Works.

A final ambitious sting in the tail added:

The engineer will delay consideration of gas lighting until next winter.

Uphill Parish Pump   [UVS]

Part 6:   Golden Decade 1880 - 1890

Chapter 57. Uphill in 1880

Foreground left: four thatched haystacks.
Behind the haystacks, the house among allotment strips is now part of Rhyne Terrace.
The roof of the second house in Frog Lane is lower than today.
The Rectory has a thatched haystack alongside.

[UVS]

Population 646: 303 Male + 342 Female
100 households in 131 houses

Rector: Rev Stephen Bennett MA
Curate-in-charge 1881 Rev Maunsell Eyre; 1887 Rev Edmund T Bennett
Parish Clerk: Robert Counsell; Old Church Sexton: Bob Jarvis
Rector's Churchwarden: John Harse; 1889 Edmund Burdge
Parish Churchwarden: CE Whitting; 1889 Henry Brown
Rate collector: Thomas Counsell; Waywarden: Obed Poole

National Schoolmaster: Henry Frith; 1888 JJ Francis
Postmistress: Mrs Mary Minifie; Postman: Joseph Williams

Lord of the Manor: Thomas Tutton Knyfton; 1887 Reginald Bennet Graves-Knyfton

Col. 1.

R. S. D.

Parish of Uphill

including part of Uphill Drove

Upper and Lower Moorland Road

The Sanatorium, Houses on the

road leading to Bleadon the Houses

on the Hill, and all other Houses or

Cottages in any Road, Lane, or Field in

and belonging to the aforesaid Parish,

of Uphill, and all persons being in any

Vessel in the Uphill Bay.

1881 Census

22% of the population was born in Uphill. Four out of 100 households, including only one complete family, were born in the village: Edward and Matilda Fear and their son Albert Edward; Hannah, Alma and George Hancock all unmarried; widowed sisters Mary Burdwood and Lavinia Smart; and Jane Binding, her son and three daughters, whose husband John was away at sea. Only one villager was over 80, Mrs Elizabeth Harrill aged 86.

Men and boys shared 27 Christian names, the most popular being William 29, John 23, George 21, Henry 18, Thomas 16, James 15, Charles 11. The most popular of 21 different women's and girls' names were variants of Mary 41, Ann 17, Elizabeth 28, Sarah 15.

Among males, labouring remained the main occupation, employing 51 (24%). 16 (7.5%) were farmers with similar numbers in skilled trades or domestic service and 9 (4%) in service trades. Most females — 32 (21%) — were in domestic service and 21 (21%) in service trades. The village had four

shops: grocer Henry Fear, general dealer John Howe, tailor George Matters and Samuel Silcox who combined a draper's store with a grocery. James Popham was one of eight village carpenters and Thomas Taylor of Southville Cottage was one of just two stonemasons.

William Minifie left his Sandcroft smithy and opened a laundry but his brothers in Walnut Cottage announced:

The enterprising firm of Minifie Bros finds its premises inconvenient for increasing trade.

To keep pace with the times and present a more business-like appearance, it is building new dwellings, combined with a workshop and foundry.

There will also be more accommodation for Post Office business.

All this is in preparation for when Uphill is annexed to Weston-super-Mare.

The Minifie family at Walnut Cottage   *[UVS]*

Mr SH Churchill now managed the brick-yard where children still enjoyed the fun and disregarded the perils of old flooded clay-pits:

> Two lads from Weston were sailing on a plank on Mr Churchill's pits when they capsized. One boy clung to the plank and after a struggle reached the bank. The other boy sank twice before being rescued by a local lad Walter Price.

The two biggest farms were in the parish but not the village. William Brooke worked 200 acres at Totterdown and Abel Young farmed 500 acres at Flat Roof Farm on the road to Bleadon. In the village, Henry Brown's Uphill Farm covered 150 acres, John Harse had 108 acres at Slimeridge while widow Eleanor Luff looked after Manor Farm's 117 acres until her son Edward was old enough to take over. Most of the other farms were of just a few acres.

The clay-pits   *[UVS]*

Uphill Farm   *[UVS]*

When John Harse died in 1882, Edmund Burdge took on Slimeridge, losing several pigs from swine fever in 1885. In the following year at Centre Farm, Frederick King's sow produced 49 pigs in ten months, in three litters of 16, 14 and 9.

William Fear had sold Uphill Farm to Henry Brown, finding more profit in a market garden. In March 1886 one of his hens "laid an egg shaped like an hour-glass with the yolk in one globe and the albumen in the other".

Centre Farm   *[UVS]*

His stepson Obed Poole left farming to pursue the business opportunities of the late 19th century. He moved to a new villa at 109 Moorland Road and set up as an auctioneer. Unfortunately he neglected to apply for an auctioneer's licence and was taken to court. The magistrates pointed out that the maximum fine was £100 but generously mitigated this to £10 and £1 costs – with the licence to be paid out of the fine money.

Obed still kept bees and, billed as "apiarist Mr Obed Poole", he gave a lecture on "An Hour with the Bees" in another new village venture, the St Nicholas Coffee House. An advertisement in March 1883 referred to:

COTTAGE to LET at UPHILL

Rent 3s per week clear.
Apply at the Coffee Tavern, Uphill.

and in August the *Mercury* reported:

A new Coffee Tavern is to be built on a part of glebe (church) land now occupied by Mr William Boley. It is to be designed by an eminent architect. The building will be substantial and commodious, including a handsome bar, smoking room and billiard room and a library. Building work is to be supervised by Mr Robert Counsell.

The name and site of the café with the involvement of the Parish Clerk, Robert Counsell, suggest it was a church enterprise. Robert's brother Thomas had a dairy in Frogmore Cottage and doubtless took on trade from William Boley who lost his dairy with his vacated premises.

The quarry changed hands:

Powell and Stone's Lime Kilns and
Quarries, Uphill.

White Lime, Brown Lime (Aberthaw
Pebbles), Lime and Building Stone.

And Charles Howe found another outlet for their white lime, taking about 5 cwt to Bridgwater every week for butchers who used it to clean and whiten tripe.

James Gould still ran his coal business:

Mr Gould of Uphill was delivering coal to Dr Rossiter on Birnbeck Road when his horse bolted and leaped over the sea wall at the entrance to Knightstone, falling 10 feet. The horse escaped with a few bruises and the cart, although nearly full of coal, was little damaged.

Widowed Ann Manley now had the licence for the Dolphin Inn and Isaac Yeo followed Joseph Turner as landlord of the Ship Hotel. In the new development at Moorland Road, William Cook's application for an "outdoor beer licence" was refused by the magistrates.

The sea remained important. William James Henderson, son of village gardener William Henderson, won 8th place among candidates for posts in HM Customs in 1883 and a former resident, Charles Wootton, retired from the Royal Navy with the rank of Commander in 1885. Equally proud of his nautical heritage was Mr Harris, tenant of Steep Holm island and inn, who had his daughter christened Beatrice Steep Holm Anne Cooper Harris.

Henry Lovibond brought the modern Victorian age with him when he bought Uphill House from John Davies Treherne in 1875. He had previously been Clerk to the Somerset Drainage Commission and also the Liberal Party Parliamentary agent in Bridgwater. A 60-year old solicitor, he moved into the village from Bridgwater with his wife, three unmarried daughters in their twenties and thirties and four maidservants. His three sons were also solicitors: George living at home and in partnership with his father, Charles in America and Harry in New South Wales. In 1880 the Lovibonds invited a "large and fashionable party" to Uphill House to take part in a New Year's theatrical entertainment including what the *Mercury* described as

a comic drama 'Little Toddlekins' and a truly screaming farce 'My turn next'.

Henry Lovibond died on Christmas Day 1884. Enjoying a morning's exercise on horseback, he was riding homeward through Hutton when his horse bolted and he was thrown. He was dragged with one foot in the stirrup, his skull was fractured and he died immediately. His funeral was in old St Nicholas Church, directly accessible from his grounds along the hilltop to the graveyard.

This was the usual route for funerals of the gentry which involved corteges of horse-drawn carriages escorted on foot by all the estate servants. A fee of sixpence was charged to prevent a right of way being established through the property.

Capt Charles Whitting of Sandcroft House retired in 1877 from the 6th Somerset Rifles after 17 years service.

His elder son Charles Edward maintained the family tradition, being promoted to Captain in 1882 as B Company Commander in the 3rd Somerset Volunteer Rifles. Charles Edward and his son Edward Jewell had left Totterdown House in 1879 when his first wife Maria died.

In September 1883, he married Sophia Julie Jane Mackworth of Glen Usk, Monmouth. He bought Uphill House a year later when Henry Lovibond died, and lived there for 65 years.

Two days before Christmas in 1880, his younger brother Edward Morgan Whitting (29) married second cousin Miss Mary Maud Harris, only daughter of Morgan Watkins Harris JP of Brecon in a stylish society wedding at St Georges Church, Hanover Square, London. Social proprieties were observed when "the principal tenantry were given a sumptuous dinner at the Dolphin Hotel while the cottage tenantry were cared for at Sandcroft House".

They settled in Totterdown House where their son Morgan Harris was born in 1882 and daughter Gwenllian Maud in 1884. Both brothers spent a lot on extending and renovating the house.

❑ ❑ ❑ ❑ ❑

Chapter 58.   Uphill Castle Gardens

In August 1882, the *Mercury* reprinted an article from the *Gardener's Magazine*:

> Uphill Castle is one of the many charming residences found on the coast of Somersetshire....
>
> The entrance is through a grove of handsome trees.... The rose garden consists of beds laid out on a well-kept lawn. There is a very choice selection of roses grown as dwarfs and standards, producing some very fine blooms....
>
> A tastefully designed set of flower beds were well filled and the colours tastefully arranged....
>
> A broad expanse of closely-shaven lawn and a wide gavel walk surround two sides of the Castle and stretching away behind the Castle are sufficient trees to add materially to the general effect....
>
> Standing about the lawn, in well chosen positions are some handsome coniferous and deciduous trees, notably a fine example of *Pinus Insignis* and several copper-coloured beeches....
>
> A broad stretch of park like scenery, which embraces rich meadows, dotted here and there with thriving trees, carried the eye to the far distant hills. A bank of evergreens in the most luxuriant condition shows how favourable is the climate....
>
> The kitchen garden is well sheltered and contain various glass structures. There are three or four vineries. The earliest crop of grapes is grown in pots; the crop I saw was very promising. Directly the fruit is cut the plants are thrown away and others grown to succeed them. The next house is planted with permanent vines bearing a full average crop. The gardener Mr Matthews said they sometimes bear bunches 7 lbs in weight, The next vinery is still later....
>
> Melons and cucumbers have a separate house devoted to them and during the winter mushrooms are grown in a house that is fitted up in the most perfect manner....
>
> The fruit and kitchen gardens are kept distinct. The crop of strawberries was excellent, the fruit being large and very abundant....
>
> Mr Matthews is a connoisseur in peas and potatoes and devotes attention to new kinds. The American Wonder Pea was sown March 12th and produced pods ready to pick in ten weeks. It was covered with well-filled pods and only one foot high. Among potatoes Mr Matthews planted 3¼ lbs of White Elephant last year from which he lifted rather more then 400 lbs.
>
> Amongst the hardy outdoor fruits is a good crop of plums and a fair sprinkling of apples and pears. Of gooseberries and currants the trees were fairly breaking down under the weight. In the middle of the fruit garden stands a substantial noble span-roof orchard house 62 feet long and 20 wide with glass down to the ground. Peach and nectarines are grown in pots. Figs are planted out and bearing well as are tomatoes. The house is not heated yet Mr Matthews is able to ripen several varieties of grape on vines which are also planted out, relying on solar warmth and controlled ventilation.

Pinus Insignis

Castle Mulberry tree
[Tony Lee]

Chapter 59.   Fun and Games

Thomas Buller was a strong influence in the movement towards democracy in the village and now moved to Chippenham to stand as the Liberal Parliamentary candidate. When the Wesleyan Methodist Sunday School of Wellington presented a Bible and an illustrated scroll of thanks to him for his liberality, he replied that he owed much to the influence of such Sunday Schools on his early life. This background had not, however, made him a pacifist. Hearing that the Weston Rifle Volunteers were in debt, he organised an entertainment in the grounds of his house The Retreat and donated all the proceeds to the Corps:

> The Ship landlord Isaac Yeo built several triumphal arches over the village's roads and residents hung out bunting. Capt Spooner and Lt Whitting led the Volunteers on a march to The Retreat where they mounted guard. At 5pm 200 select guests attended a Promenade Concert. At 7 pm the entry price was reduced to 6d and a steady stream of people came in. At 8.30 pm, 1,000 Chinese lanterns in the trees and coloured fires in the gardens were lit making a fairy land scene. The rustic bridge over the rhyne that winds through the grounds was skilfully decorated.
>
> More Chinese lanterns hung from the old church on the hill where the bells pealed. Three bands, the Orpheus Italian, the Rifle Corps and the Rhine Band, played alternately, producing a constant stream of melody. It was all on a scale of grandeur never seen before in the district.
>
> The entertainment culminated in a Pyrotechnic display by Brock and Co of Crystal Palace in London. At Mr Buller's wish, a canteen in the grounds provided by Host Isaac Yeo of the Ship Inn sold only temperance drinks. The men of the Volunteers enjoyed a cold supper provided by their officers Capt Spooner and Lt Whitting.
>
> The crowd of 2000 to 3000 people were well behaved and dispersed by 11pm.

Shortly after this event, Host Isaac Yeo who lived in Upper Moor Road, today's Moorland Road:

> was driving his horse and trap towards Uphill when the horse fell. The driver was thrown on to the horse's back and from there rolled onto the road. Police Constable Powell was passing and he helped both man and horse to their feet, more frightened than injured.

As Mr and Mrs Buller returned from a holiday tour in Devon and Cornwall, "the bells of the old church

rang merry peals of welcome". And, "even after they had left for Chippenham, the bells rang for Mrs Buller's birthday".

Plenty of entertainment was available in the village: "A large and appreciative audience demanded seven encores" at a "high-class entertainment in the commodious schoolroom". Proceeds of these concerts, chaired by the Rector, helped fund the choir, schoolchildren's teas and their annual treat. A new Working Men's Club (Hon Sec Mr Yandle, Treasurer R Minifie) provided less serious if noisier entertainment:

> Smoking Concert in Working Men's Clubroom.
> Chaired by Mr R Counsell.
> Mr Rogers on piano – readings - songs.
> Held monthly.

All levels of society sometimes came together:

> Schoolroom Uphill
> A Vocal and Instrumental Concert
> Ladies and Gentlemen Amateurs of the Parish
> Assisted by Friends of the Working Men's
> Village Club and other Local Institutions
> Admission 1s, 6d, 3d.
> All promoted by Mr J. J. Francis.

The big attraction of a Victorian sea-side holiday was bathing in the sea but an observant onlooker wrote to the *Mercury* in 1881 insisting that:

> all men and boys should be compelled to wear drawers when bathing. Men should be allowed to bathe with their wives if properly dressed in tunic and knee-length trousers, as is allowed in France. People should not be allowed to bathe naked near habitations.

Uphill Cricket Club was set up again on 21st May 1881 at a meeting in the schoolroom. The club ended the 1884 season with a match on Robert Counsell's field and a dance in a marquee. It must have been re-formed once more as it celebrated "the first anniversary of the Cricket Club" on 2nd October 1886 in the Dolphin when:

> Twenty-eight of thirty-five members attended a supper provided by Hostess Manley and genially chaired by club captain Mr CE Whitting.

The team had played nine matches and won three. Receipts were £4 4s 6d and expenses £2 10s 3d. Secretary EC Frith was elected Vice-captain. The Committee consisted of the Rev Patterson, Messrs R Masson, W Fear, W Manley, E Luff and H Henderson. The pitch was in Mr Edward Luff's Forty Acre Field and W Brown was appointed to supervise its re-laying.

Capt Whitting was again elected chairman in 1889 with the Rev W Glanville as Hon Sec and JJ Francis aS Treasurer.

Good weather attracted crowds of spectators to a Point to Point Steeplechase in November 1885. The course started in Mr Henry Amesbury's field near Uphill railway station and covered most of the parish, although "one local landowner refused to allow riding over his land". Bookmakers came down from Bristol to take bets on three main races, the Weston-super-Mare Plate, the United Hunt Plate and the Scurry Race. Musicians, minstrels and jig-dancers turned out to entertain the crowds and pass round the hat.

The success of the event prompted local gentry and hunts to patronise and financially support another Point to Point the following April.

Races started in Abel Young's field on the south side of Uphill hill. Mr FS Young dominated the field, winning the Harriers' Cup on his own horse Banker, coming second in the Somersetshire Open on Mr Stephens' Skylark and finally winning the Open Steeplechase Cup again on Banker. Bristol bookies again set up alongside the refreshment tent where bands played and people enjoyed the amusements.

When a hawk was reported to be killing many small birds in September 1885, a team of sportsmen set out to shoot it. They soon brought down a large bird but found it was a cuckoo, not the hawk. Cuckoos and sparrow hawks do look similar and the incident recalled an old belief that cuckoos do not fly away for the winter, but change into hawks, "flying like the hawk with quick shallow wing tremors, trailing the tail".

❑ ❑ ❑ ❑ ❑

Chapter 60. Church and Chapel

Not much of the above would have interested the Chapel's large congregations which saw an increase of 60 scholars and 3 teachers at the Sunday School during 1880. Vandals struck them again in March 1882 when the Chapel windows were smashed on a Saturday night, making so much mess that the Sunday service had to be abandoned. But a month later about 60 attended a Good Friday Tea and Service at the Sunday School, followed by "a musical adaptation of *Uncle Tom's Cabin* in condemnation of slavery". In 1886 one of the Minifie brothers spoke at a new Congregational Chapel in Moorland Road.

At St Nicholas Church:

> The Rev George Bennett married Miss Elizabeth Phoebe Head on 6th May 1882. Showered with rice, the couple drove to "a sumptuous and recherché dejeuner" at the Royal Hotel before leaving by rail for honeymoon in Paris and Switzerland.

The couple were both Irish gentry, the groom being the Rector's brother. A new curate moved into The Gables at Christmas 1887, the Rev Edmund Bennett, another brother of the Rector. Their father was Patron of the living.

St Nicholas went in for ever more elaborate decorations every year at Christmas, Easter and the Harvest Festival, pleasing most but not all. As one parishioner observed:

> For many years I have been pleased with the hearty manner in which services at St Nicholas have been conducted but recently I notice that the greater portion of the part singers were not present. They have resigned, not being able to cope with their onerous duties. It is time for their places to be filled lest the choir should lose their past reputation.

The choir stalls were moved into the chancel in 1886 and a new ornamental chancel screen built by Mr Frank Bell. Coloured cathedral glass had gone into the east window in 1884 and the others were now similarly replaced by Messrs Joseph Bell & Sons of Bristol. The cost was met by subscription and all was in place for the Harvest Festival in November.

More wealthy donors turned out in 1877 at a big Sale of Work in a marquee on the Rectory lawn to support Miss Cornish's Children's Convalescent Home at her house, Richmond Villa, in Moorland Road. Most of the work on display and sale had been made and was purchased by gentry from across north Somerset and Bristol and as far afield as Gloucestershire.

Miss Cornish had 9 or 10 children in her Home and during the previous 8 months had cared for another 58 children, mostly from Bristol Children's Hospital.

Easter decorations included real eggs symbolising rebirth. Sadly in 1889 "The village ladies were all too ill to decorate the church for Christmas but Mrs Bennett provided some bunches of flowers".

Easter decorations   [UVS]

Chapter 61.   Village Villains

In their different ways, both Chapel and Church struggled against the crime and poverty caused by cheap alcohol. The Methodists and the new Salvation Army were firmly teetotal while the Church of England sought to reform the lower classes without upsetting the middle-class congregations that provided their funds. Temperance movements sprang up and in April 1881 members of the Salvation Army's White Ribbon Army marched to Uphill to parade with banners through the parish before a meeting in the new schoolroom, chaired by the curate-in-charge the Rev Maunsell Eyre. Word went ahead and some villagers gathered to ambush them with rotten eggs. The White Ribbon marchers were warned and went straight to the school. Even then an objector managed to infiltrate the meeting quoting the Scriptures in support of drinking in moderation. Others burst in and threw eggs at the speakers but, perhaps under the influence, missed their targets. All this was reported in the *Mercury* which ran an advertisement in the same issue quoting from the *British Medical Journal* that the "medical profession now very extensively recommend fully matured whisky as one of the best alcoholic stimulants". Undeterred, the "Second Battalion of the White Ribbon Army" met regularly in Uphill at "Captain Bailey's under the presidency of Captain Isaac Bower" for temperance songs and talks. Once a month they marched round the village behind their fife and drum band to the tune "Hold the fort for I am coming", a battle-hymn from the American Civil War.

On the 1887 August Bank Holiday, 18,000 visitors came to Weston, 12,000 by rail, 3,000 by water and 3,000 by road. The only one charged by the police was Joseph Turner of the Ship, Uphill, who was fined 10s for leaving a horse and vehicle unattended in Regent Street. A reward failed to catch the culprit responsible for a "spate of flower stealing from the neatly kept gardens of villas near the Dolphin Hotel". Matthew Haberfield, a labourer from Locking, left his lodging with Jesse Case in Uphill on 1st January 1885, stealing an overcoat and hat worth 12s which he pawned at Mr Couch's in James Street. He pleaded guilty and was sentenced to 14 days in prison with hard labour.

Burglars broke into St Nicholas in August 1889. They stole 10s, the entire contents of the Poor Box, and found the key to the safe which contained only a few documents. A month later the Dolphin was burgled. Cutlery and sundries were stolen but

landlord Mr Manley had emptied the till. A similar attempt was made on the Ship but the new landlord, Mr Hart, woke up and disturbed the thieves.

Gypsy Henry Joules and his mother Jane Joules were regularly fined for allowing horses to stray on the highway at Hutton. Other gypsies camped near the village:

> Gypsies Harriet and Priscilla Orchard went into Mr Samuel Hammond's grocery at Uphill. They bought some goods and asked to be given a piece of cheese that was on the counter. Mr Hammond refused and they then disputed the total he was charging for their purchases. Eventually they paid and left but he then saw the cheese, value 1s 2½d, was missing. He followed them to the Dolphin where Harriet agreed to be searched but her sister walked away. Mr Frank Exon, market gardener, had come out on hearing the disturbance and found a piece of cheese dropped by his door. Mr William Howe, gardener to Capt Whitting, found the remainder by his door. All gave evidence at court where the women pleaded Not Guilty. They were fined £1 each or 14 days' hard labour.

In February 1881, repeating a similar appearance in 1873, unmarried 27-year old farmer Walter Luff:

> appeared in the magistrates' court to show why he should not contribute to the support of Jane Webber's illegitimate son of which he is the putative father. After a 3½ hour hearing, the case was dismissed.

Uphill had been some time without a butcher before Mr Henry Waterman Herniman opened a shop in time for Christmas 1886 with a fine show of his beef and lamb from specified animals bred on named farms. He soon settled in, dropping into the Ship for a drink at the end of the day. The village bell ringers held their annual supper at the Ship on 15th January 1887 with foreman ringer William Shallish in the chair and Henry Herniman as vice.

Unfortunately he settled in too well and on 29th January 1887 the *Mercury* headlined:

MURDEROUS ASSAULT AT UPHILL

Joseph Turner, landlord of the Ship Inn, appeared before Mr CE Whitting at Weston Police Court charged with unlawfully wounding and inflicting g rievous bodily harm on Henry Waterman Herniman, butcher. A large number assembled outside the court-room but only a few could be admitted.

Joseph Turner is well known and respected having worked for the Town Commissioners as a mason for six or seven years and with an exemplary record as mine host of the Ship. He is a Cornishman, married with no children. The cause of the attack was his suspicion of an improper intimacy between Herniman and his wife, like him, aged between 35 and 40. When this became known, there was general sympathy for him and several offers to stand surety for his release.

Also respected, Henry Herniman is comparatively young, with a wife, two little children and an early expectancy. His house is 40 yards from the Ship where he had recently hired stables and a slaughter-house from Turner.

Mrs Minnie Herniman told the court that her husband came home after completing his rounds He went to Turner's to put up his horse and cart and she went to bed. She was awoken at about 2 am by Mrs Turner calling from the road. She put on some clothes and ran to the inn as fast as her condition allowed. She heard her husband calling "Help" and could hear blows and her husband saying, "Don't Joe." The front door was wide open and she went down the passage to the second door on the right, into the kitchen. She saw her husband sitting on the settle and Turner standing over him with a mallet in his hand. Her husband's hands were over his head as if to protect himself. Turner struck him a violent blow on the head with the mallet. Herniman's head and face were covered with blood and there were patches of blood on the floor. He was so injured that she could recognise him only by his voice. Turner dropped the mallet and she stood between them and implored him to stop. He said, "I'll stop when I've killed him," and continued cursing him and hitting him with his fist. When she tried to stop him, he struck her down and twisted her hair "which was not done up" in one hand while hitting her husband with the other. Saying "If I could only get a knife I'd finish him," Turner went to the door. She tried to hold it but he seized by her hair again. Herniman fell from the settle and Turner kicked him.

Mrs Sarah Ann Fry, a widow from next door, came in with her son Fred and tried to stop him but failed. Eventually Fred helped Herniman out of the building and he collapsed in the road. She told the court that Joseph Turner had called her saying he had something to show her. She dressed and went in and saw Herniman soaked in blood. His apron was to one side and his clothing was disarranged. She heard him say,

"Don't Joe, and I'll give you all I've got and I'll go away."

She said that Turner told her he had suspected his wife and Herniman were too intimate to be proper. He had pretended to be asleep on the kitchen bench when Herniman came in. His wife shook him and asked if he wanted to say goodnight to Herniman but he feigned sleep. They went out and after a few minutes he f ollowed them down the steps into the yard where he caught them "in the act of immorality". He seized them both. His wife escaped but he brought Herniman into the kitchen and gave him a beating. She told him to stop but he continued his attack. Her son Fred then helped Herniman out of the inn where he collapsed. Fred King the milkman helped get him home and onto the bed.

The surgeon who had been called from Weston gave evidence that Herniman's head, face and clothes were soaked in blood. His wounds had been caused by a blunt instrument and he remained on the danger list for some hours.

At the end of the hearing, many villagers showed where their sympathies lay by offering to stand bail for the landlord. The magistrates granted Turner bail on surety of £200 from himself and £100 each from Messrs W Millard and J Willacy with the condition not to return to Uphill. The mallet was a square-edged wooden instrument used by innkeepers for tapping casks. Commenting that it was a wonder that blows with such a weapon were not fatal, the *Mercury* went on to report drily, "Mrs Turner, we understand, has left the district."

The case reached the London press where a "society journal" rejected popular support for the wronged husband in such cases and firmly put the blame on the woman for not saying "No".

Two weeks later, Henry Herniman came to court to give evidence. His head was heavily bandaged and he remained seated while giving evidence:

He had been delivering in Weston and Bleadon during the day, unloaded his remaining stock at the shop and gone to the Ship to put up the cart and stable his horse. He then went into the inn for a drink of gin and saw Turner and his wife in the long room called the tap. He helped Turner to jib a barrel of cider. Turner gave him another drink. He didn't know what it was. He didn't remember finishing it or anything more until he woke up in his bed bleeding and bruised. He had been drinking during his day's work but not so much as to stop him stabling the horse and jibbing the barrel. He had known Thomas for 3 or 4 years. They had never quarrelled. He only went to Turner's house to drink or stable the horse. He remembered no impropriety that night but would not swear on oath one way or the other.

Two months later, on 9th April 1887, the case went up to Quarter Sessions in Wells before a judge and jury. The judge emphasised that the jury must disregard any sympathy they may feel for the accused and find him guilty if they found that he had committed the attack. After hearing the evidence as before, the all-male jury found Turner Not Guilty on all four charges: malicious wounding, grievous bodily harm, actual bodily harm, assault.

The village soon settled down again. The following New Year, Joseph Turner advertised:

> ### PIGEON SHOOTING
>
> #### Open To All Comers
>
> Mr Joseph Turner begs to inform his friends that he has made arrangements for all "lovers of the gun" to have a Day's Sport in a FIELD near the SHIP INN, Uphill, when PRIZES and SWEEPSTAKES will be competed for under the following Rules:
> Double barrel 12 bore Guns 25 yards rise;
> Single barrel 12 bore Guns 23 yards rise.
>
> Shooting to commence 12 o'clock.
>
> No Dogs Allowed.

And Henry Herniman dressed his shop with a:

> Christmas display of cuts from a shorthorn heifer grazed at Mark, two heifers grazed by Mr Edward Luff in Uphill and several cross-bred sheep from Badgworth. The artistic display of joints and quarters was very effective.

Uphill provided more of the same for the *Mercury*. In March 1888:

> Hiding versus Hanging.
>
> A gentleman who for some time had shown a strong partiality for a fireside other than his own was challenged by his "better half" for his preference for another lady, also married. Saying the lack of trust made his life not worth living, he rushed off to hang himself.

On reflection, his wife thought it better to have a second-rate husband than to be a widow and sought assistance to search for him. Night had fallen and no-one wished to help until two men in the Dolphin unwillingly agreed.

> First they climbed a wall into the yard to search an outhouse. One fell, tearing his trousers, but to their relief they found no dead body. The wife then sent them to look in the well, which despite fears of success they did, again without any result. Eventually they found the missing man nearby, hiding behind a door. The search party went back to the Dolphin, demanding compensation for the torn trousers.

A week later the story continued:

> After some days at home the errant husband returned to the other lady and told her that life was not worth living and rushed off to kill himself. This time nobody, including his wife, was willing to search for him, except a stone-mason who hoped for business providing a grave-stone if the man really was dead.
>
> When the husband again emerged from the same hiding place, people said it was a great pity that the quiet of the village should be disturbed by these exciting episodes and that he should be properly taken care of.

The village took care of him with a traditional skimmity ride:

> Soon after dusk, a wagon with two effigies on a platform was drawn through the principal thoroughfares preceded by a brass band and a bodyguard of half a dozen mounted cavaliers in grotesque costumes followed by large numbers of spectators.
>
> After the parade, they assembled in Mr Counsell's field where a huge bonfire was prepared. The two effigies, previously honoured, were now burned as the band played the Dead March. The cavaliers put on a Wild West show and. after cheers, the demonstrators dispersed peaceably.

The village band, trained by coal merchant's labourer James Exon, now played flutes and fifes and was a great improvement on the traditional pot and pan ensemble.

❑ ❑ ❑ ❑ ❑

Chapter 62.   Births, Marriages, Deaths

Skimmity rides were one thing, but proper village weddings were also considered good free entertainment and large numbers turned out one day when news spread by word of mouth "that three interesting weddings would take place this morning" at St Nicholas. But they were disappointed: the day was 1ˢᵗ April 1884.

In June 1884, Parish Clerk Robert Counsell married Mrs Mary Burdwood, widow of ex-Customs Officer William Burdwood. After the wedding, "the bride gave gifts of tea and sugar to the old folk of the parish". They settled in Sherwell House and when Miss Ellen Luff of Manor Farm married Mr OH Counsell of Sussex in 1887, they invited Uphill's schoolchildren in, giving each a bun and an orange. The new Mrs Counsell also gave 40 lb of tea to her tenants and other parishioners and a "free bumper" at the village inn for each parishioner to drink the couple's health while the village church bells pealed. The bride was a member of the Church choir and they gave her "a bread platter, knife and butter cooler *en suite*".

Robert Counsell presided sadly as foreman of the inquest jury in the Dolphin after the death in January 1889 of Osgar Frank, infant son of Frank and Mary Counsell. The baby's mother said "He had been unhealthy from birth. He was screaming as if in pain and just died." Verdict: "Heart failure". When Robert Gane Gerrish Caple died suddenly aged 6½, the inquest at the Ship found that he "died of inflammation of the brain accelerated by fright caused by some older companions". And "Edward Ashill, ostler at The Ship, died very suddenly after suffering several fits during the day".

76-year old John Harse died peacefully on 30ᵗʰ December 1882 and was buried on the hill with his wife Elizabeth and son Joseph:

> Sudden death at Slimeridge House of Mr John Harse, an old and highly respected resident.
>
> After a normal breakfast, he sat in his chair and died. He retired 20 years ago after working for 30 years as a butcher in Weston and later in Worle. He will be missed as a St Nicholas churchwarden.

In April 1888 the *Mercury* announced:

> Death of William Stone aged 51, son of the late Captain Stone of Hobbs Boat Inn.
> Jesse Gould, 15, milk carrier for Mrs Boley was on his way to work at 5.30 am when he found the body by a hay rick.

He told his mistress, who asked Mr Williams the postman to tell the police. PC James Gibson of Bleadon knew the dead man had returned from America the previous November and had lost his luggage at Liverpool. The constable knew he had no home or means and was living rough. He had advised him to find shelter or he would be found dead. He applied to the relieving officer for help but continued to live rough. Verdict: "Death from exposure to cold".

The Harse family gravestone

A flippant headline opened another tragic story:

SUICIDE AT UPHILL
ENTANGLEMENTS WITH A "WIDDER"

George Ham, a young man of 23, milkman for Mr H Brown, farmer, hanged himself in a shed. He had milked the cows as usual in the morning and went to look after stock in a field near the Sanatorium. Later in the day Mr Brown went there and found the young man hanging from a rafter. He told Police Sergeant Dicks who took the body to Uphill and searched it. He found a letter from a woman at Badgworth asking for the return of some articles and threatening a breach of promise action.

Mr Brown told the inquest that George Ham and another servant, Edward Dean, shared accommodation on the farm. Mr Brown called them as usual at 3.30 am and both went to the milking. When George did not return to the farm, Mr Brown went to look for him. He found him in the shed with his black dog lying by the body preventing anyone from approaching.

George Ham had become entangled with the married daughter of Mrs M Young, 46, and under threats from them had given them money.

Verdict: "Suicide while of unsound mind".

Lord of the Manor Thomas Tutton Knyfton died in Uphill on 2nd February 1887 aged nearly 90 and was buried within old St Nicholas Church. The *Mercury* reported:

The funeral left Uphill Castle along the "chief road of the parish towards Uphill Batch, saving a steep gradient by going through Mrs Lovibond's grounds in Uphill House on to the hill". Four well-matched black horses drew an open funeral car on which lay the coffin and wreaths. Mr Knyfton's land steward, Mr Edwards of Hutton, led estate staff walking alongside as bearers. They included Mrs Cross, lady's maid at the Castle for 30 years; Mrs Smale, the cook; Mrs Gibbs, a maid; Mr Pitman, the butler; Mr Savage, the footman; Mr J Vincent, former coachman and Mr H Vincent, the present coachman. Three coaches of mourners followed, with 15 private carriages and hundreds on foot.

The body was laid in one of the two family vaults. The inner coffin was of mahogany, inside another of lead and an outer of oak, all suitably decorated and inscribed.

His widow Mrs Georgiana Sophia Knyfton rebuilt the Westbury-sub-Mendip church tower in her husband's memory and re-cast its peal of four bells into six smaller bells. When she died in 1891, the family remained a major landowner in Westbury.

As the Knyftons were childless, the estate and the title of Lord of the Manor of Uphill were left to a great-nephew Reginald Bennet Graves on condition that he added Knyfton to his name. Born in 1874 in Stoke Winterbourne, Wilts, Reginald Graves had his own estates at Charlton near Salisbury and Broadoak near Bridport.

Knyfton   vault   stone

❏ ❏ ❏ ❏ ❏

Chapter 63. Uphill National School

Still in use in the 21st century, Uphill school is a memorial to the generous public spirit of the Knyfton family. From about 1876 Henry Frith and his sister Miss B Frith were "Master and Mistress of Uphill National School", Henry Frith being also church organist and choir master. They taught children the 3 Rs (Reading, 'Riting and 'Rithmetic), scripture and singing. In 1880 the Education Act made education compulsory for all 5 to 10-year olds. Strict discipline instilled in the children an unquestioning acceptance of their place in society.

Her Majesty's Inspector reported in 1881:

> The tone and discipline are very good, the attendance good and the progress made is creditable to the teachers. Of 81 children examined, 81 passed in reading, 75 in writing and 75 in arithmetic. Walter Harvey, Abram Pople and Ellen Yeo have an honours certificate for attendance.

In 1884:

> The school numbers are over 120. The school is in excellent order and passed a most satisfactory and creditable examination. The work of teaching to all standards must be onerous to Mr Frith – more help is now desirable. The infants are in very good order and the elementary work is thoroughly good. The school is classed as excellent. An assistant teacher or transfer pupil teacher should be at once engaged.

Uphill School Committee raised the fees to match neighbouring parishes and advertised for a pupil teacher at £15 per annum. As a result in 1888:

> Work is excellent. Mr Frith deserves great credit for the discipline and attainments of the school.

But the same year he and his sister moved away:

> Mr Frith, schoolmaster and choirmaster for nearly 12 years, was presented with £10 and a very handsome clock subscribed by nearly all parishioners for his zeal, energy and success. Miss Frith, school mistress, was presented by Miss Fear, pupil teacher, with a handsome travelling bag elaborately fitted. Mr Frith is to leave Uphill for a new post in a Grammar School in Lincolnshire.

The promotion was well-deserved, but ill-rewarded. In November 1889:

> Mr Henry Frith died aged 34 after a month's illness. He had always had delicate health which was suited by Uphill's climate, but the weather of his new home had proved too harsh for him.

Compulsory schooling created an unexpected problem by exposing children to epidemics. Mumps, scarlatina, chicken pox, whooping cough, diphtheria, even swine-pox were still commonplace and many parents kept children at home to protect them. A School Attendance Officer chased up absentees: he reported one family in Uphill where two babies had died and the three other children were dangerously ill with scarlet fever. But, after calling at another house where he found no excuse, he informed the Master that "he had visited two families for poor attendance and both would go to the magistrates".

Mr JJ Francis followed Henry Frith in July 1888 as Master with his wife and sister as Mistresses. He "found children in various Standards to be backward and dull, many with no idea of sums in Practices. He therefore concentrated on Arithmetic and Grammar in all Standards". In August he "replaced slates with pens and pencils and began a thorough system of home lessons which worked well". His wife and sister made infants learn addition while "in the Upper Division boys learned to hem handkerchiefs and girls hemmed pinafores". Within one year attendance increased by 180. Her Majesty's Inspector Mr HH Barry reported:

> Good general progress has been made in elementary work. The class subjects were on the whole good, and singing by note was very good. The infants are orderly and carefully taught. Object lessons and Kindergarten exercises were very fair.

Rev WF Rose, assistant diocesan inspector, checked on scripture:

> The children knew their books well, and answered readily and with intelligence. The written work throughout the school was very good. The infants were brightly and efficiently taught, quiet, and the repetition and answering was good in general.

A report dated 14th September 1889 read:

> UPHILL PAROCHIAL SCHOOL – The number of children has increased so considerably that it has been necessary to make further accommodation. A commodious and handsome infant-room, built according to the latest improvements, fitted with the latest scholastic appliances, and capable of accommodating 60 children, has been added to the original building. This will make Uphill school one of the pleasantest and most convenient schools to be found anywhere. Mrs Knyfton of the Castle, to whom the school belongs, very beneficently bears the whole expense of the improvements.

❑ ❑ ❑ ❑ ❑

Chapter 64.   Parish Politics

During the last decade of his life, Thomas Tutton Knyfton heard new tones of voice in the village and observed new attitudes to old authority. Many of his tenants attended the April 1880 Vestry meeting, attracted more by the politics than the official business.

> Robert Minifie spoke up immediately: I object to the Rector presiding because of his autocratic manners. As there is no provision for election, I propose Mr Knyfton as chairman.
>
> But Mr Knyfton declared: The law says that the Rector must preside at a vestry meeting if he is present, without any proposition.

He nominated Messrs A Young, J Gould, J Quick and R Counsell to a list from which magistrates would choose Overseers as collectors of Land and Income Tax. This was carried and business proceeded routinely. Waywarden Obed Poole's accounts were adopted and he was re-elected. James Evans was re-elected Assistant Overseer but said he now needed more salary as rate collection was very difficult with more houses in Moorland Road. He accepted £33 a year.

> At this a voice from the floor shouted: They'll all be selling up soon if they don't get drains.
>
> Robert Minifie: If it were not for the abominable Conservative government, times would be better and it would be easier to get the money in.
>
> Obed Poole: The parish bought 400 yards of stone and laid 100 yards of it there.
>
> Another voice: It was pitched there and then shifted somewhere else.
>
> Mr Peddle: The Parochial Committee should be dissolved as it has failed to provide proper drainage in Moorland Road and has recommended that no action is needed.
>
> Mr Knyfton: This is not on the agenda – this matter is out of our hands.

Six days later another large meeting of people came to the Easter Vestry "expecting more than formal business". The Rector took the chair and appointed John Harse as rector's churchwarden. Mr CE Whitting was proposed as parish churchwarden, but Robert Minifie proposed an amendment. In a "speech of great excitement" he condemned "the ritualistic practices in the church". To secure a form of worship more tasteful to the parish he therefore proposed his brother William Minifie as churchwarden. This was seconded by Richard Minifie who read from the rubrics of the Church, proving that candlesticks on the altar were illegal.

> Voice: What would you put in their place? An anvil?
>
> The Rector: I am prepared to prosecute Robert Minifie for some of the assertions he had made.
>
> Mr Knyfton: If parishioners wish to complain about the services there is a proper Church Court they can turn to. Making unkind remarks about the Rector does not help.

William Minifie then retired from the election and Mr Whitting was elected. As the *Mercury* declared:

> One of the most exciting meetings ever held in the parish was brought to a close.

It was difficult to ignore the drains in Uphill. In July 1880 Weston Town Commissioners appointed 36-year old fisherman William Pople on £20 a year to look after the penstock where the rhyne drained into the Pill. Moorland Road residents were astonished when the Local Government Board in Whitehall promptly acknowledged receipt of the Parochial Committee's report on the "Upper Moor Drainage and Water Supply Scheme" and ordered an official enquiry. In the meantime the Parochial Committee pressed for a public pump which Axbridge Rural Sanitary Authority eventually installed in the middle of Moorland Road where "there was plenty of water for it". Axbridge also agreed to connect the road to the main sewer if Weston Town Commissioners agreed and Uphill Parochial Committee collected a rate to pay for it.

Objections to a new rate were promptly signed by those who would have to pay it: Thomas Knyfton, Charles Edward Whitting, Henry Lovibond, Henry Brown, James Evans, Abel Young, Rev Stephen Bennett, Charles Whitting, John Harse, Edward Luff, Henry Amesbury and Robert Counsell. They argued that drainage should have been installed by the original speculative building company "which chose to build on the moor because it was outside Weston thus avoiding their rates". Uphill itself was badly drained and should not pay for Moorland Road.

The Public Enquiry opened at the Ship Hotel on 10th December 1881 and the Local Government Board invited Weston to "annexe the Moorland Road area of Uphill as far as Mr Knyfton's lodge for the purposes of drainage and water supply".

In 1888, the Parochial Committee voted £60 for a new penstock "to control Uphill Great Rhyne which for several summers has produced obnoxious effluvium, being stagnant". Chairman Charles Edward

Whitting wrote to Weston Town Commissioners who on 14th September 1889 discussed:

> The Drainage of Uphill. The number of houses proposed by Mr CE Whitting to drain into the Weston-super-Mare sewer is 36; the number of persons 185, and the rateable value of such houses £327 12s; but ... as there are other properties in Uphill which also require better means of drainage ... a scheme is needed for draining all such properties into the main sewer.

Every year the Uphill and Hutton Dyke Reeves of the Jury of Sewers made their Autumn inspection of rhynes within their district and every year they:

> afterwards adjourned to the Dolphin Hotel where a capital dinner was provided by Host and Hostess Manley. After the removal of the cloth, business was transacted; and the remainder of the programme consisted of a brief toast list, interspersed with songs.

The Reeves included Messrs S Davies, F Blackmore, G Conway, Warne, W Dyer, E Luff, F Amesbury, R Counsell, A Counsell, H Hemens, J Brown, E Hemens and G Stagg. In 1888 their foreman Sidney Blades tendered his resignation:

> Much regret was expressed at losing the guidance of one who had discharged the onerous duties in a most genial manner for so many years.

Sidney Blades died a month later.

When they gave brickyard owner SH Churchill the contract to deepen the rhyne near the outfall, a contest ensued "matching the skill and activity of a resident of Uphill against one of Bleadon in boring the bed of the rhyne for blasting purposes". Bets were placed, but there is no information on the outcome. This was the same Mr Churchill who had just been called before Axbridge Highway Board to explain why his road-metalling work was so very unsatisfactory.

Uphill Batch came in for more attention. Ten years after the road was lowered by five feet, waywarden Henry Brown invited tenders to lower the crown of the road by another six feet to "improve the thoroughfare which leads to most picturesque scenery". Peter Harse was given the contract, the cost was defrayed by public subscription and the work was completed in nine weeks, "making an excellent improvement". To protect the public, the wall "round the pond at the bottom of the Batch was raised four feet for a length of 42 feet".

It was all very rural compared with Weston's career into the dynamic Victorian Eighties. A new metalled road along a new sea-front from Knightstone to the Sanatorium swept away ancient sand dunes, a pier was planned from the end of Regent Street, the Atlantic cable from Nova Scotia reached Weston beach, telephones were installed and electric light proved "as good as gas".

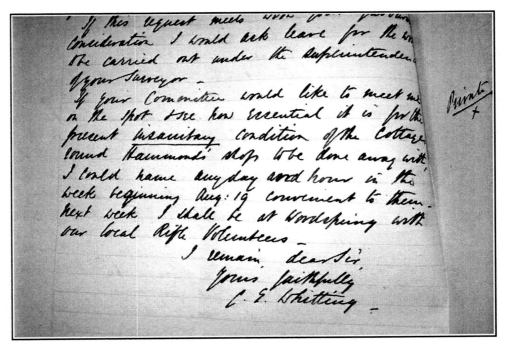

Charles Edward Whitting's letter
[Permission kindly given by SRO to use the image of signatures from file C/GP/MISC/5]

❑ ❑ ❑ ❑ ❑

Chapter 65.   Battle of the Allotments

Seventy years after the Enclosure Acts had taken away their common land, the people demanded it back in the form of allotments, while the land-owners did their utmost to keep it. Six determined, intelligent and articulate villagers — Robert Minifie, John Hayes, J Marshall, William Powell, George Staples and Frank Harvey — studied the Cottagers Allotments Act and appealed to the Local Government Board for help. The Board sent pamphlets explaining the law to the Axbridge Board of Guardians which shifted its responsibility by asking if anyone in Uphill really wanted an allotment or if they preferred to make private and local arrangements.

This led to a meeting in Uphill Schoolroom in 1887, where the original six were joined by Robert Counsell, Henry Brown, Henry Frith, G Thatcher, Richard Minifie, William Minifie, Edward Luff and Thomas Simpson. The Rector and Capt CE Whitting attended as Guardians with the Chairman and Clerk of the Axbridge Board.

> The Axbridge Chairman: Rents would have to cover all costs. Necessary roads and fences would be charged to the parish as a whole. No buildings would be allowed except tool sheds, hen houses, greenhouses and pig sties.
>
> Robert Minifie: It would be better if a local land owner offered land for village use as allotments.
>
> Charles Edward Whitting: I, my father, Mrs Knyfton and other land owners would support a local voluntary system. Mr Knyfton would have done the same when alive if the village had asked.
>
> Robert Minifie: Until the Act came, we knew nothing of what could be done.
>
> Rector: It would be best to do it voluntarily.
>
> Robert Minife: But would we have the same security of tenure?
>
> Chairman: It would be best to do it voluntarily.
>
> Charles Edward Whitting: Land in the village is valuable and would fetch £150 an acre. There is no arable land near the village. It is all pasture and if you cultivate it you destroy it as pasture for years.
>
> Robert Minifie: We are willing to pay a rent equal to the average paid by farmers, provided no further expenses are required.

Robert Minifie asked for a vote to see if allotments were wanted. 22 were in favour and they said that others not present would support them.

> Richard Minifie: From Mr Whitting's remarks, landowners would make land available.
>
> Charles Edward Whitting: No land is available at present. We would need to give notice to our tenants and pay them compensation. There is less than four acres of ploughed land in the village but 22 people would need 5½ acres.

Those present agreed to form an Allotments Committee and the meeting was adjourned. After a year of negotiation Robert Minifie reported back to the Allotments Committee:

> Mr Whitting is willing to let 3 acres of land near the school for £4 per acre, the tenant to pay all rates and taxes, but no other landowner is able to help. This would not be enough land. The committee will therefore have to go back to the Axbridge Rural Authority.

In the meantime they agreed to accept the 3 acres on offer, letting it to the original 22 applicants for twelve months to see how it worked. The Committee also heard that more villagers now wanted allotments, some as much as a full acre. Mrs Knyfton promised to offer some land in 1889 to meet demand if people still wanted it.

The year's experiment passed. On 30th March 1889, the Allotments Committee wrote to Axbridge Rural Authority that two more pieces of land had been offered for Uphill allotments but one was too small and the other too far away. They complained that villagers had asked in October 1888 for access to the land promised by Mrs Knyfton in order to prepare it for Spring planting, but were now told it would not be available until March 1889. They accepted this, but in March access was still not available. Robert Minifie signed the letter which ended bitterly:

> We feel we have been treated in a manner that we, as honest working men, would blush to imitate.

More promises followed. CE Whitting told Axbridge Rural Authority that a field adjacent to the existing allotments would be made available on next Lady Day. The field was currently rented by Mr Gould, "who would accept £16 compensation". He also pointed out that the Act authorised allotments for "the labouring classes" and not "master tradesmen" and the Authority would decide who was eligible to have an allotment. Robert Minifie said that the Uphill Allotments Committee agreed to this, to be carried out "if possible this year, 1889."

❑ ❑ ❑ ❑ ❑

Chapter 66.   Weather, Wireless and Great Western

Big hauls of sprats brought unskilled boatmen out in November 1880, working their nets below Brean Down, when a sudden storm wrecked two boats on the rocks from which the crews were rescued by soldiers from the Fort. A 36-hour hurricane and blizzard blocked roads and railways in the New Year. The rural postman from Uphill to Rooksbridge had to take cover overnight with no way of informing his family where he was. Three feet of snow embedded trains and at East Brent 200 navvies cleared the line and road of 15-foot drifts. The frost lasted eight days giving good skating on the River Avon and splendid views of a brilliant aurora borealis. Another storm the following autumn caused widespread damage in Uphill. Trees came down and rainwater undermined the road, gouging out a hole. William Boley's cart fell in but his demand for compensation was refused "as the damage was unforeseeable and apparent only when he drove over it".

February 1882 brought another gale, wrecking the French ship *Espiègle* on Brean Down. There was no local lifeboat but Chief Coastguard Officer Mr William Burt and two boatmen took an ordinary 16-foot flat-bottomed shore-boat across the bay and rescued the crew of five from the rigging. All were lucky to survive. The RNLI acknowledged their bravery with an award of £2 to Coastguard Burt and £1 10s each to the boatmen.

On 30th April, a widespread storm brought down trees in Uphill, blocking the road past the church so that travellers had to go to Bleadon via the Dolphin. A chimney stack came down through the Sanatorium roof. The ketch *Arabella*:

> sailed by Captain Sidney Camm and a crew of three with 116 tons of coal from Newport for Mr Gould of Uphill, struck Black Rock. The crew took refuge in the rigging until the tide fell and they could walk ashore. The tug *Petrel* from Bridgwater pulled her off the next day.

Captain H Silk's *Crowpill,* carrying coal from Lydney to Bridgwater, lost all her canvas save the jib and ran for the Axe where she anchored safely. The cutter yacht *Flower of the Flock* was driven ashore at Uphill but lay there undamaged until pulled off two days later. After a continuous downpour for two days in October 1882:

> water streamed down Folly Lane from the hill lik a river, flooding the principal street and leaving it almost impassable for pedestrians.

Embankments of turf and mud had to be raised in front of some of the houses to prevent the water from flowing into them, but the water found its way through the floors of the low-lying houses, the cellars being literally full.

Owing to some defect in the drain the water remained on the road for the rest of the week to the depth of two or three feet and some horses refused to go through it. The water in the rhyne was higher than has been known for several years and in several places it left the banks and flooded the fields. The road to Windwhistle was rendered impassable and the occupants had to find their way home by a circuitous route across the fields.

Parish Clerk Robert Counsell immediately complained to Axbridge Highways Surveyor who examined the road and found 74 yards still flooded and impassable. In heavy rain the water was two feet deep. He agreed to raise the road centre by six inches with broken rocks, lower the edges by six inches and dig a drain on the left side. January 1883 brought a similar complaint of floods in Moorland Road.

March, however, brought very mild weather with several tortoise-shell butterflies being seen in Uphill. They were a good sign as, if the first butterfly of the season was yellow, villagers thought it brought bad luck. The miller moth (*Acronicta leporina*) was itself unlucky as it looked dusted with flour from the mill and was killed by children who chanted:

> Millery! Millery! Dusty poll!
> How many sacks hast thou stole?

An unusually high tide backed by strong winds from the Atlantic flooded Uphill in October 1883:

> At Slimeridge Farm, home of Mr Burdge, 300 yards of stone wall, the property of Mr TT Knyfton, were washed away. The sea bank burst and the levels flooded. One of Mr H Amesbury's sheep was drowned in the field used as a rifle range. At Mr Churchill's lime kilns the water reached 3 foot 8 inches deep, destroying 100 bushels of lime and endangering the kilns which were burning at the time. Occupants of the cottages behind the weigh-bridge left before the rising water and took refuge on the house of Mr Thomas Price on higher ground. When the water receded, Mr S Body took them home in a wagon.

Their rescuer, Thomas Price, died aged 49 on 29th January 1887 and was buried on the hill.

February gales in 1884 drove hail into drifts two feet deep which froze solid. In more high winds in October, "a large tree fell on Henry Brown's Uphill Farm, a very old tree came down in the Rectory grounds and several more at the Castle".

Victorian technology was tested as heavy snow brought down telegraph wires across Somerset on New Year's Day 1887. The Royal Mail's horse-drawn cart, however, continued to run regularly and frequently from Weston to Uphill, Hutton, Locking, Banwell, Woodborough, Axbridge, Cheddar and Wedmore until March when snow fell for twenty unbroken hours:

> the deepest for half a century, more than the snows of January 18-19 1881, or those of 31st October 1878 or 3rd March 1867.The mail-cart service from Weston to Wedmore was suspended but Mr Minifie was able to send the mails by train to Banwell, Winscombe and Cheddar.

This service continued despite another 20 inches of snow a fortnight later. In March 1889:

> unprecedented rainfall and snow brought floods which filled the rhyne from Watersill to Uphill. The "vast barrel sewer" draining from Weston to Uphill coped well with the rain.

A *Mercury* leader on 8th October 1881 suggested, perhaps jocularly, that the town should not build a navigable harbour, thus forcing dirty coal barges to unload in Uphill and not disfigure Weston. Uphill ignored this and the old harbour received legal recognition:

> Port of Bristol, Limits of Port
> .... shall commence at the Westernmost part of and include the Flat and Steep Holms .... to the Most Eastern part of Brean Down at the mouth of the River Axe .... and shall include all other Rivers and Pills and all islands, bays, harbours, rivers, creeks and canals.
> Whitehall, Treasury Chambers, this twentieth day of December, 1881.

In a fiercely competitive world, the port lost trade to the new Severn railway tunnel in 1886. But the Brean Down Harbour scheme, abandoned when contractor Mr Chaplin died in 1868, was revived in 1888, adding a plan for a ship canal between the harbour and Bristol. Mr Lawson was appointed as supervising engineer and *The Lighthouse* "a shipping and commercial journal" enthused:

THE GREAT WESTERN SHIP CANAL

The proposed ship canal extending from Uphill Bay to the estuary of the Exe passing via Bridgwater, Taunton, Tiverton and Exeter would undoubtedly be one of the great requirements of modern maritime commerce. It could accommodate two steamships of say 1,500 tons passing each other. Further it would carry off the immense volume of water which, in this very rainy district, descends from the heaven and the hills, and accumulates on the low-lying lands to such an extent as to give the locality the appearance of a vast shallow sea, with hedge and trees and buildings appearing above a world of waters.

The vision widened. In May 1897, the General Post Office sent engineers to Uphill "where ferryman William Pople rowed them across the Axe", a low-tech introduction to a high-tech experiment. The aim was nothing less than to span the waters of the Bristol Channel using Marconi's still untested system of wireless telegraphy. They based themselves in:

> a Royal Artillery fort at the end of Brean Down above the site of the abandoned harbour scheme where dressed stones still lay, prepared for the pier that was never built.

Using 300-foot aerials suspended from kites, signallers successfully transmitted Morse messages across eight miles of sea to Lavernock Point in Wales, opening an unimaginable future of boundless wireless communication.

As wireless waves crossed the Channel, railway station masters decorated their platforms with elaborate flower beds. As this pleased travellers, the railway directors rewarded the best with annual prizes. The first GWR 1st Prize of £2 was won by Uphill station master Mr Baker and his successor Mr Payne won the next five. Queen Victoria appreciated the display as she passed through in her royal coach but she had the blinds drawn at Bridgwater to shut out any view of Sedgemoor, scene of the Monmouth Rebellion two hundred years earlier.

The railway also brought tragedy. In January 1886, Robert Amesbury, a 51-year old Bleadon farmer, was cut in two by a train where it passed through his fields. Only a month later:

> Miscreants laid a huge log across the railway line near Uphill Station, where the railway crosses

the Axe. The mail train engine cut into the log and then fortunately cast it aside. A derailment could have killed many passengers.

Louisa Grentner (45) of Bleadon went to Uphill Station in April 1888 to collect a parcel. She crossed the two tracks on the foot-crossing. As she walked back, she stopped between the tracks, watching a coal train on the down line but did not see the 8.40 approaching fast from Highbridge. The engine-driver sounded his whistle and the station master shouted at her, but the train hit her and she was killed. A neighbour told the inquest she was deaf although her family denied this. Verdict: "Accidental death".

Uphill Station   *[UVS]*

❑ ❑ ❑ ❑ ❑

Chapter 67.   The Volunteers

The Somerset Rifle Volunteers expanded against a background of mixed British fortunes in military operations across the world. The *Mercury* reported bloody defeats and victories in Afghanistan and Zululand, Boer attacks in South Africa, the capture of Alexandria in Egypt and complete defeat by Islamic militants in Sudan.

Twenty years after the collapse of its first gunnery unit, local men joined a new Weston Volunteer Artillery Battery, part of the 1st Gloucestershire Artillery Volunteers. Every summer over two hundred men marched from Weston station behind their fife and drum band to camp on Slimeridge Farm in sixty tents in a field facing the sea. Their beds were stuffed with "Irish feathers" — bracken or whatever else the soldiers could find. They cooked on a field oven built by a new local unit, Weston College Cadet Corps (Royal Engineers) under Lt Nunn. Mr Silcox of Uphill had the contract to supply groceries and teetotal drinks. The gunners brought their own two 40-pounder Armstrong breech-loaders which they fired from the beach at floating targets.

Every day men took the Axe ferry to Brean Down to train on the 7-inch, 7-ton muzzle-loading guns in the Fort. The unit attended a Church service in St Nicholas, the band put on a concert in the schoolroom, the officers were entertained in the Rectory and the Castle while the Dolphin and Ship welcomed the soldiers.

Other local men provided a company of the splendidly named 1st Gloucestershire (The Western Counties) Volunteer Fortress and Railway Forces, Royal Engineers, Somerset Detachment, soon to become (despite protests) the more prosaic 1st Devon and Somerset Engineer Volunteers.

Charles Edward Whitting was promoted Captain to command B Company of the 3rd Somerset Rifle Volunteers. In August 1888 he entertained them all at his house, now renamed The Grange, where they dined in his "spacious front room facing the lawn, decorated with flags, shields and flowers".

B Company Shooting team, 3rd Somerset Rifle Volunteers   *[UVS]*

Chapter 68. Queen Victoria's Golden Jubilee

In June 1887, arrangements for Uphill's celebration of Queen Victoria's Jubilee were made at a meeting "convened by postcard". The Rector and the curate, the Whittings, Robert Counsell, Henry Brown, Edmund Burdge, A Young, Edward Luff, J Gould, S Silcox, William Minifie and schoolmaster Henry Frith planned the event and did most of the work. Charles Whitting opened his field opposite the school for the occasion. The committee built an ornate arch with flags and a great crown over the gateway and others decorated a marquee with patriotic tributes.

On a day of fine weather, swing boats, athletic sports and a cricket match filled the field. Huge flags flew from both churches and bells pealed throughout the day.

In the marquee, 150 women and children attended a public tea where women "had the privilege of partaking of meat". Two hours later, 160 men went in for a dinner. Between them they consumed 260 lb of meat, supplied by three butchers including Henry Herniman. Village grocer Mr Silcox supplied sugar and 25 lb of butter. The meals were cooked in the kitchens of Mrs Knyfton, Mrs Bennett, Mrs Luff, Mrs Burdge, Mrs Whitting and Mrs Counsell and transported to the marquee by the committee, who then performed as waiters, serving the villagers at table. The Blue Cord Brass Band from Weston provided a musical background to the meal and the dancing that followed. The day ended with a bonfire on the hill. Voluntary subscriptions met the costs, Mrs Knyfton heading the published list with £15.

Uphill in 1888   *[UVS]*

❑ ❑ ❑ ❑ ❑

Part 7:   All Change 1890 - 1900

Chapter 69. Uphill in 1890

> Population: 231 male + 264 female = 495 in 103 houses
> + 340 in Moorland Road and 65 in the Sanatorium
> Rector: Rev Arthur John Burr MA
> Parish Clerk and Sexton: Robert Counsell; 1890 Frank Counsell
> Waywarden: Henry Brown; Assistant Overseer: Richard Minifie
> Old Church keeper: John Hayes
> Schoolmaster and Organist: 1891 John E Stibbs; 1896 Frederick J House ACO
> Lord of the Manor: Reginald Benett Graves-Knyfton, Uphill Castle

Villagers born in Uphill included 91 males, 94 females, 11 heads of family and just one complete family. The most popular male names were William 28, George 19, Charles 17, James 15, John 13, Henry 11, Thomas 11. The most popular female names were Elizabeth 21, Mary 20, Ann variants 15, Alice 15, Sarah 10. The oldest couple were Henry (77) and Sarah (80) Staples closely followed by James (77) and Mary (79) Evans. The oldest women were Frances Godby (89), Mary Henderson (89), Elizabeth Cavill (88), Hannah Binding (82) and Sarah Staples (80), with four more in their seventies. Five men were over 70, the oldest being Robert Vowles (81) who had investigated James Heath's box thirty years earlier. In all, 14 (nearly 3%) of the village population were in their 70s and 80s.

Of 112 male workers, 25% were labourers, as were over half the 20% who worked on the land, 15% were skilled, 16% worked in service trades and 6% in domestic service. The only professionals were the rector, schoolmaster and a solicitor. 64 women worked, 31 in domestic service and 33 in service trades including a surprising 20 laundry workers. Villagers who didn't make their own clothes could choose between four dressmakers and one tailor. Most of the flour in James Williams' bakery now came from America and cheap imports lined the shelves in Edward Hammond's grocery. But Samuel King and Elizabeth Boley sold only local milk, butter, cheese and eggs in the two village dairies. A fine shop-front display at Christmas 1890 maintained Henry Herniman's high standard, with butcher's cuts from:

> a shorthorn heifer grazed by Mr Edward Morgan Whitting, Totterdown; a Devon heifer bred and fed by Edward Luff of Uphill; a shorthorn heifer fed by Mr Frith of Brent Knoll; Welsh sheep grazed by Mr Edward Morgan Whitting, Totterdown; and Down wethers fed by W Hucker of Uphill.

In September 1892, farmer Edward Luff:

took 1st Honours at the Mid-Somerset Agricultural Show with Dainty in the class for cobs not exceeding 13½ hands.

Peter Hart took over the Ship Inn from Isaac Yeo and also managed the quarry:

> Uphill Stone Quarries
> PETER HART
> COAL, LIMESTONE MERCHANT
> Begs to inform the Public that he has opened the
> LIME KILNS at the UPHILL STONE QUARRY
> And can Supply
> BEST WHITE LIME for BUILDING PURPOSES
> AT 3d PER BUSHEL
> ALSO BUILDING STONE at LOWEST PRICES
> After the 1st of June, Machine broken Stone and Machine Gravel will be supplied at the above Quarries.
> Prompt Attention to all Orders.

Lt Col John Sheffield Gilbert Ryley, aged 83, "died peacefully in his bed, of influenza" at Sea View after a lifetime's service in the Indian Army with the 2nd and 5th Bengal Cavalry. His house Sea View, today's White House, was near Flat Roof Farm, where George and Hannah, Joseph Hancock's children, had grown up. Now aged 29 and unmarried, George Every Hancock shared the house of his 48-year old married sister Hannah James. Hannah had worked as a needlewoman and George in the grocery but both were now "living off their own means". They quarrelled and George was arrested in July 1892:

> George Every Hancock, of no occupation, living in Uphill, threatened his sister, Hannah James, saying he would "swing for her". Their neighbour Elizabeth Pople, wife of Thomas Pople, gardener, gave evidence that the prisoner asked her for some things he had given to his sister. Another sister, Alma Lucy Hancock, said the same. Mrs Hannah James said she was afraid of him and wanted him bound over to keep the peace. He was bound over for 6 months on three sureties of £5 or prison for a month.

George kept out of trouble until New Year 1894 when he was fined 5s or 5 days prison for being drunk and incapable. A few days later, he pleaded guilty to maliciously breaking a glass show case and was remanded for a medical report on his sanity. Another member of the Hancock family, John, died in Canada aged 84 in 1898:

> Born in Uphill, where his father was a prosperous farmer, he emigrated to Canada at 28 to branch out in the then almost unknown colony.

Living with Hannah James as her servant was Elizabeth Cavill. Born in Locking in about 1813, Elizabeth began a lifetime of domestic service in Farmer George Every's household, moving on to work for Joseph Hancock in the Ship and then as his dairymaid. By 1871, she shared a home with her younger brother Francis, working as a laundress, with his stepdaughter doing the ironing. Elizabeth finally returned to the Hancocks as their servant and died, senile, in her 80s. Hannah paid for her gravestone which remains in the old churchyard, fallen, eroded and trodden on, proclaiming "Her end was peace".

The village experienced a series of tragedies. 54-year old Joseph Williams retired in 1892 after 23 years as village postman. He lived with his wife Elizabeth next door to Walnut Cottage Post Office with two grown-up children and a daughter at the school down the road. He was charged with attempted suicide after cutting his throat:

> His wife said he had not been himself after being pensioned off and a friend, Charles Hayes, a railway ganger, said he had been depressed. Dr BH Andrew of Bleadon said he had treated Mr Williams and considered him then of unsound mind and that he still was. Joseph Williams was discharged.

Well known as a drinker, Florence Annie Sarson of Weston drowned herself in the Axe. She returned home one night unable to recognise her husband. As she kept wandering about the house, he locked her in her room but she climbed out of the window. Next day, labourers George Pople and James Exon saw her body in the river and towed it ashore.

A 17-year old boy drowned accidentally. Thomas William Taylor was the son of stone mason Thomas and Sarah Ann Taylor, who lived next door to Sherwell House. Quarryman Ball was working high on the quarry and saw Thomas bathing by Uphill Wharf where he sank. Mr Ball raised the alarm and went out in a punt but could not find him. Quarryman Frederick Penberthy found the body in the bed of the Pill when the tide went out. Thomas had been a regular player with Uphill Castle Cricket Club and Uphill Association Football Club. He could swim but was not expert. Verdict: "Accidental drowning". He was buried on the hill with William Minifie as undertaker. Shortly afterwards Mr Minifie himself died aged 56 and was buried in the new parish churchyard.

65-year old James King lived in 1 Hillside Cottage with his son William John, a cab-driver. His wife had died 12 months earlier and he had been depressed at times. After haymaking all Thursday he complained of a pain in the head and didn't go to work on Friday. Farmer Robert Counsell of Sherwell House saw his body in the rhyne on Saturday. As there were no marks in the reeds along the bank, it seemed he had jumped in. Verdict: "Death by drowning. Suicide during temporary insanity". A neighbour of James King, John Badman, had worked as Robert Counsell's farm hand for 40 years up to the day before he died of pneumonia aged 72. Another of the King family, Charles of Uphill Dairy, appeared at Bath Police Court on a summons by Selina Holtham as the father of her illegitimate child. She had formerly worked as a servant in Uphill but the case was dismissed "for lack of corroborative evidence".

Ordinary life also had its hazards. 49-year old Charles Howe dealt in dairy produce, principally butter. He had been buying in Bridgwater and returned down the steep Uphill Batch with his horse and cart containing over 300 dozen eggs and other dairy produce. His horse shied and ran into the wall, smashing almost all the eggs and damaging the rest of the goods. Charles Howe suffered severe cuts to the head. Alfred Counsell of Centre Farm, rebuilt in the 20th century as Centre House, had fields out at Oldmixon where his cowman James Knight:

> was attacked by a ferocious bull and tossed two or three times. He had the presence of mind to lie perfectly still which saved him from further attack. He suffered extensive bruising and was lucky to escape.

The *Mercury* reported on 28th October 1899:

ATTACKED BY A RAT

Early on Thursday morning, Mr W Manley of the Dolphin Hotel was aroused by the cries of his son, aged 6 years, sleeping in an adjacent bedroom with his little sister. The lad's head had been badly bitten by a rat, the pillow case being saturated with blood. The little girl fortunately escaped the rodent's intrusion.

Chapter 70.   Knyfton ... Graves-Knyfton

Travelling to London in November 1891, 77-year old widow Mrs Georgiana Sophia Knyfton "caught a cold and died on the arm of her faithful attendant Mrs Cross". Flags flew at half-mast on the Castle and St Nicholas Church as her coffin progressed on an open carriage to the old church through the grounds of Capt CE Whitting's Uphill Grange. She was escorted by her household staff on foot: Mrs Mary J Cross, maid; Mrs Gibbs, nurse; Mrs Ada Smale, cook; Miss Ellen Gullick, housemaid; Miss Mary Howard, housemaid; Miss Lucy May Kirby, kitchen maid; Charles Pitman, butler; John Savage, footman; Henry Vincent, coachman; the Castle's gardeners and carpenters; and AP Edwards of Hutton, her estate steward. She was buried in the family vault inside the chancel. The St Nicholas Burials Register records:

Georgiana Sophia Knyfton aged 77 - 27/11/ 1891 - Plot 493.

Mrs Knyfton left £188,000, itself a legacy from Penelope Brice, which she bequeathed to her cousin Charles Edward Hungerford Athole Colston. She gave £500 to Weston Hospital and other bequests to her god-daughter and cousins. The Castle's furniture and stock went to Reginald Bennet Graves, heir to her husband's estate.

His surname duly changed by deed poll, the 19-year old Reginald Bennet Graves-Knyfton arrived at the Castle accompanied by his mother Mrs Graves. A new life-style came with them. He was 21 in October 1894 and they invited the whole village to celebrate his Coming of Age. Gardener William Fear erected a floral arch over the road outside the Castle, where the Cricket Club and Castle servants put on displays.

Children gave a show in the schoolroom and the Town Band performed in the playground while children and parents enjoyed a tea-party. The band moved over to the Castle in the evening to play at a fancy dress ball for seventy couples. The next day Mrs Graves entertained former Knyfton tenants from Uphill and her own tenants from Graves family estates in Salisbury and Dorset.

A house party of invited guests celebrated Christmas 1895 at the Castle with a bright style of entertainment billed as a "Chamber Concert" featuring:

the Mandoline Band of the Misses Battiscombe, Cox and Bridges, songs by the Misses Helyar and Graves and comic songs from Mr Masters, while Mrs Graves' concertina solo was quite a masterpiece.

In July 1897, Reginald Benett Graves-Knyfton married Edith Mary Alston at Winscombe. Gifts included "a walrus tusk candlestick from the tenantry of Uphill Castle" and another gift from the tenantry of Charlton. Not wanting to live in a castle, his wife changed the name to Uphill Manor and the couple moved in permanently in October 1898. His mother moved out, first entertaining:

villagers to tea in the Castle where a minstrel troupe performed. This is her last such gathering. It is hoped that the young squire and his wife will follow the example.

Minstrel troupes with blacked-up faces and striped clothes provided popular summer entertainment for trippers on Weston sands, their banjos accompanying harmonious commercial versions of black slave music.

Chapter 71.   The Whitting families

Three strands of the Whitting family lived in St Nicholas Parish in 1890: Charles and his two sons Charles Edward and Edward Morgan. All had Welsh wives with estates in Wales and all were commissioned as Somerset Rifle Volunteer officers.

Captain Charles Whitting, Uphill's second oldest male inhabitant at 77, lived in Sandcroft House. On 14th April 1894, his wife Anna Harris Whitting died in her 76th year. She had lived in Uphill for 44 years and was buried in the old churchyard in a new brick grave at the west end of the roofless nave. Charles Whitting died almost exactly a year later, aged 82, on 20th April 1895 after nearly 50 years in the village and was buried in a railed-off family vault in the new St Nicholas churchyard. He left £100 as the Whitting Charity, the interest to be distributed annually to the poor of the parish by the Rector and Churchwardens.

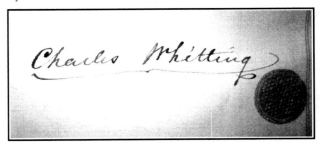

Charles Whitting's signature 1894   *[SRO]*

His first son, Major Charles Edward Whitting, now 44, occupied Uphill House, renamed Uphill Grange, with his second wife Sophia Julia.

Charles Edward Whitting   *[Sue Davis]*

His second son by his first wife, Edward Jewell Whitting, an 18-year old student, lived with them. On 2nd December 1891, a few days after Mrs Knyfton, Sophia Julia died aged 39, at Uphill Grange. True to her Welsh roots she was buried in Monmouth.

The following summer, Edward Jewell Whitting graduated with a BA from Trinity College, Cambridge and in September 1893 celebrated his Coming of Age. The family entertained two hundred villagers to tea at the Grange followed by walks through the grounds and dancing on the lawns to the music of the Somerset Light Infantry Band under Bandmaster Mogg. Later in the evening a fire balloon was floated above Uphill, inaugurating a large firework display. The young man became a good shot and in January 1899 the *Mercury* announced:

> Success of Mr Jewell Whitting at Monte Carlo where he took first place against 117 competitors in the Grand International Pigeon Shooting Meeting, winning a gold medal for England.

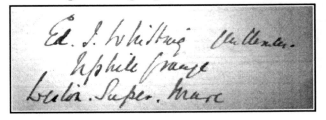

Edward Jewell Whitting's signature 1894
[Permission kindly given by SRO to use the image of signatures from file C/GP/MISC/5]

Charles Edward married his third wife, Jessie May Lilly, on 22nd September 1894. They had three children: May Lilly in 1896, Charles Edward in 1897, and Richard Harcourt in 1900. Their estate in Wales sat on rich coal seams and in 1897 they augmented the family fortunes by leasing the coal output to a colliery. At New Year 1897:

> Major and Mrs CE Whitting entertained the servants and employees of Grange Estate.

His younger brother, Edward Morgan, lived in Totterdown House, with his wife Mary Maud Harris. A son Morgan Harris was born in 1882 and a daughter Gwenllian Maud in 1884. In November 1896:

> Mr Edward Morgan Whitting of Totterdown gave a dinner at the Ship for the workmen building his mansion.

❏ ❏ ❏ ❏ ❏

Totterdown House 1903   *[Whitting family]*

Edward Morgan Whitting is the horseman on the right and Morgan Harris Whitting is in the doorway.

❑   ❑   ❑   ❑   ❑

Chapter 72.   Old Churches and New Chapel

After thirty years as Rector, the Rev Bennett retired in October 1890 because of ill-health. Over 300 donors subscribed to present him with a "handsome silver bowl and a pair of goblets".

Within a few days, the new incumbent the Rev Arthur J Burr arrived "to merry peals from the hill". Arthur Burr, aged 31, was born in Birmingham. His wife Florence, also 31, had three children from an earlier marriage: Muriel (7), Gerald (5) and Edmund (4) Wellesley. Her fourth child, Florence Burr, was born soon after their arrival at the Rectory where they were well looked after by a cook and three maids, with two nurses for the children.

At the close of his Induction service:

the Rector was conducted to the West door and, ascending the tower, rang the bell in the customary manner.

He pleased the parish at his first Christmas Communion Service by using the original St Nicholas Church chalice and paten for the first time for thirty years. The chalice, dating back to Charles I, was a narrow goblet, hall-marked 1635, 6¼ inches high and 3 inches in diameter, weighing just over 7 oz. The paten had a hall-mark and the inscription "Uphill 1742" dating it in the reign of George II. It was 6¼ inches across and weighed just over 6 oz. They had "passed into private ownership" when the old church was closed for worship and now reappeared inscribed "Restored to St Nicholas Church, Uphill, by AJ Burr (rector), Christmas 1890". On the same day, a silver and ruby glass flagon was presented to the new church by a group of communicants.

More change followed. At the 1891 Easter Vestry meeting, farmer Robert Counsell (66) of Sherwell House was presented with a gold watch when he retired after serving for 26 years as Parish Clerk and Sexton. His nephew Frank Counsell was elected in his place. A 32-year old builder and decorator, Frank lived in Myrtle Cottage next door to Sandcroft.

The new Rector reported that he had placed a board in the church porch listing the 45 Rectors of the parish, dating from the Rev Johannes de Gidding in 1318 to himself in 1891. He also announced an extensive rebuilding plan for the church, built fifty years earlier for £1,500. Renovation costs would be £1,000 but contributions had already been promised from Charles Whitting, Charles Edward Whitting and Mrs Knyfton. Fund-raising continued with an August Garden Party and Concert in the Rectory. This was a major social event, attracting gentry from across Somerset and Gloucestershire. Mrs Knyfton's family, the Colstons of Bristol, donated new oak seats for the choir and at the Harvest Festival the church, including the gallery, was full and crowds gathered outside.

By May 1892, the work was all done and celebrated with an opening service, followed by a tea and entertainment. The cost had gone up to over £2,130, "all donated by friends of the Rector":

The organ chamber, choir and clergy vestries have all been improved. One vestry has been converted into a south porch and a porch added to the north door.

The new spacious chancel measures 28 feet by 21 feet, is paved with tiles and has a panelled wooden ceiling. Seven steps lead up to the raised and extended altar and a marble square inserted. The Rev Edmund Bennett has donated an Italian altar lace, Mrs Burr has made a green altar frontal and four frontals of white, purple and crimson have been made by Tatersall's of London.

The old pulpit has a new stone base. The ancient font with its 600-year old wooden cover has been brought down from the old church. The priest's step near the baptistry is also from the old church.

The nave has been lowered by three feet and laid with a wood block floor. The old high and straight-backed pews made of deal are replaced with open oak seats, all of which are free and unappropriated to any person. The church now seats 317 people, 64 more than previously. Warm air heating and new lamps are to be installed.

In September a concert raised a further £36 to repair the tower. A year later, in 1893, Sunday School children gave a Litany Desk and a brass ewer. The rector's brother, Mr GF Burr, designed and donated wrought iron gates for the chancel. He also designed a new reredos:

Of Gothic design, the reredos was made by J Northcott of Devon from well-seasoned oak with intricate and delicate carving and five zinc panels. It was paid for anonymously.

On 25th November 1893:

New lights were installed by Mr Leaver of "The Axe", Meadow Street, Weston-super-Mare. These are the latest patent shadowless oil lamps of 100 candlepower each but costing less than ¼d an hour to run. The adjustable hanging arrangement, designed by the Rev Anthony J Burr, is simple and extremely effective.

The ancient font   [UVS]

All this cost more money and at the 1894 Easter Vestry the Rev and Mrs Burr offered to pay off the £1,000. In time for the following Christmas service, Frank Counsell installed a hot-water heating system which worked well but needed another concert to defray £10 still owing to him:

Performers included Mrs Burr and Mrs Charles Whitting who is a thorough musician and plays the 'cello with more than an ordinary taste and skill. This musical treat drew a large attendance.

Work continued into 1895 when statues of St Andrew and St Nicholas donated by Sunday School children were placed in niches "with handsome canopies and pedestals" at the east end of the chancel. The congregation were reminded that St Andrews was the diocesan saint while "churches in seafaring places were usually dedicated to St Nicholas and built on a high place so as to be the last to bless outgoing mariners and the first to welcome them home". George Coleman, Weston's new librarian was so impressed that he designed a banner of the two saints. When he died, his widow had the banner made and donated it to the church. The final refurbishment of the century came in 1896 when the original plaster ceilings of the nave, baptistry and tower were replaced with painted boards.

But all this was nearly lost. On 27th November 1897 the *Mercury* headlined:

Sacrilege and Robbery at Uphill.
Impudent Thefts.
Narrow Escape from Burning of Uphill Church.

Mr FJ House, headmaster of the National Schools and church organist, went early to the church to practise on the organ. As he approached he could smell burning and on entry found immediately that the alms boxes had been damaged. Inside the vestry the window was covered with cassocks. Other cassocks had been used to make two beds on the floor and others stuffed under the door to keep out draughts. The vestry door had been soaked in oil from church lamps and set on fire to force access.

A note left in the vestry read, "When people play 'The Blue Bells of Scotland' in church, dreadful things will happen. – The Devil"

The miscreants went on to Uphill Station where they broke the stationmaster's office window and took money from the cash drawer. This indicated previous knowledge of the station. The rest of the room's contents were upset. Other local churches and chapels have been similarly attacked.

Four youths were eventually caught and convicted for the offences.

The old church on the hill was not forgotten. During 1890, Mrs Knyfton paid for the chancel and tower of the old church to be thoroughly repaired and the walls covered with cement to preserve the building from further decay. In 1891 she funded the renovation of the belfry and restored changes made in 1847 when a door wide enough for a coffin had replaced a window in the south wall. This was rebuilt as a window with another window to match. The original porch was re-built and the Norman arch re-pointed. The roofless nave was laid with turf and paths made in the churchyard.

Immediately after his first Christmas in Uphill the Rev A Burr re-opened the church for public worship as well as a mortuary chapel, promising to hold an annual service there to preserve continuity of worship.

On Sunday 12th July 1891:

> The first Holy Communion in the old church since 1846 was attended by over fifty relatives of those buried there. It will continue to be held on the second Sunday in July.

> Mr John Hayes senior keeps the keys and will show visitors over the building for 3d each or 2d each for parties of 6 or more.

Villagers had been christened in the old church's font since the 12th century. It stood in a niche in the west wall on a 13th century base. Its bowl was probably originally cylindrical, re-shaped into an octagon in the 15th century, with seaweed carved on the panels. In 1892, the new rector exchanged it with the white 1884 font from the new church. This was cut vertically in two and the halves used as supports for the altar which had its wooden panelled frontage removed to show the new base.

The bells tolled as one of the oldest families in the parish walked up to the first funeral in the renovated old church on 28th May 1893. They mourned the death of 13-year old Lionel Francis Counsell, a chorister and assistant verger at St Nicholas and the son of Frank Counsell parish clerk and sexton.

A "popular London weekly" in 1899 admired:

"SINGULAR MONUMENTS"

In the cemetery at Uphill, Weston-super-Mare, is a grave on the top of which is mounted the model of a cannon. The man to whom the memorial is erected served his country as a soldier, and, after reading the suitable inscription, all beholders are forced to admit that a more fitting adornment to the tomb could not have been designed.

The grave-top cannon was admired throughout the twentieth century until it was stolen.

To accommodate larger congregations, the Wesleyans built a new room for their Sunday School, burying the names of donors in bottles beneath four Memorial Stones adjacent to the chapel. The room measured 28 feet by 18 feet and would hold one hundred scholars. It opened in March 1892: "Furnished by Mr Minifie of Uphill". New south and west walls were shared with Charles Whitting's Sandcroft gardens.

Two years later the congregation installed a new organ. In August 1896, the Sunday School held its annual service with children's recitations and music, attracting the *Mercury's* comment:

> Their presentation was not all that could be desired, but that ought really to be seen to in the village day school, for we believe it would not be easy to surpass Uphill children in their barbarous use of the English language.

Split font supporting the old church altar

Chapter 73.   School Report

In the village day school from 1st September 1891:

> Uphill National School will be conducted as a Free Elementary School. Children will be given a thorough, good English education and will be carefully trained in secular and religious knowledge without any fee or payment.

In November Mr John E Stibbs was appointed National Schoolmaster. Unfortunately, on 1st December:

> The Master has been incapacitated by severe lumbago. In his absence a Certificated Mistress conducted the school according to the time-table. There has been only one difficulty. When she corrected a boy for misbehaviour, he ran out of school. He will not be allowed to return until the Master comes back.

By April 1892, order was restored and Her Majesty's Inspector reported:

> The rooms are very satisfactory. A few more pictures on the wall would be a gain. The Registers are well marked and good order prevails.

The Headmaster noted:

> The Rector and Charles Whitting were much pleased with the above entry and special attention was given during the week to Geography and History.

After that, the school broke up for the Easter holiday and Mr Stibbs recorded:

> The attendance during the week has been moderate owing to Potato Planting and other causes.

After an inspection in June 1892:

> The school has been at a great disadvantage through the Master's prolonged absence on account of sickness. The want of efficient help has also been a drawback. It is however in good order and has passed on the whole, fair examination in the elementary and class subjects.
>
> Attention should be paid to the Handwriting above the second, to Spelling in the third standard, to Arithmetic in the fourth standard and Mental Arithmetic in the second and third standards. Indeed this last named subject should be more intelligently taught throughout.

The rate of school finances depended on results and the report went on:

> The historical knowledge of the boys is so limited that only the lower rate can be recommended for History and Geography combined, while the higher is recommended for Geography and Needlework without hesitation and in consideration of the difficulties during the year.

The Master should have some efficient help and the room should be more amply supplied with pictures and apparatus.

The Infant Department had its own curriculum, including Object Lessons based on prescribed topics:

Animals	Objects	Natural Products	Miscellaneous
Crow	Bottle	Cork	Sugar
Dog	Glass Tumbler	Sponge	Spring
Lion	Gloves	Sugar	Shoemaker's
Tiger	Umbrella	Storm	Shop
Sheep	Brick	River	Sea-shore
Horse	Wild Flowers	Water	Bell
Camel	Apple	Ice	
Elephant	Potato		

The Inspector reported:

> The order and elementary instruction are very creditable and the Object Lessons are given on sensible lines and are fairly successful. Owing to sickness they have been somewhat curtailed and the occupations neglected. They will, I hope, receive due attention this year and I should be glad if drawing were included among them. Form should be an important part of the infant's instruction.
>
> The note singing is very good but the ear singing seems to be somewhat flat.
>
> The children are very happy and bright and are good influences.
>
> A few more low desks are needed.

Village children had educational opportunities beyond the school. In September 1894:

> Alice Maud Fear, daughter of Mr Wiliam Fear of Rose Cottage, on the recommendation of Headmaster Mr Stibbs, has been awarded one of six Somerset scholarships to attend Gloucester School of Cookery and Domestic Economy for six months.

After three months at Gloucester, Alice won the school's highest certificate.

But standards slipped in 1895:

> There is need for improvement. Handwriting is deficient in style and uniformity and the sums are not worked by the best methods. Knowledge of Geography is praiseworthy.
>
> In lower classes, Needlework is good and Singing deserves special commendation. Hymn Singing is excellent and Repetitions are reverent and correct.
>
> Composition and Slate work are especially neat and tidy but the answering in some Standards was not nearly good enough.

At the end of the year:

Mr Stibbs, Miss Showell and Miss Stibbs are all leaving the school. After 35 years as a school-master, six of them at Uphill, Mr Stibbs is retiring on a pension.

The school's Annual Grant for 1895-6 was just ove a hundred pounds, despite some faulty official arithmetic:

Mixed Class under Master		Infant Class	
30 boys, 41 girls	71	19 boys, 18 girls	37
Grants			
Principal	14s 0d	Fixed	9s 0d
Disc and Org	1s 6d	Variable	4s 0d
Singing	1s 0d	Needlework	
Drawing	1s 0d	& Singing	1s 0d
Geography	2s 0d		
History and			
Needlework	2s 0d		
	20s 6d		15s 0d

Grants Claimable and Paid	£	s	d
Mixed under Master	72	15	6
Infants	27	15	0
Act 102	2	0	0
Amount of Annual Grant	102	10	6
Final Amount of Fee Grant	10	7	6
Total Sum Payable	112	18	0

In April 1896, Mr Frederick House was appointed to replace Mr Stibbs as Headmaster. He arrived to find:

a Kirkman Grand Piano was placed in the school for School and Concert use. This has been paid for by donations.

Not all the money came from generous wealthy villagers:

A Sale of Needlework done by children during the year raised £1 4s 8d. Sixpence was given to the girls who had sold it leaving £1 4s 2d to be given to the School Treasurer.

The new Headmaster took a grip on the school. Within two years:

Both the discipline and work are praiseworthy. The needlework deserves special commendation. A well ordered and well taught infant class. Drawing excellent. As there are more children on roll, there should be an extra teacher.

After another year:

The school has earned the highest grants in all subjects.
It is in very good order and continues to do very creditable work.
The Infants are thoroughly well trained and taught. The staff of this part of the school ought to be strengthened. Furthermore, the Infants' class room is insufficient for the average attendance. The school must either reduce attendance or increase the accommodation.

Overcrowding wasn't helped when extra children turned up unexpectedly for lessons. Some were visiting relatives in the village and they were allowed temporary admission to avoid being charged with truancy from their own school. Others, however, just arrived with a big sister when mother couldn't cope at home and in July 1896 a "Visit without Notice" order was made:

Parents will not, after this, be allowed to send children under three years of age, neither as scholars nor occasionally to sit with older sisters.

In April 1893 a father reported his absent son "to be suffering from Inflammation of the Lungs ... said by the doctor to be a very serious case". Another father reported his son's "complaint of the brain liable to cause Brain Fever". The Autumn Term had hardly opened in 1894 when "An Epidemic of Measles in Uphill" closed the school for a month. A full day's official holiday was allowed for the annual Parish Church Choir outing accompanied by all the teachers but only a half-day on July 16th 1893 for the:

Royal Marriage.

All scholars assembled at school at 3.30pm and marched in a procession headed by the Town Band to Uphill Castle Lawn. There they sang "God Bless the Prince of Wales". After tea they all enjoyed dancing and games until 8pm. Then the Band played the National Anthem followed by three cheers for the "Royal Pair" and three for the Royal Family. The children then went home.

As the century neared its end in 1899:

Schoolchildren attended the Ascension Day service in St Nicholas church. Afterwards they remained to attend the funeral of a delicate 6-year old pupil.

Chapter 74.   Village Activities

New Graves-Knyfton golf course   [UVS]

Where sport was concerned, Uphill had nothing to match a contest reported in 1891:

> a man died in London from injuries inflicted while wrestling a bear for a wager on a music-hall stage.

But within months of the arrival of the new squire:

> a Golf Course was laid out on Graves-Knyfton land near Moorland Road.

Mrs Graves, the new squire's mother, gave unstinting support to Uphill Castle Cricket Club. Their successful 1893 season closed with an all-day match between Singles and Marrieds on the Castle ground, followed by tea and a dance in the evening. This celebrated a record of Played 15, Won 11, Drawn 2, Lost 2. Runs For 961, Against 655. At their New Year dance and supper in 1894 in the schoolroom, Mrs Graves sent across food for 70 guests, prepared in the Castle kitchens by her own cook, Mrs Feadon. In May she invited the Club to tea in the Castle grounds. A Singles XI again played a Marrieds XI, followed by dancing on the lawn to Weston Town Band. The 1896 season recorded figures of Played 14, Won 6, Drawn 2, Lost 6. In 1899 they Played 20 Won 15 Lost 5 and started an Under 15 Club. In the meantime:

> St Nicholas Sunday School and Temperance Guild, secretary Mr John Stibbs the schoolmaster, has two flourishing cricket teams of 10- and 15-year olds. They play on the Recreation Ground, always losing heavily.

Uphill Castle Football Club lost its old pitch in 1897 but Henry Brown of Uphill Farm let them play in one of his fields. Mr Graves-Knyfton opened a field north of the Castle as a tented summer camp for 250 members of Bristol Boys' Brigade.

Hare-coursing remained popular:

> Clifton Foot Beagles met at Uphill Castle in January 1899, having a lavish breakfast in the old schoolroom. Following 18 couples of hounds, they found hares at Hutton. They have also met at the Grange.

Supported by gentry and clergy, Uphill Working Men's Club opened in January 1890 with a Smoking Concert chaired by the Rev Glanville with Mr Edwards on the piano accompanying songs. These included such favourites as Cottage By The Sea, A Boy's Best Friend Is His Mother, Empress Of The Waves and The Light Brigade. The singers were Sidney Francis, Fred Taylor, William Minifie and his son William, George Masters, William Henderson, A Way, C Fear and Henry Herniman. Membership was open "to any respectable person over 18" for 3d per week while boys could go in for a penny. The clubroom had a bagatelle board and a selection of books and games, periodicals and illustrated papers donated by wealthier villagers who also sent in their newspapers every day when they had read them.

Part of the purpose of this was to keep men out of the pubs, but Peter Hart countered by organising weekly Smokers at the Ship. Even respectable St Nicholas parishioners turned up at the Ship for their annual tithe-payers' dinner where:

> supper brought from the Rectory augmented Host Hart's most liberal catering.

St Nicholas bell-ringers also favoured the Ship where Edward Jewell Whitting entertained them to dinner before they rang in the New Year with a midnight peal on the hill in 1897.

Although some feared that education would give workers ideas above their station, there were genuine attempts to raise domestic standards. Mr TH Slade gave a series of talks on the culture of fruit and vegetables in the grounds of the Grange and the Castle, with lectures in the Clubroom. Mrs Graves arranged for her cook Mrs Feadon to give a series of practical cookery lessons in the old schoolroom "for girls and women in order to help the wives of working men". She donated the materials and subsidised the cheap sale of the dishes cooked. For this, girls paid 1d and women 3d with the proceeds going to Uphill Castle Cricket Club. A series of ambulance classes for villagers given by Dr Crouch, showed how to bandage a wounded head, a broken jaw, collar bones, legs or arms and how to improvise stretchers. Weston now had Technical Education Committee which sent Miss Rose to teach dressmaking classes. These were rated "very popular especially among older schoolgirls".

It was not only the gentry who helped. Mark Minifie lived in one of the new villas in Moorland Road and ran Grove Park Dairy Factory at 92 High Street in Weston. He announced a far-sighted:

> Evening Gardens Continuation Scheme for men under 21.
>
> Each man will be given 1-1½ perch of ground, all tools and tuition and will be able to keep the produce.
> The times of tuition will suit the pupils.
> The total cost will be less than 2/6 each for the season.

Another Minifie, William, described by the *Mercury* as its "energetic secretary" advertised the annual meeting in 1891 of Uphill's branch of the United Patriots National Benefit Society as:

> A public tea and entertainment in the Schoolroom under the patronage of the Rev and Mrs Bennett and other ladies and gentlemen.

The entertainment resembled that of the Working Men's Club with the added attraction of ladies: Mrs Alfred Counsell, Miss Dorvill, Mrs Statter and Mrs Bennett all joined in. The following year, the event began with a Choral Evening in the church before moving on to "a substantial tea in the schoolroom for 130". The Rector urged the society to remain a voluntary organisation to insure working people:

> We do not want a compulsory insurance scheme which would end Friendly Societies and pay those who have not worked. Hard working men grudge Poor Law payments to paupers and criminals. Now that education is free, you no longer have to pay to send your children to school. What have you done with the money saved?
>
> Voice from the floor: Spent it.
> Rector: Yes – you should put the money saved into the United Patriots National Benefit Society.

The Methodists had their own scheme, the Independent Order of Good Templars which met without entertainment:

> The anniversary meeting was held at the Wesleyan schoolroom and Brother Jones DCT took the chair.

Cheap rail travel extended the scope of village outings. In August 1890, members of St Nicholas Choir went to Bournemouth. They were:

> taken to the station by the new horse-drawn Weston Omnibus Company's "easy and comfortable" Parisian Car which announced itself to the village by bugle at 5.15 am. Unfortunately this was one of the wettest and roughest days of the summer.

The following year, the Rector's wife, Mrs Florence Burr, planned the annual Sunday School treat. Gentry drove their coaches from Weston to watch and spectators lined the village streets. At 2 pm, over a hundred children marched from the school lustily singing hymns, including the popular All Things Bright And Beautiful with its socially definitive third verse:

> The rich man in his castle,
> The poor man at his gate,
> He made them, high or lowly,
> And ordered their estate.

Mrs Burr accordingly placed her own three children at the head of the procession with the honour of carrying the Sunday School banner. The children reached the church at 3 pm, where the Rev Burr spoke to them. After tea in the Rectory garden they played games in the adjoining paddock. Prizes were presented to Bessie and Florrie Radford and Herbert Pople for regular attendance and to Edith Shallish and Ernest Skyrme "for reverence in Church". For New Year 1892, a rich young couple Herbert and Annette Wootton of Riversdale House invited the same hundred children to a:

> Magic Lantern entertainment presented by Professor Carl Merton of Weston-super-Mare. His slides were much admired especially one that displayed the motto, "Success to St Nicholas Sunday School" in large letters on the sheet.   After the show, the children were given buns, oranges and New Year cards.

Wearing the white ribbons of St Nicholas Temperance Guild, eighty youngsters tasted all the delights of modern transport in 1893. They caught the 10.31 am train from Uphill Station, arriving at Temple Meads at 11.45 am. A steamer took them through the busy docks to Hotwells. There they crossed the road and entered a door in a rock-face much higher than Uphill quarry. Inside they clicked through an iron turn-stile that counted them as they passed. The Cliff Rocks Railway swept them upwards and they walked out into daylight onto the Downs. After an afternoon at the Zoo, they went back into the Cliff Rocks Railway and down to the road. Two chartered trams were waiting to take them to the train which dropped them back in Uphill at 8 pm.

More was to come in October when the choir outing to London left Uphill Station on Monday morning at 3.30 am on Lever's Fast Excursion Train. In London, described to them as our "modern Babylon", they travelled on the Underground Railway, by bus and on steamers on the river. The highlight was a choral service in Westminster Abbey. Mrs Burr provided the Christmas treat for St Nicholas Sunday School and the Temperance Guild. Children loudly cheered:

> a very beautiful Christmas Tree literally covered with handsome and useful presents. Numberless wax candles and reflectors sparkled brilliantly as if imported from Fairyland.

Mrs Burr answered the cheers with a reminder of her earlier promise to provide the tree "for every deserving scholar". Therefore, if anyone present did not receive a present, it was their fault and not hers. She gave treasures from the tree to about 90% of the children.

Older villagers were not forgotten. In June 1892, the Rev and Mrs Finlayson provided a treat for the twelve oldest ladies of the parish. Their ages totalled 887 and ranged from 52 to 90. They averaged 74 and ten were over 70:

Well-appointed conveyances drove them to Weston Hill, Kewstoke and Worle, returning to Southfield for high tea with the Town Band playing on the lawn.

At Christmas 1894, old folk and widows were given coal by Edward Morgan Whitting of Totterdown, the Rector and Churchwardens. Other gifts came from Mr and Mrs Charles Edward Whitting of the Grange. All the big houses entertained their servants and families giving them food and clothing. In the village however, Christmas was reported as:

> very dull, there being no entertainment of any kind during the festive season. Unfortunately for the parish, Miss Graves being so ill, the parishioners have missed the usual Bank Holiday entertainment so much appreciated by the people as they are always free for all, unlike some that are for a select few.   Christmas appears to have been celebrated in its good old style at the Castle as the servants, their wives and children were all kindly and liberally supplied with joints of beef beside some valuable and useful presents from Miss Graves and the squire.

Forty families were assisted from the Harrill Charity, a £100 bequest in Mr T Harrill's will in 1888. With the Whitting Charity it was invested as a mortgage on Hagley Villa and Hampstead Villa in Moorland Road, paying 4% every Christmas to the Rector and Churchwardens to distribute annually to the poor of the parish.

At Weston-super-Mare Christmas Cattle Market auction in 1899:

> Capt EM Whitting, Totterdown, sold West Highlander cattle for £18, Devon steers for £26 and fat sheep for 46s 6d. Mr Luff, Uphill, sold fat heifers for £23.

In the village:

> The catering of Mr Herniman for his numerous customers was publicly displayed and induced universal admiration. Included in his stock was a Highland ox, grazed by Captain Whitting; Shorthorn heifers, grazed by Mr E Luff, Manor Farm, Uphill; and a splendid fat lamb, fed by Mr Graves-Knyfton, of Uphill Castle. The decorations of the establishment were exceedingly pretty.

By 1890 Weston had its own horse-drawn omnibuses and was planning a tramway down the sea-front, but neither ran as far as Uphill. Nevertheless, anyone with business in London could catch the train at Bleadon and Uphill Station at 8.31am, arriving at Paddington at 12.25 pm. The 3 pm train back reached the village promptly at 7.22 pm. The trains ran on time, even on 24th January 1891 when:

An outhouse at Uphill Station caught fire. Being made of sleepers it soon burned to the ground. The flames spread to the house roof but were put out by Station Master Mr Payne and helpers before the Weston Fire Engine arrived.

Mr Payne was a keen gardener with a prize-winning station flower plot. In the winter he stored pots of plants in the shed and had put a stove in there to protect them from frost. A cat and a dog slept in the shed and it is thought that the cat's fur may have caught on fire. The animals died and the pots and plants were destroyed. The building was not insured.

Henry Brown of Uphill Farm was appointed Waywarden at the 1892 Vestry Meeting held in the Coffee Tavern. His first job was to deal again with the "very poor condition of Middle Bow near the Post Office and ask for it to be widened". Middle Bow was the bridge at today's Rhyne Terrace. Within days he reported that Axbridge Board would widen and improve the bridge and that he would donate £7, half the cost.

As the century ended technology transformed the people's transport. In thirty years the velocipede had developed into the boneshaker, the ordinary and the penny-farthing, to the safety bicycle, recognisable today with its chain-drive and two equal wheels:

❑   ❑   ❑   ❑   ❑

Chapter 75.   Democracy and Drains

All male householders over 21 could now vote and national politics came to the village for the first time in the General Election of 1892. Uphill's Liberals "met in strong force to support their Parliamentary candidate Mr Beaumont Morice" and in response Sir Richard Paget the Conservative MP spoke in a marquee on Major Whitting's field opposite the school:

> Sir Richard met rowdy opposition by juveniles, non-voters and non-residents.
> After his speech, Robert Minifie mounted the platform to shouts of "Good old Moses". He asked the MP how many allotments had been provided in the Wells Division by the Conservative Government.
> Sir Richard: I don't know exactly.
> Robert Minifie: You should.
> Sir Richard: the government has provided as many places as possible across the country.
> Robert Minifie: Allotments are needed in Kewstoke, Weston-super-Mare, Uphill and Bleadon but people are charged £5 an acre whereas farmers pay only £3 10s. The House of Lords has defeated the purpose of the Allotments Act.
> Sir Richard: You only know half the story – you stick to your forge and I'll stick to politics.
> Mr Richard Minifie (in a somewhat excited frame of mind) rose to shouts of "Cheers for Aaron".
> He shouted: Now my friends, if you want to hear the High Priest of Liberalism, keep quiet.
> Laughter, derisive cheers and shouts of "Get your hair cut".
> Richard Minifie: The people want peasant proprietorship of the land. It is the fault of the House of Lords.
> Chairman: You have taken ten minutes and said nothing.

When Beaumont Morice returned to Uphill a vast crowd waited an hour for him. They cheered as he came down the hill from the station in a wagonette to tell a meeting in St Nicholas Coffee House that he would work for "one man, one vote".

Although Sir Richard Paget was re-elected, the 82-year old William Ewart Gladstone's Liberal Party took power at Westminster.

At an earthier level, Uphill's drainage was still a matter for the unelected Axbridge Board of Guardians which decided that drains needed a special rate borne by Uphill. The 1892 Easter Vestry Meeting agreed and Richard Minifie was re-appointed Assistant Overseer with an extra £35 on his salary to prepare a new rates valuation list.

The Rector had sunk two new wells in his grounds but the Axbridge Board found that:

> Analysis of water from wells adjacent to the Rectory shows that it is quite unfit for human consumption. There has been extensive pollution with sewage which has percolated through the soil even though there is no drain in the garden. Mr James's well opposite the Rectory is also largely polluted with sewage. The Castle wells give a good water for dietetic usage as does the village pump. Mr Wootton's well at Riversdale is dangerous for dietetic use and the well for nine cottages near William Minifie's the blacksmith, belonging to Mr C Whitting senior, is impure with sewage and unfit to use.

Three out of five samples and six out of eight wells were condemned and Uphill hastily elected a Parochial Committee for water and drainage comprising the Rector, Edward Luff, Henry Brown, Robert Counsell, William Minifie, Charles Whitting, Edmund Burdge, Charles Edward Whitting and Robert Minifie.

This alliance of gentry and people proved unstoppable. When Robert Minifie complained that Axbridge had closed their well without providing a water supply in its place, Charles Edward Whitting commented "That's the way they work in Axbridge" and immediately wrote to Weston Town Engineer to ask the cost of extending the town's public water supply to Uphill. A quotation of £550 was accepted, with the Whittings and the Rector offering to pay for five years the difference between this and the amount produced by a parish rate. Assistant Overseer Richard Minifie required a rate of sevenpence in the pound for the half-year to pay for the new water supply "as far as Peter Hart's on the west and Mr Brown's farm on the east. The supply to the school would be metered." Another penny in the pound was needed to extend the mains along the main road past the Ship Inn to Slimeridge Farm. A further extension took the pipe "from the Post Office westward 400 yards to Hart's Coal Wharf, and in the east of the parish to Mr Brown's corner and his gardener's cottage just beyond". To help matters along, Capt Charles Whitting guaranteed to pay the Water Board 10% on their outlay for five years.

On 13th March 1893 the committee engaged its own engineer and submitted full plans to Weston for Uphill's "96 houses to be drained into the main outfall sewer as the village wished to do away with cess-pits".

A year later Charles Whitting connected Sandcroft and many of his other properties to the main drain. These included nine Sandcroft Cottages with their row of outdoor privies at the west end alongside

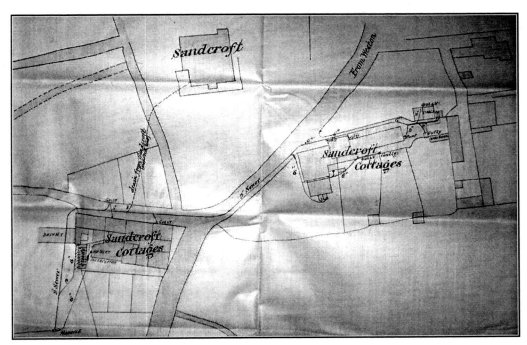

Sandcroft drainage plans   *[Permission kindly given by SRO to use the image from file A\AKH/6/7/1-6]*

the Minifie forge. They were occupied by William Minifie, George Staples, Robert Minifie, Robert Jarvis, Charles Hollier, George Avery, Jane Nash, Frank Harvey and Edmund Lang. Across the road were five Russell's Cottages occupied by John Jones, Mrs Sarah Harvey, John Yandle, James Williams and Henry Fear.

Near the school Mrs Harriet Demack rented Westfield House, sub-letting part to George Owen. George Wadham had the tenancy of the neighbouring Westfield Cottage. All these properties with

Coastguard Cottages, Coal Wharf Cottage, and six Brickyard Cottages were connected to the sewer.

Uphill's sanitation was now better than that of the Queen when she came to the throne, but rate collector Richard Minifie reported that Moorland Road householders still refused to pay anything as they already paid a rate to Weston.

Uphill Parochial Committee accepted this, but refused Richard's request that he should keep any balance of profit between the rate collected and the outgoings.

The Minifie family, 9 Sandcroft Cottages   *[UVS]*

❑ ❑ ❑ ❑ ❑

Chapter 76.   Parish Council

Until now, such local decisions had been taken by Church Vestry Meetings, held at a time and place that excluded ordinary working people. The rector was always in the chair and voting was by a show of hands. The 1894 Local Government Act swept this away and established civil Parish Councils that were elected annually by rate-payers. A parish like Uphill of over 300 people could elect between six and eight councillors. The council controlled education, waywardens, overseers, even churchwardens on non-Church matters. It had power to compel land-owners to let land for allotments at a fair price. A single councillor could demand a poll of the parish on any issue. Every rate-payer valued at under £50 pa had one vote, plus an extra vote for every £25 over this, to a maximum of six votes per voter. Major property owners could amass twelve votes each.

Axbridge Board of Guardians became an elected District Council and Weston an Urban District Council with Uphill Castle wall as its southern boundary. This split the ancient parish, defined by the Rev Burr as:

> Its ecclesiastical boundary on the North side ran from the Sanatorium, along the sandy lane opposite out as far as the railway bridge and along Uphill great rhyne. On the East side, from the rhyne to Totterdown House which is within the parish, up the lane at the side, almost to the top. On the South side, from Sea View or White House which is in Bleadon parish, across the road embracing Flat Roof Farm, alongside the home field of the Grange, down to the quarry.

Uphill embraced democracy. Rate-payers met on 8th December 1894 to choose five members for their first Council. Major Charles Edward Whitting seconded by Robert Minifie proposed the Rector as chairman and a traditional show of hands elected five of seven candidates. The unsuccessful candidates immediately demanded a poll of the whole village. They titled themselves Progressives while the successful candidates were termed the Church party. The *Mercury* deplored this intrusion of party politics into local government.

The village poll confirmed the first result and the Parish Council met in the Schoolhouse on 5th January 1895. It elected Charles Edward Whitting as chairman, Edward Luff as vice-chairman and Mr Ransom, the manager of Wilts and Dorset Bank, as treasurer. He arranged an overdraft to cover expenses until April when the first rates would be collected.

The first business concerned allotments, inviting new applications and transferring the tenancy of existing allotments to the Parish Council. They next considered the Parish Cottages near the village well. These were parish property let to the poorest parishioners. Overseers Robert Counsell and William Minifie were now to pay the rents into the Council bank account. They had to inspect the cottages and report on their condition at the February meeting. They also had to "remind the tenant of the Parish ground opposite Wheatstone Houses that his tenancy expires next Lady Day and it will not be let again".

At their February meeting, Councillors agreed that "Parish houses have been a disgrace for many years. All necessary repairs are to be carried out by 1st May." In March they offered a "Parish cottage to Widow Pople at 1/6 a week". They noted "The Parish Enclosure near the Ship is now occupied by Mr Frederick King. The sheds in it are let to Mr Edward Luff and Mr Frank Counsell" and agreed to "improve the Enclosure by raising its walls and installing a couple of gates and seats".

Parish Cottages   [UVS]

When the Council received "eleven new applicants for allotments, nine for more land and two for smallholdings of three acres each", members had to demonstrate their ability to find land for them. Mr Nantes, agent for the Graves-Knyfton estate, said he could not reduce the rent of £20 on the existing allotment field but he was willing to pay the tithe and transfer the tenancy to the Council. The Council then asked him for "two closes adjoining the north side of the present allotment fields for new allotments and smallholdings". Mr Nantes agreed "to let 2 acres at £4 per acre, the Parish Council to fence it". The Council offered £3 and half the cost of fencing and this was accepted by Mr Graves-Knyfton. Finally, "all allotment tenants living outside Uphill are to give up their tenancy".

George Masters, tailor, and Henry Waterman Herniman, butcher, were appointed Overseers in April but trouble came when the Council decided to advertise for an Assistant Overseer. Unsurprisingly Richard Minifie asked if this meant that his present appointment was being revoked but the Chairman refused to hear him because he was not an Uphill ratepayer. His brother Robert spoke on his behalf and the Chairman ruled him out of order because "that was a parish matter and not on this agenda". Robert claimed that the meeting had the right to decide its business – and to elect its chairman. At this the Chairman closed the meeting.

Richard Minifie duly applied for the post of Assistant Overseer, asking for extra salary to cover new duties as Clerk of the Council. Charles Stuart, grocer, said he would do it for £15 while John Smith asked for £18. After a ballot, Mr Stuart was elected. That was not Richard Minifie's only problem, as the Council had limited its 47 new allotment tenancy agreements to residents only. He protested that it was hard to lose his allotment as he worked in Uphill although he lived in Moorland Road. The Council agreed to allow him and Mr Popham, also of Moorland Road, to continue their tenancies.

New faces appeared on the Council in 1896 when "quarryman Frederick Penberthy and squire Reginald Graves-Knyfton" were elected but Robert Minifie was not. He promptly demanded a parish poll. All 122 ratepayers voted, returning Reginald Graves-Knyfton, Major CE Whitting (who had not stood) and Thomas Counsell instead of Frederick Penberthy. The *Mercury* again complained about "too much politics in the election" but gleefully noted that "all who deemed themselves Radicals failed".

At the first meeting, Major Whitting was voted chairman with Reginald Graves-Knyfton as vice. Richard Minifie turned up, objecting to his removal as Assistant Waywarden. When the Chairman would not allow him to speak as he was not a resident elector, Robert Minifie produced a "formidable looking handbook on the Local Government Act 1894" which he said would prove that the Council procedures were incorrect.

The Chairman: I don't think you had better read that.

Robert Minifie: But I *will*.

Chairman: It's no use quoting from that book. You must give us the Act itself. I am legally Chairman. If I am wrong, somebody must resolve that I vacate the chair.

Thomas Counsell, seconded by Henry Herniman, moved that Major Whitting should retain the chair and there was an overwhelming vote in his favour. Richard Minifie cried "*My* hand is up," but Major Whitting again refused to allow him to speak, supported by cries of "Turn him out." Still seeking to discredit Council procedures, Robert Minifie demanded that its minutes and papers should be available to the public, not kept in the Clerk's house. The meeting agreed to make papers available for seven days in the Schoolhouse. That was Robert's final fling. Following the death of Councillor William Minifie at 55 in January 1897, the Council elected 50-year old Robert in his place but he declined owing to ill-health and Frederick Penberthy was at last elected.

The road up to Bleadon remained a private road known as Uphill Toll Bar. Without tolls it was "in anything but a satisfactory state" and in 1896 the Parish Council asked the County Council to take it over as a public road. The council also complained to Axbridge "of the deplorable state of the footpath from the church past Sandcroft". In 1897 Weston agreed to designate Uphill Road as a main road. With no decent road in or out of the village, the Parish Council asked the Post Office to lay a telegraph wire to Uphill. This, however, required a guaranteed payment of £24 a year for 7 years, which the Council thought too dear. Instead, and perhaps more realistically, the Council "placed a few oil lamps at dangerous points in the parish and painted the post in Church Path white". Looking across the bay to the glittering street lights of Weston, the Council asked how much it would cost to extend the gas supply to the village.

The Rev Burr unwittingly provoked another confrontation in March 1898 when he asked the Council to:

> vote a little money to repair the wall of the old church which was in a sad state of decay. This would be in the interest of all parishioners as this was the only burial ground for all denominations.

The request was approved by 13-2. Henry Brown and William Manley voted against and Robert

Minifie wrote to the *Mercury* expressing:

> vehement opposition as a Nonconformist to us-
> ing money from the rates for ecclesiastical pur-
> poses. If the Rev Burr handed the church and
> churchyard to the Parish Council for all to use, I
> would support the payment. If the Council helps
> the Rector, what is to stop him asking for funds
> for our school which is fast going to the dogs
> with a miserably restricted curriculum which is
> a disgrace to our 19th century civilisation. The
> Wesleyan chapel could say the same, that it is
> open to all, and also ask for funds.

Mrs Graves wrote from "Charlton", Weston-
super-Mare, generously praising Robert Minifie
as "an earnest and public-spirited man" and
gently regretting "the damage caused to himself
by his tone of bitter personal resentment". She
believed "the church was worth preserving for
its own sake as an ancient landmark, seen as such
by all of any or no religion" and added that Mr
Minifie had no right to use this matter to attack
the school. She concluded:

> Every man deserves respect who has the
> courage to defend the right and expose the
> wrong, but he must attack measures, not men.

Robert Minifie's reply was courteous but
vigorous:

> The school curriculum from the 1870 Education
> Act to 1885 covered reading, writing, arithmetic,
> drawing, poetry, human physiology, history, ge-
> ography, grammar and sol-fa types of music. Now
> it covers only reading, writing, arithmetic, a little
> music and much catechism. As a result I am teach-
> ing my youngest child myself.

❑ ❑ ❑ ❑ ❑

Chapter 77.   Wild Life and Wild Weather

In April 1893:

> Many gathered to hear the rare sweet song of a nightingale which for some nights had taken up its position in a tree near the Wesleyan chapel.

A gannet was shot on Black Rock in January 1894 and the Rev Burr observed in 1895:

> Wild asparagus grows here, known only in three other places in Britain. Also Twiggy Mullein, Broad-leaved Cress and Rock Hutchinsia. Evening Primrose grow in the sand-dunes. There are abundant snowdrops and bluebells in the Rectory gardens and in the beautiful field opposite the Manor House. Black moles thrive in the sandy soil. Two cream coloured moles have been caught and killed by a cat. I have had them stuffed. Three large badgers were killed in the plantation opposite the Manor. Two are preserved and kept by Mr Graves Knyfton.

Heavy snow smothered the village and birds died in the hedges as New Year 1891 opened with 23 consecutive days of frost. On 10th March:

> Today occurred one of the severest snow storms ever known in Uphill. The snow was blinding and the wind so boisterous that all the roads became impassable. Total school attendance was 9 with 1 in the Infants Department. The school closed in consequence. The road north to the Sanatorium was completely blocked and conveyances and pedestrians were obliged to go to Weston by way of the sands.

After two days of Spring-like weather, a gale and more blizzards left drifts several feet deep. Weston improvised a snow plough drawn by three horses to clear the streets. The driver of the Wedmore mail-cart ventured out but the mist was so thick that the cart overturned into a snow-covered ditch. Drifts blocked the railway line at Uphill and a train was snowed in at Brent Knoll. Two men brought a breakdown engine from Bristol to rescue the passengers but a newspaper train followed at high speed. Fortunately the men heard it and jumped off into deep snow just before it smashed into the back of their engine.

In November 1891, a storm rose to hurricane strength:

> At its height and on the full tide, a brig rounded Brean Down, her canvas showing the effects of the storm. She ran before the wind for the safety of Uphill River. Weston lifeboat crew stood ready but the gale moderated and she was able to enter the river safely.

A 48-hour November gale in 1893 tore the top from Mr Herniman's butcher's van. Joseph Ellard and George Fisher were drowned in December 1894 when a squall hit them while fishing off Steep Holm. They were in a 13-foot punt, of the type often used for fishing. Joseph Ellard's body was washed up at Berrow and identified by his brother, George, an Uphill carpenter.

February 1895 brought 28° of frost (-17C), the severest for 40 years, but in 1897:

> In unparalleled mild weather, allotment holders were digging potatoes on New Year's Day.

In March 1898:

> A blizzard of great violence blew the snow almost horizontally. The incoming tide was caught by the violence of the wind and temporarily checked forming a bank of curling waters, several feet in height, much like the bore on the Parrett. In the storm, the vessel *John* foundered off the Holms. The crew were picked up by the *Osprey*.

A letter in the *Mercury* pointed out that sewage pollution in rivers and the sea was destroying fish and birds: "There will soon be no salmon caught in Weston Bay."

Yet another Brean Down Harbour and Railway Scheme planned a fleet of transit boats with rails on the lower decks to hold 3-4 parallel rows of passenger coaches and freight wagons so that they could transfer from the Great Western Railway system in Wales to the South Western Railway in Somerset without unloading. But that required co-operation between two railway companies and as the Victorian business instinct was to compete, the scheme collapsed.

The Bay's defences remained essential to national security, with Germany rather than France now seen as the enemy:

> Steep Holm is a rock about a mile and a half in circumference rising perpendicularly out of deep sea to a height of 400 feet so steeply that in many places it overhangs the water. It is inaccessible except by narrow passages very difficult of access. It is certainly as strong as Heligoland and far more important to us than Heligoland is to the Germans. The present armament of Steep Holm consists of a few light muzzle-loading guns of a very antiquated type mounted on batteries almost unchanged since 1859. The are three batteries at most and are manned by a weak detachment of Marine Artillery.

HMS *Arrogant*, a 5,750 ton cruiser, enlivened the August holiday in 1898 with:

> an experimental bombardment of Steep Holm fort to test new steel plates used as gun shields. The ship's armament consists of four 63 breech-loaders, six 4.73 quick-firers, eight 12lb quick-firers, three 3lb quick-firers and five machine-guns. The plates were found to be entirely effective.

Chapter 78.   Victoria's Diamond Jubilee

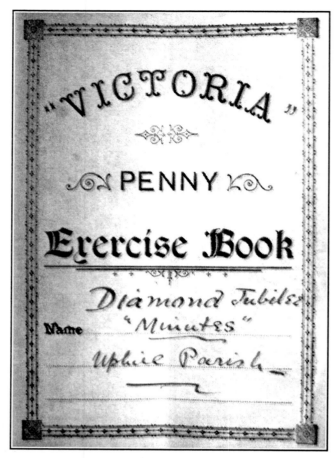

Jubilee Committee minutes   *[NSM]*

The village celebrated the Queen's Jubilee in June 1897 with segregated charity:

> Bunting and flags flew round the village and Major Whitting opened his field for sports, dancing and other entertainments. Unmarried women and nearly two hundred children were given a great tea and a Jubilee mug in the schoolroom at 4 pm. Parish householders, wives and young men over 14 enjoyed a substantial cold collation in the marquee at 6.30 pm. There was dancing to Spencer's Band in the evening and a bonfire and fireworks on the Old Church Hill. The fireworks cost an extra £3 making the total cost £43 3s. Donors had given £42 6s 6d and Mr Huntley generously allowed 14/6 discount from his bill to meet the deficit.

The Queen herself visited Bristol in 1899 to open the Royal Convalescent Home. The Volunteers lined the streets with troops as their bands played martial and patriotic music. Three Whittings checked the dress of the 3rd Volunteer Battalion Prince Albert's Somerset Light Infantry: Captain Edward Morgan Whitting, Captain Edward Jewell Whitting commanding A Company in Burnham and Major Charles Edward Whitting commanding B Company in Weston. On parade with the Weston Company was Lieutenant Reginald Benett Graves-Knyfton. They were resplendent in:

> Review order, with greatcoats rolled and the ends neatly fastened with the mess tin strap. Helmet, tunic with belt, frog, pouch. Shoulder pads will be carried in the pouch.

Near them the 1st Gloucestershire Artillery Volunteers wore:

> Busby, tunic, trousers, black laced boots, belt, frog, pouch, gloves, carbine with sling, bayonet, greatcoat rolled and slung over right shoulder. Special attention must be paid to the condition of the belt, gloves and buttons. The edges of the belt must be clean.

It was all very splendid and it was all about to end.

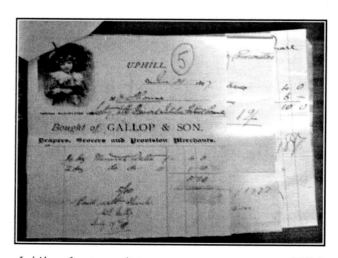

Jubilee feast receipt   *[NSM]*

Chapter 79.   War in South Africa

A few weeks after that great parade in Bristol, the *Mercury* published an aggressive leader headed WAR IN THE TRANSVAAL. Transvaal was a province of South Africa where Boer settlers were seizing independence from British rule. With no war correspondent, the *Mercury* gave authentic colour to its reports by quoting serving soldiers:

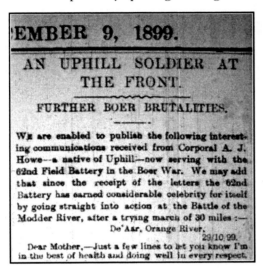

AN UPHILL SOLDIER AT THE FRONT
FURTHER BOER BRUTALITIES

Cpl Alfred J Howe is a native of Uphill serving with the 62nd Field Battery in the Boer War. We may add that since the receipt of the letters, the 62nd Battery has earned considerable celebrity for itself by going straight into action at the Modder River after a trying march of 30 miles.

Alf was the second son of Charlie Howe, Uphill's butter dealer:

De Aar, Orange River 29/10/99
Dear Mother,
Just a few lines to let you know I'm in the best of health and doing well in every respect....
This is a funny country. We have seen a few Boers and had a few shots with them. Our fellows did some splendid work last week, scaling a hill 1,000 feet high, and capturing the place, losing 12 men. We advance on Kimberley this week.
Our cavalry scouts this morning brought in an English woman and four children – they were turned out of their farm by the Boers, and the husband turned adrift naked. The officers surrounded them as soon as they came in, collected around and gave her £10, sending her on to Cape Town. It was the most pitiable case I ever saw, and every man swore he would show no pity to anyone after it....

The Boers have also started stripping our dead and robbing our wounded, so that you can guess we feel mad. We get on well with the friendly natives here – they all want to fight for us, but we wish to do all that ourselves.

We have one blanket to sleep on and have not undressed since we got off the boat; and don't expect we shall until it is all over. We sleep with our pistols and swords on us, and the harness all ready to put on the horses. They want a lot of us to join the police out here, but they won't have much trouble after this is all over.

I like the country for getting about; you can go for miles here without seeing anyone; save monkeys and ostriches and goats in a proper big drove of 100.

Back in Weston, heavy headlines proclaimed:

WESTONIANS BOUND FOR THE TRANSVAAL
LOCAL ARMY RESERVISTS CALLED OUT
LOCAL YEOMANRY VOLUNTEER FOR ACTIVE SERVICE

The *Mercury* named "R Softly, who previously served with the Somerset Light Infantry in India, now coachman of Mr Reginald Graves-Knyfton JP" as one of fifteen soldiers cheered off by crowds at the station as Volunteer bands played:

THE SOMERSET REGIMENT AND THE WAR

The 2nd Battalion Somerset Light Infantry embarked at Southampton for South Africa on the Union liner *Briton*. They numbered 961 men, half of them Reservists. A good crowd assembled to wish "the gentlemen in khaki going South" God-speed and a safe return as the Regimental band played "Say au revoir but not goodbye".

Some of the men had small Union Jacks attached to their rifle barrels, and all seemed to be in the best of spirits. Some made jocular remarks to the bystanders. Others had a grim determined look, showing they felt the separation from their wives and children and the uncertainty of seeing them again. But all swung by with a go that left nothing to be desired.

They were all dressed with khaki puggrees and puttees – the former being a covering over the pith helmet, and the latter a khaki coloured bandage round the legs in place of leggings – and overcoats. The khaki uniform will be donned en route to South Africa. On the left side of the helmets was the arms of the regiment, white on a red ground. The advantage of the khaki as a dress could be observed at great advantage in the first dull glimmer of dawn. The overcoats showed up dark, but the helmets and puttees could hardly be seen.

There appears to be an endeavour on the part of the authorities to make as much distinction as possible between the dress of the officers and men. Th helmets even differ, those of the officers being considerably broader at the back, and the difference can be detected at a great distance. The knapsacks, cross-straps, and sword further accentuate the difference.

Khaki was a good idea, but distinctive dress for officers was not, as Alf Howe observed:

Orange River, Cape Colony, South Africa. 14.11.99

I expect this will be the last letter I shall be able to post for a bit as we move tomorrow at day-break.

We had a fine old skirmish last week. The 75th (the old Bristol Battery) was sent out and they only fired ten shots before the enemy were cleared out of the hills altogether.

Our Infantry Officers are dying off fast out here. In one small fight we lost four Officers, who had galloped out to the front to lead the men into the thick of it and they were knocked over in about ten minutes. One of them, a young Lieut. who was shot down, afterwards took a rifle off one of the horsemen and shot four Boers, and then lay down and said, "I am satisfied." Those were his last words at the hospital. We buried them here with full military honours; they had one gun and team from us and one from the 75th Battery to carry them on.

We are getting a lot of prisoners here every day. I hear that some more of my chums are for the front; it is the finest camping life I have ever had, and I would like to stop in this country all my life. We are going to work our way on this week. You would not know me now if you saw me; everybody has got to wear a beard, and I have got a big Buffalo Bill hat to wear to set myself off.

More troops landed:

SOMERSET LIGHT INFANTRY AT THE CAPE

HM Transport *Briton* arrived at Capetown on Monday and has completed by far the fastest passage by any of the chartered transports. The *Briton* has on board 50 officers and 1,116 non-commissioned officers and men, with six officers' horses. The troops include the 2nd Bn Somersetshire LI, under the command of Lieut-Colonel EJ Gallwey.... The *Briton* also conveyed a number of 12-pounder quick-firing guns, a quantity of ammunition, revolvers etc.

As the men joined their units they met old friends:

Orange River 25.11.99

Dear Mother,

Just a few lines to let you know I am in the best of health ...I had a surprise last Saturday; who should come up and tap me on the shoulder but Bert Dart of the Coldstream Guards who came home to Weston on sick furlough when I was at Aldershot. He went up to the front with me on Monday ...

I never felt more pleased in my life than I did when we started the fight at daybreak on Thursday morning: 10,000 infantry marched into the field, and a grander sight I never wish to see, as they went along almost racing to see who could get in first — to either win a soldier's name or death.

Anyone would have thought they were going to a dancing party when they were told off to their posts. The night before when they were told they were going to fight at 3am, every man in the field lifted up three cheers for our Queen and Country, but I am sorry to say many of them did not live to come off the field. One of Dart's regiment, who was the first to get over the barricade, got shot after tackling five men, four of whom he killed, but the fifth shot him. The

Mounted British soldiers

Boers flew the white flag again on Thursday, and on Dart's adjutant galloping up, he was shot. The Boer that shot him, however, got captured and was also shot. This is the third time the same thing has happened. Our killed and wounded number about 260, and the Boers are estimated at 2,000.

I hear that several large firms are sending every soldier and sailor in S Africa a present for Xmas; our Queen is also sending us a present. We are treated by the people of S Africa just as if we were their own sons – we can say this much for them, they are doing everything they possibly can for our comfort. I expect by the time you get this it will be Xmas – so I wish you one and all a "Merry Xmas and a prosperous New Year."

I have a splendid collection of ostrich feathers in my bag, and an ostrich's toe-nail for a keepsake. I captured a nice little Arabian pony – my section officer has it now....

Your ever-loving son,

Alf

Tobacco tin sent by Queen Victoria

The *Mercury* published:

AN APPEAL FOR THE SOMERSETS

As Christmas approaches we are asked to send ½lb of tobacco to each man of the Somerset Light Infantry at the front. It is the most useful present, and if it can be extended to 1lb, we will do so. Some have sent between 1 and 2lb. Another suggestion is a box of presents, such as woollen caps, jerseys, socks, comforters, pipes, tobacco etc. The War Office points out that tobacco is one of the most useful presents.

Alfred Howe fought in several engagements, keeping up to date with the *Mercury*:

Modder River Dec 16th 1899

Dear Mother and Father

I take the pleasure of writing a few lines to you just to let you know a little bit about this affair. I received the Mercury all right yesterday (15th), and see that there is a Sergt Baker belonging to Weston in S Africa.... No doubt it pleased the Weston folks to read of his doing 64 miles in 5 days.

We have had a rough time of late. We left Orange River on the 26th Nov for Modder River, and did a march of 26 miles the first day, and on the second day we had 56 miles to cover. We got into action at about 2pm on the 28th, after a trot of 10 miles through dead sand. We lost eight horses going into battle over the last 10 miles, and 3 horses and 3 men wounded in crossing the field. It was a hard fight for 14½ hours, and we were without food and water for a complete day and night. We had about ten days' rest after that, and then our battery had to relieve the Northamptons, 210 of whom held their own against 1,000 Boers for 7½ hours. We did that march – about 15 miles of sand – in two hours.

We cleared them out, and then four of our guns left the next day for Modder, leaving two guns behind belonging to my section. We stopped there two days and then we had to move back for another hard fight. We left Graspan about 2 o'clock and got to Modder River about 6 pm in time to hear that the battery was heavily engaged some five miles away. We had our tea and left that night for the front at 12 o'clock. We opened fire at daybreak, and kept it up till dark without any food. We got to sleep about 10 pm, but soon after were woke up again with the horses stampeding all over the show. At daybreak we opened fire again, and then we left them to bury their dead, which amounted to over 2,000 killed and 1,400 wounded. Our losses were also heavy – about 800 to 1,000 killed and wounded....

Your loving son

Alf

The war was not going well. The *Mercury* boosted morale with the story "as told by himself" of Winston Churchill's escape from Boer captivity and appealed for more volunteers:

LOCAL VOLUNTEERS FOR THE FRONT
PATRIOTIC RESPONSE TO THE CALL BY YEOMANRY, RIFLES AND ARTILLERY.

A special parade of the members of "B" Co. of the Rifle Corps was convened at the Drill Hall. The muster was some 80 strong, the officers present comprising Lt Col Perham, Capt and Adjutant Brocklehurst, Major CE Whitting, Capt RF Duckworth and Lt Graves-Knyfton.

Capt Duckworth mentioned that the Somerset Regiment were now situated at a point just below Colenso and to this regiment the 3rd Battalion volunteers would be attached. He called upon volunteers desirous of serving at the seat of war.

The following responded: Lt RB Graves-Knyfton,

Sergt EW Wilcocks, L/Cpls Lethebe and Withyman, Cyclists W Saturley, AWH Marshall, F Hutchings and AE Brown, L/Cpls Frost and Masters, Privates CG Moule, Wilcox, P Webb, M Frampton, A Raines, A Major, Smart, A Weare, Hathway, Hodder, Brunton, Leach and Gagg.

Led by Lt Col Perham and Maj Whitting, the entire remainder of the company volunteered for garrison duty to release regulars for the front.

Major Whitting was 55 and Lt Graves-Knyfton was 26. Alf Howe was 20 when he posted his Christmas letters:

Modder River, S Africa. Xmas day, 1899.

Dearest Charlie

We are having a very good Xmas, better than I expected – but there, Tommy Atkins can make himself happy anywhere, and more so on this sort of life, for we know what we are here for, and don't care a jot for anything that comes in our road. We are having high jinks here between fights.

We have not done any fighting for about a week. We are getting reinforced ... and every man has vowed to stand to the last but what they will relieve Kimberley. The Boers are getting captured here every day in mobs. ... I have just come in from scouting after a rather narrow escape of getting popped off by our own men. I have captured about 20 horses since being out here. I went five miles from the Battery to get the last lot I had, and did not know the Battery had stopped so far away. I got a good "telling off" for being so fearless, but when scouting like that we never think of getting captured or shot. ...

My first experience of war was at Belmont. Then came Graspan. The next was Modder River, and I hardly know how to explain it – it was nothing but pure slaughter for the Boers. We also lost a fearful lot of men. This fight will be remembered by all here – "the fateful 28th day of November" it is called. It was the hardest fight England has had since the Crimea – nothing but one continuous hail of bullets from daybreak to dark. The field next morning was strewn with dead and wounded. The Boer losses were never known properly – some were left dead for us to bury and the rest they buried themselves or carried away. What they could not get rid of any other way, they tied large stones to the bodies and threw them into the river to poison the water.

The next battle was at Graspan. Our battery was sent to shell them out of the hills, and in less than

four hours we could see nothing but dead and wounded Boers and ponies. We only had 11 slightly wounded and all are back again. The next battle was at Magersfontein. There we had nearly two regiments cut up. You must excuse me for not telling you more about it. It is too dreadful to mention. I shall, perhaps, be able to tell you more when I come home...

Many thanks for the writing paper. It was very acceptable: we have an awful hard job to get any here.

From your ever loving brother
Alf.

Modder River, South Africa, December 30th 1899.

Dearest Father,

I am very pleased to tell you our battery is in the best of health as yet. The only thing that troubles us out here is our poor horses. They get lame areas in their feet from the long marches they have to do: it almost knocks them up, especially the forced march we did from Orange River to Modder River. That was a 26 hours' good hard forced march; it is stated to have been the hardest and most marvellous performance ever done. We used to think we did some long marches at home, and no doubt they were, but we had not the heat to put up with.

The day we marched into the battlefield we met two despatch carriers coming to look for us about nine miles from the fighting line, and the news they gave us livened us up a good deal when we found out we were having the good luck to "muck in" with a bit of a "rough house" for the good of our Queen and Country. I think myself a lucky fellow to take part in these hard and fearful battles, which through the help of God we intend to fly our good old Union Jack over the country. We are having a hard struggle for it and I am sure it will be our side that will win. We lost nine of our best horses during the last nine miles of the march. With only water, we trotted and galloped through dead sand for about seven miles, the horses dropping down in the road. All we could do was cut them loose, leave them on the road, and get along without them.

We did fine work that night. It was fine sport to see the Boers among our shells: they fell in all directions, but they gave us a very warm reception. It was almost like being in a band-room to hear the bullets whistling over our heads.

From your ever loving son,
Alf

Field Battery at the Modder River

Part 8:   New Century, Old Queen 1900 - 1901

Chapter 80.   Uphill in 1900

Pony and trap at Donkey Field   *[UVS]*

Village population: 242 males + 276 females = 518 in 107 houses + 781 in Moorland Road area
= 1299 in ecclesiastical parish
Ecclesiastical area 1077 acres; village area 1024 acres

Rateable value of agricultural land in village £1,417; of buildings £2,638
Total value £4,055

Rector: Rev Arthur John Burr MA; Churchwarden: George Masters; Verger: Frank Counsell
Schoolmaster: Frederick J House ACO; Average school attendance: 44 infants + 78 aged 7-14

Lord of the Manor: Reginald Bennet Graves-Knyfton of Uphill Manor

Signatures of new Parish Council
[Permission kindly given by SRO to use the image of signatures from file C/GP/MISC/5]

Just under half of the population had been born in the village, but only five full families: the Harveys, Staples and Minifies, all living in Sandcroft Cottages, the Exons in a Dolphin Cottage and the Poples at 1 Hillgrove Terrace. Ten villagers were over 70. Living with the Poples was 84-year old Henry Whimple, an uncle from Devon. Next door at 2 Hillgrove Terrace, Henry Staples (86) was the oldest man in the village and nearby at the Dolphin the widowed Ann Manley (72) lived with her son William the new licensee. Round the corner at Walnut Cottage Post Office, Mary Minifie was the oldest woman at 83. Across the road in Rhyne Cottages lived William Webber (76) and his sister Louisa Walsh (71), near Thomas (73) and Caroline (75) Penberthy. The oldest couple were Thomas (82) and Mary (78) Russell in 3 Hillside Cottages.

Favourites among 83 different first female names were Alice 16, Mary 16, Ann variants 15, Edith 14, Florence/Florrie 14, Elizabeth 11. Victoria Sheppard, month-old baby in a family of nine living in a Brickyard Cottage, was the first village female in the queen's reign to be given her name. 34 of the 68 working women (52%) were now in service trades with 25 (38%) in domestic service. Six taught in the school and one was resident governess in the Rectory.

Most popular of 55 different first male names were William 25, Charles 19, James 14, Fred / Frederick 11, George 11, Henry 11. The quarry employed a quarter of all working men, reflecting the need for stone in new building developments. Various aspects of transport, ranging from horses to the railway and a traction-engine, occupied 21 (14%) men. 12 (8%) were in specific building trades and Peter Hart of the Coal Wharf brought his younger brother William up from Cornwall to run a contractor's business. He perhaps employed the man who later recalled working on Uphill's roads at that time:

> Well the village had three, what you would call muddy lanes, in much the same places as where the three main roads now are. I can mind how a fellow used to come down from Axbridge and rake over the surface and rake back the mud. Then 'er 'ad a load of stones big as yer vist, tip 'em in and leave me and the 'orses to do the rollin'.
>
> Of course, we 'ad a lot of footpaths, rights of way, across the fields to the Church and to and fro across the village, and a goodish road up to the windmill near the old church for the farmers round about to bring their corn for grinding.

The number of new shops showed there was money to spend. Perhaps the most significant sign of a new age was Uphill's first newsagent's, opened by 23-year old Noah Gould, probably on the same site as today's newsagent's in Old Church Road. Almost opposite, grocer Charles F Turner (31) and his wife Laura ran The Stores in today's Laburnum House. They had two daughters, a lodger Edith Wood who taught at the school, and two servants, 16-year old William Stone from Bristol and 14-year old Annie Berry from Hampshire. Nearby George Masters (41) was the village tailor, as well as church-warden and secretary of Uphill Castle Cricket Club.

60-year old Charles Howe ran a poultry and butter business from one of the new Rhyne Cottages:

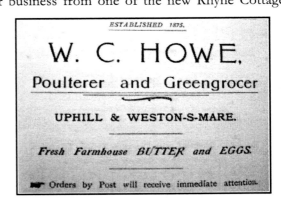

ESTABLISHED 1875.

W. C. HOWE,
Poulterer and Greengrocer
UPHILL & WESTON-S-MARE.
Fresh Farmhouse BUTTER and EGGS.

Orders by Post will receive immediate attention.

Round the corner past the Dolphin, Henry Herniman now 40 and his 19-year old son, also Henry, displayed their usual fine selection of butcher's meat for Christmas 1900. People in Uphill Road bought their groceries from 74-year old Francis Fear's shop in the front room of his home in Russell Cottages.

Five old farms remained: Henry Brown's Uphill Farm, Edward Luff's Manor Farm, Abel Young's Flat Roof Farm, and George Smith's Slimeridge. Robert Counsell's land was around his home in Sherwell House. Between them they employed 14 men. A sign of the times was that 15 others worked as gardeners. Samuel Frederick King (53) ran his dairy from Centre Farm. His elder son Charles had left home:

UPHILL – ACCIDENT

On Tuesday whilst engaged upon works in the course of construction at The Wharf, Bleadon, Charles King – son of Mr Fred King, dairyman of this parish – sustained serious injury necessitating subsequent treatment at the Weston Hospital. It appears that whilst holding a bolt in position in order that a fellow employee might hammer in the rivets, his comrade on swinging back the hammer accidentally dealt him a severe blow in the forehead, inflicting an ugly wound and rendering him temporarily unconscious. He was subsequently removed to the Hospital, where the wound was dressed but his detention was not ordered.

More happily, a year later:

> Wedding on Whit Monday 1901 at Uphill of Mr William King, second son of Centre Farm, and Miss Edith Florence Brimble, grand daughter of the late Mrs Brimble of Uphill. Mr Fred King Jun was best man. The wedding breakfast was held at Centre Farm and merry peals were rung from the belfry of the Old Church.

Whereas one baby in four had died in infancy in 1800, the infant death-rate had fallen to 1 in 60 in 1900. But early life was still uncertain. At New Year 1900:

INQUEST AT UPHILL

> An inquest was held at the Ship Hotel, Uphill, on the body of Evelyn Rose Burden, aged 5 weeks infant daughter of Edwin and Louisa Burden, 6 Hillgrove Terrace, Uphill, who was found dead in bed by her mother on Sunday last. Mr R Counsell was foreman of the jury. Both parents had slept in the bed with the child. The mother had given her milk in a bottle before going to bed and again during the night. She woke at 6 o'clock and found the baby dead. She was well up on the pillow and not under the clothes. Verdict: "Death was caused by convulsions brought on by the irritation of the mass of undigested milk in the stomach".

When three children turned up at school in October with sores on their lips and hands, schoolmaster Frederick House sent them home immediately and closed the school for one and a half days while floors, desks and slates were scrubbed with carbolic soap.

Yet again, the Parish Council complained to the Uphill and Hutton Sewers Jury:

> For several summers, there has been obnoxious effluvium in Uphill Rhyne between Middle and West Bow because the water is stagnant. The penstock should be lifted once a fortnight next summer, for half an hour each time, to let the stagnant water out. Another penstock is needed above Middle Bow.

But Weston had mains sewerage and a good water supply, opening Uphill Moor for profitable development. Weston Council soon questioned why they should pay their Clerk of Works to supervise laying drains through new "Whitting" and "Knyfton" estates in the area.

When Uphill coal merchant Peter Hart started building a new house in Moorland Road he met a different problem:

> A pair of wagtails, locally known as "dish washers", flew in and built a nest in the fireplace of an upstairs room. Workmen found them there, sitting on three eggs. They propped bricks round the birds for protection and worked elsewhere until the eggs were hatched.

In July 1900, figs ripened on Edward Luff's tree in:

> a heat wave of unprecedented severity. On Tuesday, the highest temperature in the sun was recorded at 140 degrees and on the following day 131 degrees.

Two weeks later:

WESTON AND THE GALE

> The town experienced a gale of abnormal severity. Under normal circumstances the morning tide (which attained its maximum at 11am) would have been moderately low, but with a half hurricane driving from the west, it speedily attained the dimensions of a flood tide. The wind attained its maximum velocity soon after noon, at which time the Channel was a racing mass of "white horses". Three steamers, bound down Channel and due to call at Weston were unable to make the Pier. On the Sands, the fragile structures erected by the itinerant entertainers and refreshment vendors came in for the full force of the gale, to the unfeigned glee of scores of juveniles who lost no time in conducting salvage operations.

> The gale blew away two marquees at the Boys' Brigade camp at Mr George Smith's Slimeridge Farm. The entire camp of the Church Lads' Brigade in the field adjacent to Uphill Castle was demolished. The boys rescued their possessions and slept in the schoolroom and the old schoolroom. The following day the tents were re-erected in the Rev Burr's sheltered paddock.

The storm roused village boys to add to the chaos causing the Rev Burr to write to the Mercury:

> With reference to the noisy band which paraded round the village in the early hours of Thursday, the Church Lads' Brigade were in no way connected with the disturbance.

New Year's Day was rung in as normal, 1900 not being considered the first year of a new century:

> The bells of the old parish church rang out merry peals on New Year's Eve, when our "local medallist" made his third appearance. A few minutes before twelve, the bells were muffled, and afterwards rang the Old Year out and the New Year in. On New Year's Eve, the ringers were entertained to supper, as usual, by Host and Hostess Smith at the Ship Hotel and a very enjoyable evening was spent.

A few weeks later:

> The ringers of the Parish Church, Weston, paid a visit here and went through a course of change ringing under the able leadership of Mr Ball. After a couple of hours ringing they adjourned to the Ship Hotel to a smoker. During the evening the ringers gave a special performance on the hand-bells interspersed with various patriotic songs, including "The soldiers of the Queen" and "Sons of the Sea" sung by Mr Milton Jones.

When summer came:

The Choir and bell-ringers enjoyed an outing in a 4-horse brake to Dunster and Minehead.

In October 1900, William Fear was presented with an elegant silver watch when he left the choir after over 35 years. Another villager well-known in church and chapel remained active:

A vigorous anti-Catholic lecture was given in Weston by the Rev WC Minifie BD, who has local connections and who exercised considerable powers of oratory.

St Nicholas Church hit the headlines in November 1900:

SACRELIGIOUS ROBBERY
A SMART UPHILL LAD

Edward Diamond (17), Edward Byrne (17), Thos Feeney (17) and Jas Feeney (15) were charged with feloniously entering Uphill Church on the 9th inst and stealing 12s 10d the property of the Rev AJ Burr.

James Fear (15) residing at Rose Cottage, Uphill, deposed that he saw Diamond, Byrne and James Feeney enter the church, Thomas Feeney remaining outside. The three remained in the church about five minutes, and then came out and spoke to Thomas Feeney and afterwards returned into the church. They remained in the church about ten minutes, and on returning outside, showed Thomas Feeney some money. Witness sent a messenger to Rev Burr.

All the prisoners then walked away in the direction of Bleadon. Witness went into the church, and noticed that the padlocks of both the alms boxes had been forced, whereupon he informed PC Palfrey stationed at Bleadon.

He found the prisoners in the tap room of the Anchor Inn, Bleadon. They admitted the robbery and said they had been prowling the country for a long time, living on robberies. All were sentenced to one month's hard labour.

The previous day, the Rev Burr had given them food at the Rectory and two of them had stolen his galoshes from the porch. For this they received another 7 days' hard labour.

Two months later:

ANOTHER ROBBERY AT ST NICHOLAS

Robbers found the keys to the safe, stealing objects from it but not the papers. They also took the sacramental plate, preventing the holding of communion. Fortunately the real silver plate had been removed to the Rectory and this was an electro-plated nickel silver plate of little value. They also took half a bottle of sacramental wine and a silk handkerchief from a surplice.

Within days:

THE ROBBERIES FROM UPHILL CHURCH
TICKET-OF-LEAVE MAN COMMITTED

John Payne alias John Murphy alias John Barrow alias Wilkinson was charged with having feloniously stolen from Uphill Church an electro-plated Communion Cup; an electro-plated bread plate; a half-pint bottle of sacramental wine; a bunch of keys; and a pen-holder, of the total value of £1 10s, the property of Rev AJ Burr, Rector of Uphill. Also a white linen handkerchief value 6d property of Frank Counsell. The prisoner had been arrested at Trowbridge on another charge and the police found the stolen goods in his possession Enquiries showed they came from Uphill.

The Rector and the verger (Frank Counsell, builder of Uphill) confirmed the property was theirs. William Fear, gardener, identified the man who had called at his house with a woman who was selling lavender.

The man was sentenced to 5 years imprisonment.

St Nicholas   *[UVS]*

Not all village children appreciated the good work of the village ladies who ran St Nicholas Sunday School:

UPHILL ENTERTAINMENT

The Sunday School tea and distribution of prizes was followed by an entertainment consisting of recitations, dialogues and musical pieces performed by the children. A most successful

Maypole dance was executed by the elder girls, under the superintendence of Miss Byrnes and Miss Joyce. "The Absent-Minded Beggar" was recited by Miss Nellie Foster, who afterwards collected 18s for the Boer War Fund.

Prizes given by Mrs Graves-Knyfton were for regular attendance and good conduct; also for good behaviour in church specially given by Mrs Burr. Mrs Vawdrey gave prizes for the best needlework done in the day. The performance closed with the National Anthem.

The tea was supplied by Mr Turner of Uphill and gave great satisfaction.

It was a pity that the bad behaviour of some of the big lads at the back of the room spoilt the pleasure of others who had come to enjoy themselves and it is hoped that it will not happen again.

Chapter 81.   Clubs and

❏ ❏ ❏ ❏ ❏

Village Dinner

[UVS]

Cricket

Sunday School met a need, but at a time of great and growing national wealth, universal literacy and political awareness, people needed more. In November 1900:

> Through the kindness of Mrs Graves-Knyfton, the old schoolroom has just been re-opened as a place where the residents of the parish may spend enjoyable and profitable evenings three times weekly. The room, which is well heated and lighted, is liberally supplied with current literature and bagatelle and other games, provided free to all males over 15 years of age. The room is well filled each night it is opened. Between 40 and 50 attended the opening of the club.

> Messrs Fear, Masters, Shallish, Taylor, Hayes, Masson form a Committee to attend, open up, light up and be responsible for the conduct of members.

> The room adjoins the Castle grounds and was once the village schoolroom. It is well suited for the present purpose being lofty, well ventilated and lighted by three hanging lamps. Two long tables are arranged along each side of the room for newspapers of which there are three dailies, Tit-Bits, Answers, and other popular papers such as Graphic, Strand, Badminton, and quite a library of various books, some of the latest. The games consist of bagatelle, chess, draughts, dominoes, ludo, fish ponds, and various others for younger members. Writing materials are provided for any member who may wish to use the same.

> The want of such an institution has long been felt, and we feel the greatest admiration for Mrs Knyfton for the kindness and interest she is taking in the working classes, and it now lies with the members to show their appreciation by attending as often as convenient, as their attendance means the success of the kindly undertaking.

A woodworking class gave an exhibition of work and Wilfred Smith, Fred Patch, William Howe and Robert Jarvis won prizes. In April 1901 both activities closed for the summer. At the same time Robert Minifie stood for election to the Parish Council promising to work for a public library in Uphill but the village wanted neither him nor a library and he was not elected. He then requested a grant of £5 to set up a library but only one councillor voted in favour.

Sport was better supported. As President of Uphill Castle Cricket Club, Reginald Graves-Knyfton entertained members to a New Year dinner at the Old Schoolroom:

> A large company sat down including the Rev A Burr, Messrs W Luff, HW Herniman, R Counsell, F House, GR Masters (hon sec), P Hart and G Purnell. During the evening the health of Private A Weare, a member of the local Rifle

> Corps and also a member of the Uphill Castle Cricket Club – who has been accepted for service in South Africa – was heartily drunk followed by the singing of "The Soldiers of the Queen."

In August:

> Playing for Uphill Castle Cricket Club against Banwell, Mr A Russell accomplished a splendid performance with the ball, taking six wickets for 5 runs. J Hicks took 7 for 6 against Congresbury.

In April 1901:

> The balance sheet showed a most satisfactory balance of 17s 9d. The Club played 15, won 8, lost 5, drew 2. Mr Graves-Knyfton presented a bat for the highest batting average to Mr Cox and Mr Morgan Whitting presented another for the highest bowling average to Mr A Russell.

Set up by William Minifie ten years earlier, the Uphill branch of the United Patriots' Benefit Society was supported by all levels of society. The Rector presided with Major CE Whitting as his vice-chairman at the annual dinner at the Ship in November 1900. The large attendance included:

> Messrs RB Graves-Knyfton JP, J Hayes secretary, HW Herniman,, W Fear, P Hart J Hart, E Hart, F Taylor chairman Uphill branch, E Bailey, F Pearce, W Shallish, FJ House, GR Masters, A Counsell, H Hemens, D Lloyd, F King, W King, J Watts, J Porter, C Porter, R Jarvis, W Hollier, W Minifie, R Minifie, W Marshall etc. A most excellent repast was served in Host Smith's usual style. The Society now has 40 members. Mr Graves-Knyfton offered the Old Schoolroom for the Society's quarterly meetings.

During the speeches:

> Major CE Whitting read a telegram from his son Capt EJ Whitting who sailed from South Africa for England on 6th November. The rest of the Volunteer Service Company was not coming home yet.

❏ ❏ ❏ ❏ ❏

Chapter 82.   Fish and Fowl

As the 19th century ran into the 20th, soles, plaice, shrimp, herrings, sprats, conger eels, salmon and cod were still being taken in the bay with eels, mullet and sea bass in the Axe. Sprats remained the most popular:

> Whitings want zummat to cook 'em wi' an' make 'em good. They bean't the poor man's fish, but sprats be. They doan' want nothin' to cook 'em wi'. Dap 'em in the pan jest as they be. There never 'ave been shrimps and sprats same as what used to come into Uphill. How we watched mother boil they shrimps. We could hardly wait for 'em to turn red.

Fishermen sold some on the Wharf for a penny a pound as they landed, with cats and children scavenging any overflow, but the bulk went to London's Billingsgate Market. Working in back yards and behind the Ship, women sealed the catch into barrels to be carted to the station for despatch by rail. Their payment was a basket of sprats, whiting and shrimps.

The fish were followed by several thousand gulls, feeding round fishing nets and the new sewage outfall. The *Mercury* commented:

> It is a pity these handsome feathered bipeds, which are encouraged at other seaside resorts, should here meet with a reverse reception. For dietary purposes they are absolutely worthless, yet shooting, trapping and otherwise snaring gulls appears to be a favourite pastime in this district.

Another favourite was the annual rook-shoot on the Grange and Manor estates on May 12th, the traditional date for shooting fledgling rooks for rook pie. If there was no shoot, folk said, the rooks would leave.

Thanks to Victorian industry guns were better and cheaper than they had ever been:

Below the heronry in Grange wood, the muddy shores of the Axe regularly attracted curlew, redshank, dunlin and ringed plover with snipe and water-rail on the salt moor. The commonest duck were teal, widgeon and wild duck, some breeding. Sheldrakes from Brean Down occasionally led their brood up the Pill nearly to Uphill Wharf. Knot, sanderling and purple sandpiper were observed, with cormorants, razorbills and guillemots as occasional visitors from Wales. Common tern and grey phalarope sometimes put into the river on their way south in the autumn and a flock of snow buntings usually wintered in the sand dunes. Hard winters brought geese, swans, scaup duck, pochards, golden-eyes, scoters, and mergansers. In really violent weather Great Northern Diver, Little Auk, Storm Petrel, Leach's Petrel, Manx Shearwater and Pomatorhine Skua dropped in. Some were shot; all were carefully observed and noted by amateur naturalists.

Regular packet boat services ran out of the Axe to France and South Wales. One of these was the 21-ton sloop *Swansea Packet* operated by James Knight of Bleadon until 1917 when it hit the Wolves rocks near Flat Holm, sinking with all 60 passengers and crew. Some farmers transported produce in their own boats. Banwell farmer Thomas Hewlett owned the small schooner *Swallow* of 23 tons, Henry Jones owned the 23-ton *William and Mary* and Peter Neathy of Brean owned *Three Brothers*, 27½ tons.

❏ ❏ ❏ ❏ ❏

Chapter 83.   Guns and Rifles

A thunderous rumble disturbed Uphill early on 16th April 1900:

MAGAZINE EXPLOSION AT BREAN DOWN
SOLDIER BLOWN TO ATOMS
ANOTHER SEVERELY WOUNDED
GREATER PORTION OF THE FORT WRECKED
TWO GUNS DISMANTLED

An appalling catastrophe occurred in the early hours of Wednesday, when a terrific explosion of the powder magazine situated at Brean Down Fort took place. Shortly before 5 am a heavy rumbling report from the direction of the fort aroused no suspicion of any sinister significance. Shortly after eight o'clock however, news arrived of a momentous catastrophe, involving the destruction of a considerable portion of the fort as well as the loss of one life, and severe injury in another case. How the magazine was exploded is a mystery; but rumour attributed the disaster to deliberate intent on the part of some person.

The contents of the magazine included 5,000 lbs of powder in cases. Had the whole garrison – which was temporarily considerably augmented by the presence of a number of men intended to participate in heavy gun practice – been annihilated, one could not have been surprised. Immediately after the explosion Sgt Major Withers, who is in charge of the garrison, attempted to telephone from the Fort to Weston-super-Mare for assistance, but the force of the explosion had destroyed the communication with the result that a messenger had to be despatched per cycle via Berrow, Brent Knoll and Bleadon, in order to communicate with the Governmental Officer (Surgeon-Col Phelps of Weston) and the local Police.

During Wednesday morning a *Mercury* representative found that portion of Brean Down adjacent to the fort was covered with wreckage, huge coping stones weighing upward of 2 cwt being found 200 yards from the scene of the disaster; whilst at intervals were scattered iron girders twisted into every conceivable shape, and the debris of the zinc powder cases were freely scattered around. The wall separating the fort from the moat in the south west corner had been demolished and with the force of the explosion a considerable portion of the barracks had been destroyed. From the top of the hill the interior of the fort could seen. Here an awful scene of wreckage met the eye and the only thought that passed through the mind was how so very few were injured. Two of the 7-inch guns were dismantled and lay amidst heaps of debris, the working portions being twisted and broken almost beyond recognition, whilst masses of concrete and ironwork were scattered in all directions.

In October 1900, the Government cut its losses:

The officers at Brean Down Fortress received an intimation that Her Majesty's Government intends to demolish the buildings there so that it shall cease to be a fortified rock. Since the "Bristol Channel Defence" question cropped up, and the neighbourhood was visited by a man-of-war, great alterations and improvements have been in course of completion; but now, after great expenditure of money, the Government do not see the importance of fortifications.

By June 1901, the great Brean Down enterprise was over:

The Fort has been permanently dismantled and the guns sold to a Birmingham company. A road has been built for a traction engine to travel from shore to summit and thence to the fort. With its help, the gun carriages were dragged away through Burnham.

Only one commissioned officer was available for the Weston Rifles' summer camp at West Down on Salisbury Plain in June 1900. Capt R Fagan Duckworth took over command from Major CE Whitting who announced his retirement and Lt Graves-Knyfton was commanding Burnham Company while Capt Edward Jewell Whitting was at the front in South Africa:

LOCAL RIFLES ON SALISBURY PLAIN
CAMP EXPERIENCES
TROPICAL WEATHER RESPONSIBLE FOR QUEER SCENES

Lt Col Perham commanded 3rd Volunteer Battalion Somerset Light Infantry at West Down Camp. Speaking to the officers he referred to "disgraceful pro-Boer riots" in Weston. His men beat the Bristol Rifles at cricket with Pte F Taylor, captain of Uphill Castle CC, bowling a hat trick.

Bowler Frederick Taylor was a 32-year old stone mason. Having qualified at the Army School of Musketry, Hythe, Lt Graves-Knyfton was appointed Instructor of Musketry. He also helped recruit for the band which played at Weston Company's farewell to Major Charles Edward Whitting, Commandant of the Corps for 18 years:

After the toasts Major Whitting read a cablegram dated November 5th: "Capetown. To Whitting, 'Grange', Uphill. Somersets sailing today, transport Fort Salisbury." Loud cheers greeted the news. He told the gathering that he was proud that a Whitting had served in the Company since its formation. He was presented with a massive silver punch bowl inscribed: Presented to Major CE Whitting by the officers, non-commissioned officers and men of B Company, 3rd Volunteer Battalion Somerset Light Infantry, as a slight token and in recognition of his kind and generous support during his 18 years' command – November 12th 1900.

The *London Gazette* of 16th February 1901 announced his retirement promotion:

Major CE Whitting 3rd Volunteer Battalion Prince Albert's Somerset Light Infantry has been granted the honorary rank of Lieutenant Colonel.

Chapter 84.   Boer War

Meanwhile Pte William May, 1ˢᵗ Coldstream Guards, wrote a Christmas letter from the front to his sister in Uphill:

Modder River Jan 2ⁿᵈ 1900

My dear sister

I received your letter on the last day of the old year ... I thank you very much for the socks – they are just what I wanted, as we have to do a lot of marching; the sweets were also very nice. We cannot get anything out here yet, but there is a lot of things coming up by train. We are 500 miles from Cape Town and the trains are very slow; we were three days and nights in the train. We have been here at Modder River now for five weeks waiting for more troops.

We fought three great battles and drove the Boers back with heavy loss, but were checked three weeks ago. We started on the Sunday night at 6.30, and were fighting all day Monday; we were holding a hill, but had to retire for want of more big guns. We are 15 miles from Kimberley, and if we get there alright our Division will have done its share.

I am keeping very well out here – it is hot by day and very cold at night, and we are out as much by night as by day, as we get a lot of outpost duty. We have lost a lot of men, but it's all chance, and I do not see much fear as most of the work has to be done with the big guns. The Boers never fight in the open, they are always behind big hills, and that is the reason it is taking us so long to beat them.

We had a very poor Xmas this year, but I hope to have a better one next. I was pleased to get the newspaper, as we get nothing to read out here. You know better than we do what is going on. I don't think there is anything I want. Hope to have more news to tell you next time.

Your affectionate brother

William May.

A Weston boy wrote sadly home about his Christmas:

The only things we got out here was one pint of beer and a bit of Xmas pudding, that is all we were allowed, and we had to pay 3d for the pint of beer. Things are very dear – we have to pay 3s 6d a pound for tobacco, 2d for a clay pipe, 1d a box for matches, eggs 3s 6d a dozen, 2s a pound for butter. You want plenty of money to live out here.

Alf Howe did better:

Dearest Mother,

.... I received a most handsome present from Mrs Whitting, consisting of two woollen helmets, a muffler, and some splendid books which came in

very useful to the whole of the men under my charge. I have lent one of the helmets to a chum: we wear them at night to keep the insects from getting in our ears – there are hundreds of different sorts and sizes, from the ant up to the snake. One of our men got out of bed one night and found he had a scorpion keeping him company – they are fearful things, and if they bite you, cause unmentionable pain for 48 hours – but he managed to get free. He hadn't been in bed again about half-an-hour when he had a nice fine snake crawl in under his blanket. You can't think how comfortable he felt for a little while! We all have a good look around now before we make our roost.....

We have been very quiet on our side here, and have provisions enough to last six months.

Alf.

More men joined them:

LOCAL VOLUNTEERS DEPART
FOR THE FRONT

Seven volunteers from the local Rifle Corps left Weston Station to report to the Somerset Regimental HQ at Taunton. They included Pte A Major, boot and shoe maker of Moorland Road, Pte A Weare, native of Uphill, son of Mr Frank Weare. They were cheered off by big enthusiastic crowds and the Regimental band.

Four Royal Engineers volunteers included Sapper BD Butt of Uphill, labourer for Mr HC Sleep, decorator, plasterer. They received a send-off by a crowd of 600.

Somerset LI Volunteer Company Soldier

The volunteers steamed south to the Cape on the troopship *Tintagel Castle*. Putting in to Gibraltar for coal they passed Cape Trafalgar, scene of Nelson's victory almost a century earlier. At the equator the soldiers went through the ritual of "Crossing the Line" being shaved with a huge wooden cut-throat razor by a sailor dressed as Neptune and tipped backwards into a canvas tank of cold seawater. Alongside them, they recognised their escort vessel as the cruiser HMS *Arrogant* which had bombarded Steep Holm two years earlier.

They landed in May 1900 and were posted to the 2nd Battalion SLI as the Somerset Volunteer Company commanded by 28-year old Capt Edward Jewell Whitting. The Battalion marched 80 miles across Orange River Colony, eventually taking up guard duties to defend the Kimberley-Mafeking Railway from Boer guerrillas.

Other local volunteers in the Imperial Yeomanry joined Field Marshal Lord Roberts as his bodyguard and were the first to enter Bloemfontein in April 1900.

Sapper Butt's widowed mother Jane lived in Uphill Grange as the Whitting family nurse. Seeing the *Mercury* headline TWO WESTONIANS MISSING AT FRONT she found it was about her son. With three Weston men he was with 43rd Royal Engineer Company repairing bridges and culverts on the Rhenoster River. They were attacked while working on Leeuwsprit bridge, losing many captured or killed. The Volunteers remained under fire all night defending the train which held their workshops and stores. Next day Sappers BD Butt and FG Kerton of Weston were reported missing. In the dark and confusion, they had mistaken Boers for British and were captured. Two months later the Boers released them unharmed.

Alfred Weare wrote home:

> Volunteer Service Company, 2nd Somersets,
> Vryberg, May 31st 1900
>
> Dear Mother,
>
> Just a few lines to let you know I am alright up to now.
>
> We have been travelling a bit since I wrote last. We left Smithfield on the 23rd May for Bethulie. We thought we should be in Smithfield for the Queen's Birthday, but we had to be on the march. We had a drop of rum served out to us and a bit of jam extra that day – we had a long march and we wanted it. Some of the fellows got served out with new boots and new clothes and they wanted it. About a hundred of our fellows had to ride on the wagons from Smithfield, having scarcely any boots on their feet and trousers broken all to pieces.

> We left Bethulie about two o'clock in the afternoon and had a comfortable carriage to ride in – a second-class sleeping compartment. It was nice and easy travelling, especially at night. There are four shelves where you can get up and lie down and then two can lie down on each seat; it was the softest bed we had had for some time. We had two nights in the train.
>
> At Burghersdorp, we came across a Weston chap – Sam Tozer, who used to be in the Rifles at Weston, and when we got to Dectar I saw a man named Palmer who used to live at Oldmixon. I knew his face directly I saw him. He was in the Welsh Militia stopping there. He went out and got me a big bag of cakes – they went down alright, I can tell you.
>
> When we got to Vryberg I got four letters and one paper. Someone had torn the stamp off the paper and I had to pay twopence for it but I did not mind that. We had a draft here waiting for us, from England, under Major Lloyd and Captain Brocklehurst who used to be Adjutant of the Rifles at Weston. We were paid at this place for the first time since we have been out here.
>
> Dear mother, remember me to all enquiring friends and thank Noah Gould for sending me the papers: it is kind of him.
>
> Sixty of our chaps and the officers are gone back down the line guarding the bridges and the rest of us are left here, four Companies going up the line somewhere towards Mafeking.
>
> Dear mother, I must close now, with fondest love from your loving son,
>
> Alf.

In his next letter, Alfred Weare remembered his time with Uphill Castle Cricket Club:

> Vryberg, Orange River Colony,
> June 11th 1900.
>
> Dear Mother,
>
> Just a line in answer to your letter which I received this morning, dated May 17th. I noticed in the paper that Uphill Castle let Worle beat them in the first match. We are having some nice weather here – rather warm by day and cold by night. We have no outpost duty to do here, so we don't feel the cold so much. We have plenty of work to do at the station, unloading the trucks and camp fatigues. We have not got much time for writing.
>
> I don't think I want any clothes sent out here – the only thing I want you to send is some tobacco, if you have not sent any. We have to pay about 7d per ounce for English tobacco, you can get it out of the stores, then they keep it back out of your month's pay.
>
> The first train from Mafeking came down through here yesterday. The line is open now right up to there, and the relief force came down through here about two or three days ago.
>
> We are having pretty good living now with what we buy and get served out with, and there are

about half-a-dozen coffee stalls alongside the camp.

I suppose there was a general holiday home in England when Mafeking was relieved and when Roberts entered Pretoria. We had a drop of rum on the strength of it. You ought to have seen the relief force and their horses that came back from Mafeking; they left their horses here. They looked half-starved, and some of them were so weak they could not get up once they got down.

Remember me to all my friends at Uphill....

I have not taken off my clothes to lie down since we landed out here – it would seem good to take them off once.

From your loving son

Alf.

By August 1900 Alfred Howe had fought in 35 actions with the Royal Field Artillery and was promoted full corporal. In September the *Mercury* ran the optimistic headline WAR NEARING THE END but admitted in December:

THE SOMERSETS BESIEGED

WESTONIANS UNDER FIRE FOR 27 DAYS

Colonel Chanier's force of 250 men, including a strong draft from the Somersets and the Volunteer Company in which several Westonians are serving, are besieged at Schweizwer Reneke by 1250 Boers under Commandant De Beer. The garrison had only rations for 35 days, but possessed sufficient cattle to last until Christmas. It had maintained a gallant defence and had erected such splendid defences that its safety is practically assured, as Lord Methuen and Col Settle are within a few days march of relieving it, only one man having been killed. The Boers who have bombarded the town for 27 days past have twice demanded the surrender of the little force, but the demand was scornfully rejected. Bravo Somersets! The force was duly relieved with one man killed and a captain wounded during the withdrawal.

But Capt Edward Jewell Whitting was not with his men. He was already on his way home from South Africa and the *London Gazette* dated 4th December 1900 announced:

Capt Edward Jewell Whitting, 3rd Volunteer Battalion Prince Albert's Somerset Light Infantry, removed from the Army, Her Majesty having no further occasion for his services.

The Somerset Volunteer Rifles Company followed on the trooper *Templemore* in May 1901 having lost 16 men from accident or enteric fever. While on active service they were paid 1s 1d a day and now received a civilian suit or 13s 6d gratuity. Bands played and councillors led a big crowd at Weston station to welcome the first group of nine Riflemen wearing their South Africa Medals.

More great crowds cheered the later arrivals of four Engineers and then six Yeomanry, but no councillors turned up.

At Burnham Edward Jewell Whitting welcomed his returning soldiers. In his speech he referred to "my dispute with the War Office ... I might have made a mistake, but others had done far worse ... I have been treated badly and hope to be reinstated".

South Africa War Medal

In December 1903 a Somerset memorial window was dedicated in Wells Cathedral and Col Long unveiled a memorial brass to the dead in Weston's new Town Hall.

❏ ❏ ❏ ❏ ❏

Chapter 85.   Death of Queen Victoria

Before the Boer War ended, Queen Victoria died on 26th January 1901. General Post Office telegraph wires carried the news across the land instantly. In black-edged columns the *Mercury* announced:

RECEPTION OF THE NEWS AT WESTON-SUPER-MARE

At 7.45 pm hosts of enquiring residents at the Post Office were confronted with an official announcement that "Our beloved queen passed away this evening at 6.30 pm" with almost simultaneously a muffled peal from the Parish Church.

The blinds of the Post Office and at such business establishments as had not closed for the evening were immediately lowered. In the following days blinds and curtains were drawn in private houses and businesses, flags flew at half mast, the wearing of mourning was wide-spread and sports, diners, entertainments were all closed.

At Uphill, directly the news of the Queen's demise reached the village the bells rang muffled peals and a bell tolled all day.

An order from the Duke of Norfolk, Earl Marshal, proclaimed:

> **ROYAL MOURNING**
> **Order in Council**
> **It is expected that all persons upon the present occasion of the death of her late Majesty, of blessed and glorious memory, do put themselves into deepest mourning.**

Some Weston traders rose to the occasion:

> E Hawkins & Co 33 High Street
>
> Large stock of Black kid, suede and wool Gloves.
>
> Black hatbands. Black neckties.

But Weston's big new department store just got on with business:

> LANCE and LANCE'S
>
> Great Dawn of the Century Sale is now in progress.

The *Mercury* ran a Special Offer:

> A Lasting Memento of our Beloved Queen
>
> Life-Like Portrait in Colours Size 35in x 26in at a reduced price of 1/6 each.
> Post free to Country Subscribers.

On 9th February 1901:

On Saturday, the day of the Queen's obsequies, flags floated at half-mast from both the old church on the hill and the present edifice, as well as at the Castle and other private residences, the village throughout presenting signs of general mourning.

At St Nicholas Church, a communion service was held at 8.15 am and a crowded congregation assembled for the memorial service at 2.30 pm. Among the hymns were Now The Labourer's Task Is Over, There Is A Blessed Home and Ten Thousand Times Ten Thousand. The Burial Service was sung to Tallis' setting and the lesson read by Major CE Whitting. Organist Mr FJ House ACO played The Dead March.

Throughout the afternoon, muffled peals were rung on the bells of the old church and a bell tolled through the day.

The bell that had pealed for Victoria's birth now tolled for her death with its inscription:

> I to the church the living call and to the grave summon all

Bibliography

Austin, Brian: *Facts Index 1843-1850*,
Petty Sessions Cases 1844-6; Family Trees.

Baker, Ernest E, FSA: *Old World Gleanings*.

Chapman, RB: *The Warden of the Road – A Dreamland Cavalcade of Opopille and Weston-on-the-Moor*. 1920s. [RBC]

Curtis, CD: *Calendar of Treasury Books 1685-1689* and *Mercury* material.

Davis, Sue: *Broadway Lodge*.

Directories:
    Harrison, Harrod Bristol Post Office Directory 1859.
    Post Office Directory 1866 Uphill.
    Morris & Co's Commercial Directory Somerset 1872.

Kelly's 1861, 1875, 1883, 1889, 1894, 1897, 1902.

Farr, Grahame: *Somerset Harbours* Christopher Johnson 1954 12s 6d.

Fisher, WG: *History of Somerset Yeomanry, Volunteer and Territorial Units*.

Frith, Colin Col: Records of the Knyfton and Graves-Knyfton families and Uphill Castle.

Gloucester and Avon Life

Goulthard, Alfred J and Watts, Martin: *Windmills of Somerset and the Men who made them*.

Kinglake, Robert Arthur: *Somerset Archaeological Society Proceedings* Vol xxxiii.

Richards, Chris articles: *Bristol Evening Post* and *New Scientist*.

Richards, Chris: Knowledge of the quarrying industry.

Skinner, Rev John: *Journal*.

Van der Bijl, Nicholas: *Brean Down Fort* Hawk Editions 2000.

Warre, Rev F: 1849 paper on old St Nicholas, Somerset Archaeological Society:

Weston Family History Society: St Nicholas Church Baptisms and Burials 1813-1837; Burials 1837-1916.

Watts, Martin: *Somerset Windmills*.

Weston *Mercury* files:
    News reports.
    Various memoirs of 19th life by the Oldest Inhabitant, Samuel Norvill, and AM Griffin.
    Many correspondents' letters.
    Various *Roundabouts* by John Bailey.

Williams, Peter on Edward Luff: *Bristol Evening Post*.

Uphill Village Society Archive
Permission has been given to reproduce the images which are acknowledged by [UVS] where they appear.

North Somerset Museum [NSM]
    Picture and Cuttings collection.

Somerset Record Office Files [SRO]
Permission (Reference EO/68918/perm) has been given to reproduce images from the asterisked files. Those images are acknowledged by [SRO].

Allotment Plan ... relating to Inclosure Act 1813.

Alfred Bennett *Parish of Uphill* ...1828

Brean Down Docks and Axe roadway 1865.

Chancery Bill 1813 Uphill inclosures and claims of Simon Payne Lord of Manor.

*Martha Coates' scrapbook 19th century.

Railway: Bristol and Exeter Book of Reference, engineer IK Brunel 1835.

Railway and Pier 1854.

Railway: South Wales and Southampton 1854

Railway: Bristol and Exeter loop line 1874.

*Road: Uphill and Bleadon 1854, 5.

St Nicholas Church 19th Century to present.

*Sewer: James Evans 1869.

Simon Payne's title to the Manors of Uphill and Christon 1811.

Simon Payne, plan of sea-wall work, court orders 1801-1831.

Slimeridge Farm plan 1850.

Somerset Rifle Volunteers: nominal roll 1866, Service agreement 1870, Rifle Butts Uphill 1874, Volunteers' Handbook 1880s.

Surname index to Uphill Census returns 1841, 1861.

Uphill – 18th century deeds, common fields, Bleadon windmill 1791.

Uphill Castle history and ownership by Colin Frith 1991.

Uphill House (Grange) papers and sketch 1853-1854, inventory 1855, plans 1853.

Uphill Parish Records 1696-1963.

*Uphill parish tithing 1756-1864.

Uphill tithe map 1840.

*Weston UDC dispute with Uphill Lord of Manor 1898.

*Weston and Charles Whitting, drainage 1894, 1870-1914.

*Whitting, Capt Charles: papers, including Somerset Rifle Volunteers 1860-1999.

Whitting, Thomas, yeoman: will 1865-1870.

Attempts have been made to contact the holders of copyright of images drawn from any other material.